THE ULTIMATE GUIDE
to preserving vegetables

Canning, Pickling, Fermenting, Dehydrating
and Freezing Your Favorite Fresh Produce

ANGI SCHNEIDER
Creator of SchneiderPeeps

PAGE STREET
PUBLISHING CO.

PAGE STREET
PUBLISHING CO.

Copyright © 2020 Angi Schneider

First published in 2020 by
Page Street Publishing Co.
27 Congress Street, Suite 1511
Salem, MA 01970
www.pagestreetpublishing.com

Distributed by Macmillan, sales in Canada by The Canadian Manda Group.

24   23   3 4 5

ISBN-13: 978-1-64567-009-4
ISBN-10: 1-64567-009-0

Library of Congress Control Number: 2019951508

Cover and book design by Laura Benton for Page Street Publishing Co.
Photography by Dennis Burnett, Styling by Darcy Folsom

Printed and bound in China

This book is dedicated to my
husband and children,
whom I collectively call "my people."

Y'all are truly the best people a girl could ask for, and my
heart swells with gratitude when I think of all the taste
testing, errand running, dish washing, floor sweeping and
encouraging you have done to give me time and space to
put my words onto paper. Thank you!

contents

introduction

Along with clothing, shelter and water, food is essential to life. It's only been in recent history that people have been able to rely on someone else to grow and preserve food for them and not have to worry about doing it themselves.

Many see this as a huge advancement in society, but it comes with high costs to our health, our finances and the environment. As consumers, we demand low prices and beautiful produce; any fruit or vegetable with a blemish is discarded and, when food prices rise, we complain about those who grow our food. In order to fulfill the consumer demands of blemish-free, cheap food, farmers are forced into monocropping and using many pesticides and herbicides in order to get the largest, most perfect harvest per acre.

There is certainly no simple solution to this quandary we've gotten ourselves into. But I firmly believe that each of us can be part of the solution by growing some of our own food, purchasing food from local farmers and preserving food. When we do grow and preserve our own food, our health, our finances and our environment benefit.

Growing up, I knew only one person who grew and preserved her own food, and that was my paternal grandmother, Granny. I have fond memories of us gathered in her kitchen eating homemade biscuits slathered with homemade jam. She would let the older grandchildren go into "the backroom" and pick a jam or two off the shelves. Then she'd pop off the lid, or remove the wax, and serve jams in delicious flavors you could not find in grocery stores.

The backroom was a fascinating place, filled with jars of food Granny had "put up" and baskets of garden produce, like onions and potatoes, that would keep for a while. While the backroom was fascinating, I never dreamed I would one day have my own backroom filled with food I put up for my family. And yet here I am with a similar backroom in my home.

It all started innocently enough, when my husband found a wild blackberry patch soon after we were married. He excitedly brought home some berries and said we should make jam. So, I did what any newly married woman would do: I called Granny to ask for her super-secret way of turning blackberries into jam. I was so excited!

And this is what she said, "Buy a box of Sure-Jell® and follow the instructions."

What?! No super-secret recipe? Surely, she must be mistaken. So, I asked if there was another way.

She replied, "Yes, dump a bunch of sugar in with the berries and boil them 'til it gels, but Sure-Jell is faster."

Honestly, I was a little disappointed in the answer. All this time I thought putting up food was hard and confusing and only certain people had the skills to do it. But it's not. I'm so thankful to Granny for not making a big deal out of canning blackberry jam. Her matter-of-fact answer gave me confidence; she knew canning wasn't hard and that I was capable of canning jam, simply because I could read and follow directions. Truly, you can learn anything if you can read and follow directions.

Expanding the Pantry

Little did I know, 28 years ago, that wild blackberry jam would be the beginning of a journey toward simple living and a DIY lifestyle. I bought the most current edition of the *Ball® Blue Book® Guide to Preserving,* and I was inspired. With the right equipment and instructions, I could preserve all kinds of fruits and vegetables!

At about that time, we also started growing a small garden, and I began to realize how much more cheaply we could feed our growing family by gardening and preserving the harvest. This motivated me to learn how to use every edible part of the plant and to expand my idea of a pantry from just dry goods and shelf-stable canned goods to include frozen and fermented foods.

I want to encourage you to think about your pantry as more than just the place you store dry goods: it's all the food you have available. Your pantry is unique to your family, and the things you stock it with will also be unique.

You might want to put up 100 quarts (100 L) of canned green beans to ensure you have green beans during the long winter, when the garden is under several feet of snow. Or, if you live in a climate where you can garden all year, like I do, you might want to put up only 30 quarts (30 L) of canned green beans, just to fill in any gaps for when the garden isn't producing much. Or maybe your family doesn't like canned green beans, so you choose to preserve them by freezing them instead of canning them. There is no one way for every family.

The goal of preserving food isn't to have a backroom full of jars of food. The goal of preserving food is to feed your family. It's super important that we take our family's likes and dislikes into consideration and preserve food in such a way that they will eat it.

Most of my family members do not like pickles of any kind, so I don't need to make more than a few jars of Canned Granny's Bread-and-Butter Pickles (page 151) each year. Once I get those put up, I slice and freeze any cucumbers (page 149) we don't eat fresh. I use these all year to infuse water, add to smoothies and make Frozen Cucumber Tzatziki (page 158). As the only pickle lover in my family, I often get a bit jealous when I see other food preservers who have shelf after shelf full of various pickles. I could make all kinds of pickles to fill my shelves, but that would be a waste of food and time, because my family won't eat them, and I can't eat that many.

Preserving food isn't a competition. It's not about who has the fullest shelves or the prettiest preserves. All that matters is that your family eats what you put up.

Reducing Waste

One way to reduce waste and save money is by using all the edible parts of a plant. I'm always amazed when people choose to toss out or compost perfectly edible "scraps." I've found that when I use all the edible parts of a plant, I can harvest more and grow less than if I use just the primary edible part.

Many vegetables have edible leaves that we harvest from the garden while we're waiting for the main crop to develop. Broccoli and cauliflower leaves taste just like the flower head and are a nice treat in the early fall or spring. I like to preserve carrot and radish tops by making pesto for the freezer. Don't overlook the usefulness of the leaves.

Stems are another part that many people toss without realizing that they can be transformed into something wonderful. I like to peel the tough skin off thick asparagus and broccoli to reveal the mild, creamy interior. The peels make great spreads and dips.

Any root vegetables that are going to be canned need to be peeled before canning. I freeze these peels for making broth in the future. I keep a freezer bag or two in my freezer and add the peels to it as I'm preserving. If I have a lot of potato peels, I usually freeze those separately for making potato broth. Potato broth is thicker than regular vegetable broth and can be used to thicken other soups.

If a vegetable has secondary edible parts, I've listed them in that vegetable's section. If there is a preserving recipe that I use these parts in, I've shared that too.

How to Use this Book

This book is based on my desire to preserve vegetables in ways that my family will eat and do that as efficiently as possible. When possible, I preserve vegetables in a meal-ready way. Instead of canning a bunch of carrot slices in quart (1-L)-sized jars when I bring in a large carrot harvest, I'll make a batch of Canned Spice Carrot Soup (page 112) and a couple of jars of Fermented Mexican Carrots (page 119). Then, I'll use the tops to make Frozen Carrot Top Pesto (page 115) for the freezer. The carrot soup is the only time-consuming item; the other two can be put together while the soup is processing.

The first part of this book is an overview of food preservation methods: canning, both water bath and pressure canning, dehydrating, fermenting and freezing. You'll find the basics of how to use these methods to safely preserve vegetables, but you won't find details for every scenario that could happen while preserving vegetables. I've written these chapters with enough information to get you started preserving the harvest, but not so much information that it leads to confusion and information overload.

The rest of this book is focused on growing and preserving the most popular vegetables and herbs that are grown in the home garden. Each vegetable has its own chapter and, in that chapter, you'll find instructions on how to grow, purchase, can, dehydrate, ferment and freeze that vegetable. You will also find recipes that highlight the vegetable; most of these recipes are for preserving the vegetable, but some recipes use the preserved vegetable.

Most of the recipes are written so that you'll preserve small batches at a time, simply because I find that adjusting recipes to scale up is easier than scaling down. If your family likes a recipe, or if you have enough of one vegetable to make two batches of a recipe, just double the ingredients and it will work out fine. *The exception to this is any of the jam or jelly recipes; don't ever double a jam or jelly recipe or you run the risk of it not setting up.*

I hope you read through the whole book to get a vision for how these different preservation methods can work together to stock your pantry with food your family will eat. Then, when a vegetable is in season, I hope you reread that vegetable's chapter and make a plan for preserving all of the harvest in a variety of ways. Of course, I hope that some of our favorite preservation recipes become your family favorites, too.

The Recipes

When choosing recipes to put in this book, I wanted to make sure that the recipes are ones that my family eats, are useful and have ingredients that are easy to find.

For a recipe to make the cut, more than half my family needed to love it. However, I did make some exceptions for the pickled and fermented recipes, since I'm surrounded by vinegar haters. But here's the deal: not everyone in your family will love every recipe. That's OK. Use what you know about your family's preferences and start with recipes you think most of your family members will like.

The recipes also had to be useful. I don't want shelves full of ingredients or preserves that are so odd that no one wants to eat them. These recipes fill the real need for feeding my family. For sure, there are some fun preserves that will be eaten as treats, but mostly these are recipes that will help you feed your family on a day-to-day basis.

Lastly, I like to use simple ingredients that are easy to find, and I give preference to those ingredients that I can grow myself. Occasionally, there will be a recipe with a spice such as cardamom in it, but for the most part, all the ingredients can be found in your garden, at the farmers' market or at your local grocery store.

I truly hope you enjoy and have fun with the recipes. I hope that the information in this book inspires you to tweak flavors and experiment with various preservation methods to preserve the harvest to enjoy all year long.

PART 1

preservation methods
The Best Ways to Preserve All the Harvest

Most of us think of canning when we think about preserving the harvest, but there are other ways to preserve food: dehydrating, freezing and fermenting. Many food preservers have one main way they preserve food and are happy putting up food in that one way. I'm not that kind of person or food preserver.

I'm more of an experimenter and generalist, and I like having food preserved in a variety of ways. The only stipulation is that if my family won't eat it, I won't preserve it that way in the future. I can't emphasize this enough: the goal of preserving food is to feed your family.

Definitely experiment with new recipes and different ways of preserving food, but there's no sense in dehydrating 20 pounds (9 kg) of corn if your family doesn't like the texture once it's been rehydrated. My family is pretty good about trying new things and eating what I serve, even if the texture is a little off, so I'm not suggesting that we cater to super-picky eaters. But I am saying that you should try new things in small amounts and then make adjustments based on feedback from your family.

I know food texture is a big deal for a lot of people, and you should be aware that preserved food will always have a different texture from fresh food. Different doesn't mean bad, it just means different. I tell my family when I'm making something with preserved food when the texture will be different from what they're used to. For instance, if I sauté Frozen Summer Garden Mix (page 170) instead of fresh vegetables, I tell them so they can adjust their expectations. I've found that if they don't expect it to taste like fresh sautéed vegetables, they like it. However, if they expect it to taste like fresh, they're often disappointed.

If your family is used to eating store-bought canned and frozen food, it will take some time for them to get used to home-preserved food. Go slowly and be sensitive, but keep moving forward because it's important.

Freshness and Cleanliness

For all preservation methods, it's best to use fresh produce. Most vegetables start to lose nutrients and, often, sugars will convert to starches within hours of the vegetable being picked. If you're preserving vegetables that you're harvesting from your garden, harvest only what you can preserve that day, then harvest more the next day.

Each vegetable in this book has specific information in its chapter on when and how to harvest that vegetable, what to look for if you're buying the vegetable and how to store the vegetable to retain the most nutrients until you can preserve it.

It may seem obvious, but I'll say it anyway: you need to keep a clean kitchen when you're preserving food. All the equipment should be washed before using; as should the countertops. There's no need to use antibacterial soap or to try to sterilize the whole kitchen with bleach or cleaning wipes. Regular old soap works just fine.

canning vegetables to keep a well-stocked pantry

There are two main types of canning: water bath canning and pressure canning. Water bath canning is for high-acid foods that have a pH of 4.6 or lower, and pressure canning is for low-acid foods with a pH higher than 4.6. As a general rule, fruits are considered high-acid foods and vegetables are considered low-acid foods. However, we can safely water bath can some vegetables by adding acid to them and making pickles or jam. While sugar certainly plays a role in the preserving process, it's the addition of an acidic ingredient that makes a vegetable safe for water bath canning. Both water bath canning and pressure canning will be covered later in this chapter.

The canning process was developed in the early 1800s and glass bottles were used initially. Soon, tin cans became the standard, as they are cheaper to make and easier to ship. In the mid-1800s, tinsmith John Landis Mason invented the Mason jar, and canning became something you could do at home. While the basic principles of home canning haven't changed, the safety guidelines have changed over the last 150 years. And, as more research is done, I'm sure there will be changes in the future.

Whenever these changes come, there's usually a big controversy over whether or not they truly need to be followed. After all, no one ever died of eating my Granny's jelly that was sealed with paraffin wax. But that doesn't mean someone couldn't have died or gotten sick, just that they didn't, as far as we know.

By nature, I'm resistant to change. However, I choose to follow new safety guidelines for preserving food when they come out. Rarely do these guidelines create more work, and the risk is just not worth it. I realize that other countries may have different guidelines for food preserving, and if you live in one of those countries, you should follow their recommendations, especially if they are stricter than the ones from the United States Department of Agriculture (USDA). The canning processes and recipes in this book are based on current USDA guidelines for safe home canning.

Pros and Cons of Canning Vegetables

Canning vegetables is the most versatile way to have shelf-stable food. Vegetables can be canned plain or with herbs using a pressure canner, and they can be pickled or made into a jelly or jam and processed in a water bath canner.

Canning food retains most of the food's nutrients, which pretty much stops the food from losing any more nutrients while on the shelf. Contrast this with fresh vegetables, which continue to lose their nutrients even while in cold storage. There's no doubt that eating fresh, just picked vegetables will give you the most nutrients. However, there are studies that suggest that eating vegetables that are canned soon after harvest are just as nutritious as eating fresh vegetables that have been stored for days.[1]

---

1   http://ucce.ucdavis.edu/files/datastore/234-779.pdf

One of the biggest benefits of preserving vegetables by canning is that the food is shelf-stable. As long as the food was properly canned and the jars are sealed, canned goods can last for years.

The downsides of canning are that it does require specialized equipment and the jars take up a lot of space. However, most of the equipment is a onetime purchase, and the jars don't have to be stored in the kitchen if you don't have room there.

Equipment Needed for Canning

In order to preserve food by canning, all you really need are jars, lids and a canner. However, there are additional supplies that are inexpensive and make the process much more enjoyable.

Jars—For canning, you want to be sure to use jars that have been tempered so that they won't break under the high heat of the canning process. Mason jars with two-piece lids—sold under the brand names Ball®, Kerr® and Golden Harvest®—are the standard jars for canning in the US. In Canada, Bernardin® sells Mason jars. In the UK and Europe, Kilner® is a popular Mason jar brand. You can also find Weck® canning jars that are made in Germany and can be ordered online. These are not Mason jars, and, because they aren't widely used in the US, the USDA has no guidelines for using them. If you use Weck jars, you'll need to follow the manufacturer's instructions for properly using them for canning.

Lids—Mason jars have a two-piece lid system; a flat metal circle with a rubber gasket on the underside and a metal band that screws on over the metal lid onto the jar. The round metal lid is a onetime use product, but the bands can be used many times. There are also reusable plastic lids that come with a separate rubber gasket that can be used instead of the metal lid. You'll still use the metal bands with these. I use the reusable plastic lids for most of my canning, and I use the onetime use metal lids for canned goods that I'm giving away.

Canning supplies clockwise: pressure canner, jar lifter, jar funnel, water bath canner, Mason jar with lid and band.

According to the National Center for Home Food Preservation, jars from store-bought products can be safely reused for canning if the two-piece lids will fit on them.

"Most commercial pint- and quart-size mayonnaise or salad dressing jars may be used with new two-piece lids for canning acid foods. However, you should expect more seal failures and jar breakage. These jars have a narrower sealing surface and are tempered less than Mason jars, and may be weakened by repeated contact with metal spoons or knives used in dispensing mayonnaise or salad dressing. Seemingly insignificant scratches in glass may cause cracking and breakage while processing jars in a canner. Mayonnaise-type jars are not recommended for use with foods to be processed in a pressure canner because of excessive jar breakage. Other commercial jars with mouths that cannot be sealed with two-piece canning lids are not recommended for use in canning any food at home."[2]

[2] https://nchfp.uga.edu/how/general/recomm_jars_lids.html

Water Bath Canner—A water bath canner can be any large pot that has a lid and something to keep the glass jars from touching the bottom of the pot. There are some very inexpensive enamel canners that you can buy online or at larger grocery stores. There are also pricier stainless-steel canners and even electric water bath canners. All of these come with a rack to keep the jars from touching the pot. If you don't have one of these but do have a large stockpot with a lid, you can put a kitchen towel in the bottom of the pot to keep the jars from touching the pot. This is messier, but it will work.

Pressure Canner—If you want to can low-acid food, you have to use a pressure canner, which is not the same as a pressure cooker. The lid on a pressure canner locks onto the pot and may have a gasket but most certainly will have a weighted gauge or dial gauge to measure the pressure in the canner. This is the one piece of equipment that I highly recommend you buy new. If you decide to buy a used one, make sure that it has the owner's manual with it. If it has a gasket, make sure you can get a replacement, and, if it has a dial gauge, be sure that you can have it serviced. I have a 21-quart (21-L) All American® 921 pressure canner that doesn't require a gasket and has both the dial and weighted gauge, and I love it. Regardless of which pressure canner you use, you'll need to defer to the owner's manual for proper usage when using the recipes in this book and recipes found elsewhere.

Jar Lifter—A jar lifter is a large pair of tongs that wraps around the jars for lifting them out of the hot water. This is a necessity for water bath canning, since the hot water completely covers the jars. It's also super handy for pressure canning. But, if you don't have a jar lifter, you can use an oven mitt to remove jars from the pressure canner, since the water does not cover the jars.

Jar Funnel—A jar funnel has a wide top opening just like regular funnels, but instead of a tiny bottom opening, it has a bottom opening almost as large as that of a regular-mouth jar. This is great for keeping the mess to a minimum.

Bubble Remover and Headspace Tool—This tool is used to slide between the jar and the food to dislodge any air bubbles trapped in the jar. You can use a thin plastic spatula or wooden spoon, but don't use anything metal or you run the risk of the jar breaking. One end of the tool is stair-stepped and is used to check the headspace. Find the correct headspace notation on the tool, then put that stair-step on the rim of the jar; the contents should just barely touch the tip of the tool. The headspace is the space between the rim of the jar and the food it's containing; this gives the food room to expand when heated. If you don't have a bubble remover and headspace tool, a chopstick and a ruler will work just fine.

Other equipment you'll need for canning you probably already have: sharp knives, cutting boards, a food processor, a mandoline, a ladle, oven mitts and kitchen towels.

How to Store Canned Vegetables

After canning, leave the jars undisturbed until they cool down; at least 12 hours is recommended. When they're completely cool, remove the bands and check to make sure the lids sealed properly. Gently press on the center of the lid. It should not pop or move up and down and the lid should be completely still when you push on it. Now, gently try to remove the lid with your fingers. I do this by simply picking up the jar by the lid. Every once in a while, a lid will come off. The food is still good; the jar just didn't seal properly. Put that jar in the refrigerator to use first.

Wipe the jars with a clean cloth, then wash and dry the bands. The jars can be stored with or without the bands. My preference is to store them without the bands, so I can use the bands for other canning; if you choose to put the bands back on, make sure that they are completely dry or they will corrode on the jars.

Always label the jars with the contents and date before storing. You can write directly on metal lids with a permanent marker, buy cute sticker labels or just use a piece of masking tape. For jars with reusable lids, I use masking tape.

If you have a large pantry, you can store the canned goods in it. However, most of us don't have a pantry that large. If that's your situation, store the canned goods in any cool place, out of direct sunlight. I've stored canned goods in the mudroom, in closets and even under beds. If you aren't able to store the jars on shelves, put them in crates so they are protected. Also, keep a list of what you've stored and where.

How Altitude Changes Things

Canning recipes in the US are developed using processing times that are correct up to 1,000 feet (304 m) above sea level. If you live above 1,000 feet (304 m) sea level, you'll need to adjust each recipe for your altitude.

For water bath canning, you'll need to increase the processing time based on the chart on the next page.

For pressure canning, you don't increase time to adjust for altitude, you increase the pressure. If you're using a dial gauge, you'll increase the pressure by 1 psi (7 kPa) for each 1,000 feet (304 m) above sea level. If you're using a weighted gauge, you'll increase the weight by 5 psi (34 kPa) for elevations higher than 1,000 feet (304 m) above sea level. You can use the chart on page 25 for a quick reference. *However, it's best to check the instructions that came with your pressure canner.*

If you aren't sure if you need to adjust for altitude or have other questions about growing or preserving food, contact your local County Extension Office and ask. Every county in the US has a County Extension Office that works closely with state universities to provide resources, experts and education in agriculture and food safety. This is a free resource whose purpose is to serve the residents of that county, so don't hesitate to reach out and ask questions.

Water Bath Canning Process Step-by-Step

Most people start out their food preservation journey with water bath canning, and for good reasons. It's easy, quick and safe. Water bath canning is for high-acid foods with a natural pH of 4.6 or lower and for foods that have had enough acid added to them to decrease the pH to 4.6 or lower.

Fruits, with the exception of figs, rhubarb and tomatoes, are considered high-acid foods. Fruits can be preserved a number of ways, including jam, jelly, butters, conserves and in a syrup. But this book is about preserving vegetables, not fruit.

Technically a fruit, tomatoes are really in their own category because some tomato varieties have a natural pH of 4.6 or lower, and some have a natural pH higher than 4.6. We use them like a vegetable, so we included them in this book but treat them differently. Tomatoes can be preserved in a water bath canner if adequate citric acid, vinegar or lemon or lime juice is added to the jars. We'll discuss tomatoes and how to handle them in the tomato section (page 269).

Vegetables are low-acid foods, but some of them can be preserved using a water bath canner under two circumstances. The first is adding enough vinegar to pickle them. The second circumstance is that some vegetables can be used like fruit in a jelly or jam if vinegar or lemon or lime juice is added.

We'll talk in general about pickling and jam making in a moment and then go into more depth for each vegetable in its section. But first let's talk about how to prepare the water bath canner, jars and lids for canning.

Water Bath Canning Altitude Chart

Altitude in Feet	Increased Processing Time
0–1,000 (0–304 m)	None
1,001–3,000 (304–914 m)	5 minutes
3,001–6,000 (915–1,829 m)	10 minutes
6,001–8,000 (1,830–2,438 m)	15 minutes
8,001–10,000 (2,439–3,048 m)	20 minutes

Preparing for Water Bath Canning

Before making the pickles or jam, it's best to get all of your supplies ready, including the water bath canner, jars and lids.

Wash the water bath canner, its rack and the lid with hot soapy water and then fill the canner about halfway with clean water. The water needs to be high enough to cover the filled jars by at least 1 inch (2.5 cm). Some of the water will get displaced and the water level will rise once the filled jars are in the pot, so the water doesn't have to be at the right level to begin with. I've found that if I put a water-filled jar, the same size that I'm going to use for canning, in the pot and the water level is about three-quarters of the way up the jar, it will be good once all the filled jars are in the pot. If I need to remove some water because the pot is overflowing when full of filled jars, that's easy to do. If I need to add a little hot water because it's too low, that's easy to do, too.

Put the jar rack in the pot and put the lid on it. Then put the pot on the stove, turn on the heat, and bring the water to a simmer.

TIP: If you have hard water, you can add ½ cup (118 ml) of white distilled vinegar to the canner to keep mineral deposits from forming on the outside of the jars.

Wash the jars in hot, soapy water or a dishwasher. While washing the jars, check the rim and look for any chips or cracks. If the jar has just a small chip, it won't seal properly and shouldn't be used for canning. I keep these jars for storing dry goods or for using in the freezer.

The jars do not have to be sterilized if they will be processed in the water bath canner for at least 10 minutes. They just need to be kept hot. All the recipes in this book are processed for more than 10 minutes, so you will not need to sterilize the jars. If you washed the jars in a dishwasher, leave them in the dishwasher to stay hot until you need them. If you washed them by hand, put them into the water bath canner with the simmering water to keep them hot. I know some people store the jars in the oven at 200°F (93°C) to keep them warm. You can do that, but there is a greater chance of them breaking than if you put them in the water bath.

The lids—both the metal and reusable ones—will also need to be washed in hot, soapy water and rinsed. Years ago, the recommendation was to put the lids in boiling water, but that is no longer the case for most lids. It's best to read and follow the manufacturer's instructions that came with the lids you have.

Wash the bubble remover tool and make sure you have the jar lifter, a ladle and some clean kitchen towels available.

Pickling

There are two ways of pickling food: using a brine solution or a vinegar solution. Both kinds need to be processed in a water bath canner to make the pickles shelf-stable. Brine pickles are fermented pickles that use some vinegar in the brine and get processed in the water bath canner instead of being stored in the refrigerator. Since the good bacteria is killed in the process, I prefer to just make fermented pickles, such as Fermented German Mustard Pickles (page 154), and store them in the refrigerator. We will not be covering canned brine pickles in this book.

To make fresh-packed pickles, we cover vegetables with a hot vinegar solution and process them in a water bath canner. Some vegetables, like cucumbers, will be salted and allowed to sit for 1 to 24 hours to create a brine solution from their own juices. After that, the brine is drained and the vegetables rinsed before packing them into a jar with the vinegar solution.

With fresh-packed pickles, you're not limited to cucumbers. You can pickle almost any vegetable, including corn, as in the Canned Sweet and Zesty Corn Salad (page 138) or broccoli, as with Canned Asian-Style Pickled Broccoli Stems (page 87). Some vegetables can be pickled alone and others, such as zucchini, benefit from being pickled with other vegetables. Pickling is a great way to stock your pantry with relishes, sauces and cold side dishes.

To make vinegar pickles, you need vinegar. The standard pickling vinegars are white vinegar and apple cider vinegar and both have 5 percent acidity. White vinegar is sharp and pungent, while apple cider vinegar has a more mellow acid flavor. However, apple cider vinegar may discolor some vegetables, so if the color is important to you, don't use apple cider vinegar.

But you're not limited to white vinegar and apple cider vinegar. You can use any vinegar that has 5-percent acidity or 5-percent acetic acid. Now, you have to be absolutely sure the vinegar has 5-percent acidity, so homemade apple cider vinegar can't be used for canning. There are some wine vinegars and rice vinegars that have 5-percent acetic acid and can be used for pickling. In the US, vinegar makers are required to list the percentage of acetic acid somewhere on the label. If the label doesn't list 5-percent acidity or 5-percent acetic acid, don't use that vinegar for canning.

If you think the vinegar solution is too sour or pungent, you can mix vinegars, say, half white vinegar and half apple cider, or you can add some sugar. But, do not dilute the vinegar with water or any other liquid that will reduce the acidity level. Diluting the vinegar will compromise the ratio of low-acid to high-acid food that's needed to safely pickle vegetables.

Dry herbs can be adjusted without altering the ratio but fresh herbs cannot (page 309). Feel free to add more, or less, dried dill, celery seed, mustard seed or any other dry herb. But be aware that powdered herbs can make the liquid cloudy; the pickles will be fine to eat, just not as pretty.

If the recipe calls for salt, make sure that you use a salt that does not have any additives or anti-caking agents in it. You can buy canning salt that is just pure salt. You can also use sea salt or any other pure salt. If you use salt with iodine or anti-caking agents, the liquid will get cloudy.

Step 1: Prepare the Vegetables and Pickling Brine

For pickling vegetables, you will wash and prepare the vegetables according to the recipe instructions. In a medium pot, you will mix the vinegar, with any sugar or herbs, and bring the mixture to a boil. At this point, you will pack the vegetables into the prepared jars and then ladle the hot vinegar mixture into the jar OR you will put the vegetables into the hot vinegar mixture and bring it back to a boil. After the mixture boils, you'll pack the vegetables and the hot vinegar mixture into the prepared jars. The recipe will have the instructions for that vegetable; just follow the instructions.

Step 2: Filling the Jars

As you're filling the jars, you need to leave ½ inch (13 mm) of headspace. I like to fill all the jars first and just estimate the headspace, then go back and check each one with the headspace tool. If any jars don't have enough headspace, use a spoon to remove some of the contents. If any jars have too much headspace, add more of the vinegar solution. If all the vegetables and vinegar solution have been used in other jars, simply top off any jars that need it with straight vinegar. Most of the time, it's just a little bit that's needed, but if a jar is really short, I process that jar like it is, then put it in the refrigerator to use first.

Use the bubble remover tool and gently slide it around the inside of the jar. It will dislodge any bubbles trapped in between the vegetables. Recheck the headspace after removing the bubbles.

See step-by-step images on the following pages.

Step 3: Processing the Jars

After the jars are properly filled, wipe the rims with a clean, damp cloth and put the clean lids and bands on the jars. Using the jar lifter, put the jars into the water bath canner, making sure they are covered by at least an inch (2.5 cm) of water, and bring the water to a boil over high heat. Once the water is boiling, set the timer for whatever time the recipe calls for; pickled products are usually processed for 10 to 15 minutes. Be sure to adjust the times for your altitude (page 17), if needed.

Step 4: Testing the Seals

After the jars have been boiling for the correct amount of time, turn off the heat and let the jars rest in the canner for 5 minutes. Use the jar lifter to remove the jars from the water bath canner. I like to have a clean towel laid out on the counter and put the jars on that.

Let the jars cool for at least 12 hours, then check the seals (page 15) and store the jars (page 16).

Pickling Recipes

- Canned Dilly Asparagus (page 68)
- Canned Asian-Style Pickled Broccoli Stems (page 87)
- Canned Sweet and Tangy Slaw (page 99)
- Canned Spicy Cauliflower with Turmeric (page 128)
- Canned Sweet and Zesty Corn Salad (page 138)
- Canned Granny's Bread-and-Butter Pickles (page 151)
- Canned Three Bean Salad (page 165)
- Canned Snap Pea Pickles (page 203)
- Canned Whole Pickled Peppers (page 220)
- Canned Sweet and Spicy Radishes (page 256)
- Canned Squash and Pepper Chutney (page 297)

Jam and Jelly Making

Most jams are made with fruit, but there are a few vegetables that can be used to make jam when adequate acid and sugar is added. Jalapeño jam or jelly is a popular savory jam, but any pepper can be substituted for the jalapeño. I love to make Canned Banana Pepper and Mint Jam (page 217) for those who like the pepper flavor but not the spice of jalapeños. Carrots, beets, zucchini and cucumbers can also be used to make jam or jelly.

The main difference between jelly and jam is that jelly is made with just the juice of the fruit or vegetable and jam is made with the whole fruit or vegetable. The combination of sugar, acid, pectin and heat is what makes them gel.

Carefully fill the jars with vegetables.

Carefully add the liquid to the jars, leaving adequate headspace.

Slide a non-metallic spatula between the jar and vegetables to release air bubbles.

Using a clean, damp cloth, wipe the rims of each jar.

Add lids and metal bands to the jars.

Using a jar lifter, put the jars in the water bath canner. The water should cover the jars by at least 1 inch (2.5 cm).

After the jars are processed and removed from the canner, let them cool for 12 hours. Then gently press down on the lid to check the seal. There should be no movement.

Remove the band and gently pick up the jar by the lid to double check the seal.

In fruit jams, pectin is not essential, as most fruit has some pectin and will eventually gel if cooked long enough. However, Granny was right. Adding pectin speeds up the process. Pectin will need to be added to vegetable jams, since vegetables don't have much, if any, naturally occurring pectin. Pectin will also have to be added to jellies, since the whole fruit isn't used. For simplicity, all the jam and jelly recipes in this book were developed using Ball® Real Fruit Classic Pectin. If you use a different pectin, especially a homemade pectin, you might need to do some adjusting. It's perfectly safe to adjust the amount of pectin, as it's only in the jam to make it gel.

Step 1: Cooking the Jam or Jelly

Whenever you make jam or jelly, you'll add all of the ingredients, except the sugar, to a pot and bring it to a boil. Then, add the sugar, bring the mixture back to a boil, and boil for 1 minute. Remove the pot from the heat and ladle the jam or jelly into prepared jars. The recipe will have the exact instructions, so be sure to follow them.

Step 2: Filling the Jars

As you're filling the jars, you need to leave ¼ inch (6 mm) of headspace for jams and jellies. I like to fill all the jars first and just estimate the headspace, then go back and check each one with the headspace tool. If any jars don't have enough headspace, use a spoon to remove some of the jam. If any jars have too much headspace, add more jam, if there is some available. If there isn't enough jam to properly fill the last jar, put a lid on the jar and put it in the refrigerator to use first.

Step 3: Processing the Jars

After the jars are filled, wipe the rims with a clean, damp cloth and put the clean lids and bands on the jars. Using the jar lifter, put the jars into the water bath canner, make sure they are covered by at least an inch (2.5 cm) of water and bring the water to a boil. Once the water is boiling, set the timer for whatever time the recipe calls for; most jams and jellies are processed for 10 minutes. Remember to adjust for your altitude (page 17), if necessary.

Step 4: Testing the Seals

After the jars have been boiling for the correct amount of time, turn the heat off and let the jars rest in the canner for 5 minutes. Use the jar lifter to remove the jars from the water bath canner and put them on a towel on the counter.

You'll let the jars cool for at least 12 hours, then check the seals (page 15) and store the jars (page 16).

Jam and Jelly Recipes

- Canned Beet and Orange Marmalade (page 79)
- Canned Carrot-Jalapeño Jam (page 111)
- Canned Spicy Corn Cob Jelly (page 142)
- Canned Cucumber-Jalapeño Jam (page 156)
- Canned Banana Pepper and Mint Jam (page 217)

Other Water Bath Canned Recipes

- Canned Caramelized Maple Onions (page 192)
- Canned Hot Pepper Sauce (page 218)
- Canned Whole Pickled Peppers (page 220)
- Canned Marinara (page 277)
- Canned Mexican Salsa (page 278)
- Canned Rosemary-Squash Glaze (page 304)

Pressure Canning Process Step-by-Step

For years, I wanted a pressure canner. Then, when I got one, I was terrified to use it. It sat in my pantry for almost a year before I had the guts to try it. I read the instruction book several times and then decided the only way to learn how to use a pressure canner was to use it.

That first go-around was a little nerve-racking, and I held on to that instruction book reading the instructions over and over the whole time. My husband and children took turns poking their heads in the kitchen asking if it was "supposed to make that noise." Why yes, it *is* supposed to make that noise. And it's a good thing: it's how the excess pressure escapes.

The next time I used the pressure canner, I didn't need to hold the instruction book like a security blanket and read the instructions over and over. And my family felt like they could safely come into the kitchen and not just pop their heads in.

Now, the pressure canner is just another appliance that I use to stock my pantry with home-preserved food; it's no longer scary for me or my family. I still use the instruction book. After all, there's no way I could remember all the processing times for every food. But, I no longer have to re-read the instructions like a crazy woman.

For me, the beauty of pressure canning is being able to preserve low-acid food in a way that doesn't have vinegar or sugar in it. Most foods preserved in the water bath canner are for snacking or eating with crackers or bread. But with a pressure canner, you can preserve a side dish, a main dish or a whole meal in a jar!

Preparing for Pressure Canning

Preparing the supplies for pressure canning is almost identical to preparing them for water bath canning. The only difference is preparing the canner.

Because there are several different kinds of pressure canners, it's important that you read the instructions that came with your pressure canner. If you don't have them, look online or contact the manufacturer and ask them to email them to you.

Wash the pressure canner and its rack with soap and water, then put the bottom rack in it. Fill the canner with the amount of water the manufacturer recommends, and put the canner on the stove to heat up. The jars going into the canner will be hot, even if they've been raw packed (see page 24) . The water in the canner needs to be 140°F (60°C) to 180°F (82°C) before you can put the jars in the canner.

Wash the jars, lids and bands in hot, soapy water and rinse them. The jars need to stay hot, but don't need to be sterilized (page 17). The lids probably don't need to be heated, but check the instructions that came with them.

Wash and rinse the bubble remover tool and have the jar lifter, oven mitts and clean kitchen towels available.

Pressure Canning Vegetables

Most pressure canners will hold seven 1-quart (1-L) jars or nine 1-pint (500-ml) jars in each batch. While you don't have to make a full batch each time you use the canner, you do have to have the equivalent of two filled quarts (2 L) in order to safely use a pressure canner. If you're canning pints (500 ml), you need four filled pints (2 L).

Step 1: Prepare the Vegetables

All the vegetables will need to be washed and cut according to the recipe instructions. The root vegetables need to be peeled before pressure canning; this includes potatoes (page 226).

I like to keep a large teakettle of water simmering on the stove when I use the pressure canner; this water will be used to fill jars as needed. If you don't have a teakettle, put a stockpot of water on to boil. If the recipe calls for broth instead of water, put that on to boil, too.

Step 2: Pack the Jars

When the vegetables and the liquid are ready, it's time to pack them into the jars, using the hot-pack or raw-pack method.

Hot-Pack Method—When a recipe calls for packing the jars, you will add the prepared vegetables to the broth/water, bring them to a boil and then simmer. The recipe will tell you how long they need to simmer. The hot vegetables and liquid will then be put into the jars, leaving 1 inch (2.5 cm) of headspace. I like to put the solids into the jars first, then add the liquid, so that each jar has about the same amount of solids. Using the bubble remover, remove the bubbles and then check the headspace. Remove or add liquid to the jars as needed to get the proper headspace. If you've run out of the liquid you've prepared, use the water in the teakettle to top off the jars.

Raw-Pack Method—When the recipe calls for raw-packing jars, you'll put the prepared vegetables into the hot jars and then pour the hot liquid into each jar, leaving 1 inch (2.5 cm) of headspace. Use the bubble remover to remove any bubbles and check the headspace. There will be more bubbles that need to be removed when raw-packing than when hot-packing, so take a little more time with it. You'll notice that the vegetables will start to settle some and, if you have more prepared vegetables, you can add them to the jars. Add or remove liquid from each jar until you have the proper headspace.

Step 3: Processing the Jars

Once the jars are packed and have the proper headspace, wipe the rims with a clean cloth and put the lids and bands on the jars. Put the jars into the prepared pressure canner, and put the lid on the canner, following the manufacturer's instructions.

When the lid is securely on the canner, turn the heat up to high. Leave the vent port uncovered; if you have an older model, you might need to manually open the petcock, the valve that vents the canner. After a few minutes, you'll notice that steam is coming out of the vent on the canner. This is called *venting*. In order to properly pressurize the canner, you need to let it vent for 10 minutes. So, set a timer and tell your family not to worry. After 10 minutes,

Using a jar lifter, put jars into the pressure canner. The water will not cover the jars as it does in the water bath canner.

place the counterweight or weighted gauge over the vent port to pressurize the canner; if you have an older model, close the petcock.

You'll need to check the recipe to see what pressure is needed; most vegetable recipes are canned at 10 psi (69 kPa) up to 1,000 feet (304 m) above sea level in a weighted-gauge canner and 11 psi (76 kPa) for up to 1,000 feet (304 m) in a dial-gauge canner. Check the manufacturer's instructions for adjusting for altitude (page 25), if needed.

If you have a weighted-gauge model, the gauge will begin to jiggle and you'll know that it's reached the correct pressure. The beauty of a weighted-gauge canner is that you can now set a timer for the correct processing time and you don't have to keep watching the canner. As long as the weight is jiggling, it's at the correct pressure. You probably won't need to leave the heat on high; I can turn the burner on our stove to medium and it will still hold pressure. If you turn the heat down, make sure the weight still jiggles. The downside of the weighed-gauge model is that it can't precisely correct for higher altitudes; instead of 1 psi (7 kPa) increments, you'll adjust in 5 psi (34 kPa) increments.

Pressure Canning Altitude Chart

Altitude in Feet	Weighted Gauge	Dial Gauge
0–1,000 (0–304 m)	10	11
1,001–2,000 (305–609 m)	15	11
2,001–4,000 (610–1,219 m)	15	12
4,001–6,000 (1,220–1,829 m)	15	13
6,001–8,000 (1,830–2,438 m)	15	14
8,001–10,000 (2,439–3,048 m)	15	15

If you have a dial gauge canner, you'll need to watch the dial gauge and adjust the heat until the gauge stays at the correct pressure. It's OK if the pressure is a little high, but it's not OK for it to be even 1 psi (7 kPa) low. When the canner is maintaining the correct pressure, set the timer for the correct processing time. The downside of the dial gauge model is that it takes more babysitting than the weighted gauge canners.

Regardless of the type of canner you have, if the pressure drops below what it's supposed to be, you will need to adjust the heat and bring the pressure back up. Then you will have to reset the timer for the full amount of time again. This will probably overcook the vegetables, but it's what needs to be done to ensure that the food was properly heated throughout.

Step 4: Opening the Pressure Canner

When the timer goes off and the processing is finished, turn the heat off and let the canner depressurize slowly. This will take 30 to 60 minutes; refer to the manufacturer's instructions for a more accurate time for your canner. Do not try to force-cool the canner. Don't cool it by running cold water over it or by opening the vent port before it's fully depressurized. This can damage the canner and compromise the safety of the food.

After the canner has depressurized, remove the weight from the vent or open the petcock. Let the canner sit for 10 minutes before you remove the lid. When you do remove the lid, lift it away from you, so the steam does not get in your face. I let the jars rest for another 5 minutes before I remove them from the canner. Using the jar lifter, remove the jars from the canner and put them on a towel with at least 1-inch (2.5-cm) spaces between them. Let the jars cool for 12 to 24 hours, then check the seals (page 15) and store them (page 16).

Pressure Canned Recipes

- Canned Asparagus Soup (page 63)
- Canned Spice Carrot Soup (page 112)
- Canned Corn Chowder (page 137)
- Canned Lemon-Garlic Green Beans (page 169)
- Canned Kale with Lemon (page 182)
- Canned Peas and Carrots (page 204)
- Canned Potato Soup (page 229)
- Canned Potatoes with Herbs (page 231)
- Canned Butternut Squash Soup (page 240)
- Canned Sweet Potatoes in Spiced Syrup (page 268)
- Canned Tomatoes, Onions and Garlic (page 275)
- Canned Tomato-Basil Soup (page 282)

Filling the Pressure Canner

I mentioned earlier that it's not necessary to have a full canner to safely use a pressure canner: you need only the equivalent of two filled 1-quart (1-L) jars in the canner. However, it's more energy efficient to run the canner when it's full instead of half full.

This chart will help you know how much of each vegetable you need to start with to end up with nine pints (500 ml) or seven quarts (1 L) filled. The weight recommendation is before the vegetables have been peeled, so if you're buying produce, this is how much you need to buy.

You can also use this chart to help you pressure can jars of different vegetables in the same load. As long as the processing time is the same, it doesn't matter what vegetable is in the jar or what size the jars are.

The processing times are for weighted-gauge pressure canners at 10 psi (69 kPa) and dial-gauge pressure canners at 11 psi (76 kPa) for up to 1,000 feet (304 m) above sea level. You will need to adjust the times and/or pressure for your altitude according to the instructions that came with your pressure canner.

While most vegetables can be preserved in the pressure canner, it's not recommended for broccoli, cabbage, cauliflower, cucumbers, onions, radishes and summer squash, as they cannot withstand the pressure canning process and will turn to mush.

Pressure Canning Vegetable Amounts and Processing Times

Vegetable	Amount for 9 pints (500 ml)	Amount for 7 quarts (1 L)	Processing time for pints (500 ml)	Processing time for quarts (1 L)
Asparagus	16 pounds (7.25 kg)	25 pounds (11.34 kg)	30 minutes	40 minutes
Beans	9 pounds (4 kg)	14 pounds (6.4 kg)	20 minutes	25 minutes
Beetroots—without tops	14 pounds (6.4 kg)	21 pounds (9.5 kg)	30 minutes	35 minutes
Broccoli—not recommended	N/A	N/A	N/A	N/A
Cabbage—not recommended	N/A	N/A	N/A	N/A
Carrots—without tops	11 pounds (5 kg)	18 pounds (8.2 kg)	25 minutes	30 minutes

Pressure Canning Vegetable Amounts and Processing Times (continued)

Vegetable	Amount for 9 pints (500 ml)	Amount for 7 quarts (1 L)	Processing time for pints (500 ml)	Processing time for quarts (1 L)
Cauliflower—not recommended	N/A	N/A	N/A	N/A
Corn—whole kernel	20 pounds (9.1 kg)	32 pounds (14.5 kg)	55 minutes	85 minutes
Corn—cream style	20 pounds (9.1 kg)	Not recommended	85 minutes	N/A
Cucumbers—not recommended	N/A	N/A	N/A	N/A
Kale and other greens	18 pounds (8.2 kg)	28 pounds (12.7 kg)	70 minutes	90 minutes
Onions—not recommended	N/A	N/A	N/A	N/A
Peas—shelled English or green	20 pounds (9.1 kg) (in pods)	32 pounds (14.5 kg) (in pods)	40 minutes	40 minutes
Peppers	9 pounds (4 kg)	Not recommended	35 minutes	N/A
Potatoes	13 pounds (5.9 kg)	20 pounds (9.1 kg)	35 minutes	40 minutes
Radish—not recommended	N/A	N/A	N/A	N/A
Summer Squash—not recommended	N/A	N/A	N/A	N/A
Winter Squash (including pumpkins)	10 pounds (4.5 kg)	16 pounds (7.25 kg)	55 minutes	90 minutes
Sweet Potatoes	11 pounds (5 kg)	17½ pounds (7.9 kg)	65 minutes	90 minutes
Tomatoes—crushed, no added liquid	14 pounds (6.4 kg)	22 pounds (10 kg)	15 minutes	15 minutes
Tomatoes—whole or halved; packed in water	13 pounds (5.9 kg)	21 pounds (9.5 kg)	10 minutes	10 minutes
Tomatoes—whole or halved; packed without added liquid	13 pounds (5.9 kg)	21 pounds (9.5 kg)	25 minutes	25 minutes

freezing vegetables for maximum freshness

Chances are you're already familiar with freezing food and have the most important piece of equipment: a freezer. Most of us regularly use our freezer as short-term storage for meat, fruits, vegetables and prepared foods. The freezer is also a great place to store vegetables for long-term storage and create a second "pantry" full of home-preserved food.

When most of us think of freezing vegetables, we think of the freezer aisle in the local grocery store. And, while we can freeze bags and bags of plain veggies to use as ingredients, we can also freeze the vegetables as prepared foods that are complete as they are. This is my favorite way to use the freezer.

Pros and Cons of Freezing Vegetables

Of all the preserving methods, freezing retains the color of the vegetables best. The texture will be different from that of the raw vegetable, but the texture is different for all of the preservation methods. Because we use our freezers daily and are comfortable with them, freezing vegetables is an easy starting point for someone who wants to learn more about preserving food.

The main drawbacks to freezing food are that you're limited by how much freezer space you have and the food is not shelf-stable. If you have a prolonged power outage, you can lose all the food you worked so hard to preserve. We've had this happen only once, in 2017 when Hurricane Harvey hit, and we were without power for 8 days. Fortunately, our insurance company was great and covered the replacement cost of the food, including the homegrown vegetables that filled the freezer. That was the first time I had calculated how much it would cost to purchase all the vegetables and vegetable products we freeze each summer. The amount for just the home-preserved foods was more than $1,000.

Choosing a Second Freezer

At some point, you'll probably want more room than the freezer part of your refrigerator provides. If you're also fermenting food, then you might want to get a second refrigerator/freezer before buying a stand-alone freezer. There's no need to spend a lot of money on a second refrigerator/freezer. You can find good used ones for a fraction of the cost of a new one. Since this refrigerator will likely be in the garage or mudroom, it doesn't need to look good. It just needs to keep food cold or frozen.

When you're ready for a stand-alone freezer, you have two main choices: an upright freezer or a chest freezer. There are positives and negatives to each one; the best one will be the one that fits in the space available and is within your budget.

An upright freezer is easier to organize than a chest freezer. You don't have to dig around as much for items and it's harder for food to get lost at the bottom of the freezer. Food can still get lost; it's just easier to prevent it. Also, upright freezers defrost themselves. Chest freezers need to be defrosted at least once a year, because ice crystals form on the sides.

However, an upright freezer is more expensive to buy, uses more electricity and the door is more likely to accidentally be left open, although many newer models have alarms if the door is open too long.

With chest freezers, you get more freezer space for your money and they're less expensive to run than upright freezers. If you happen to overpack the freezer, the lid may not shut all the way. Although the food probably won't melt if the lid is cracked open, ice crystals will form in the freezer and on the food.

I've always had chest freezers simply because they're less expensive than uprights. When we bought our current chest freezer, I bought the largest one that was made at that time. I have a large area in our garage where it fits in perfectly. It has dividers and baskets, and I love it.

However, it's not what I would buy again or suggest for others to buy. For the same amount of money, I could have purchased two medium chest freezers that would have fit in that same space. There are several months out of the year when my large freezer is filled to the brim. But there are just as many months when it's only half-full. Having two smaller freezers would allow me to unplug one in the lean months and not pay to keep empty space cold.

Managing the Freezer

If you're not careful, the freezer can get unruly, just like the pantry can. A lot of people use a freezer inventory to keep track of what's in their freezer. This is a really good idea. I'm not disciplined enough to keep track of an inventory, but that doesn't mean I don't have a system. If a written inventory works for you, that's great, but if not, you need to figure out something that will. I'll describe what works for me.

I like to freeze vegetables in ways that are similar to how I'll serve them. For instance, instead of freezing a bunch of bags of sweet potato chunks, I like to freeze them par cooked and wrapped in foil (page 261) for

baking or as pecan-encrusted Frozen Sweet Potato Balls (page 265).

Whenever you put food in the freezer, make sure it's not hot. If I'm freezing something I cooked, like Frozen Summer Squash Soup (page 301), I always cool it off in the refrigerator before I put it in the freezer. Believe it or not, it's possible to thaw out frozen food by putting too much hot food in the freezer at once.

If you're using freezer bags, lay them flat for freezing. Once they're frozen, they can be stored upright, if necessary. This will make organizing them so much easier and save a lot of freezer space. You can corral the bags using cardboard boxes or plastic storage containers. If you use plastic, be aware that it can become very brittle from the extreme temperature in the freezer and will eventually break. You can buy plastic containers made specifically for the freezer, but they are quite expensive.

Whenever you put something in the freezer, make sure it's labeled with what it is, when it was frozen and how much is in the container. This is important for both solids and liquids; I know you think you'll remember all these details but, take it from me, you probably won't.

Also, put like items together. If you have ten bags of Frozen Snap Beans and Tomatoes (page 171), then put them all in one spot.

The most important thing I do to manage my freezer is to completely clean it out twice a year. I do this in the early spring, before we start the bulk of our freezer-preserving, and again in the early fall, when most of the freezer-preserving is finished. This only takes about an hour, and it will keep you from losing food in the freezer.

First, take everything out of the freezer and put it in ice chests or freezer shopping bags. If you have a chest freezer, unplug it and defrost it. To speed things along, use a windshield ice scraper to scrape

To easily fill a freezer bag, put it in a wide-mouth Mason jar and turn the top down.

To remove the air from the bag, gently press on the bag while closing it.

any ice buildup from the sides, and let the ice fall to the bottom of the freezer. When the sides are scraped, use a clean dustpan to scoop out all the ice in the bottom of the freezer. Then, wipe all of the freezer surfaces with a towel.

Once it's clean, you can put everything back into the freezer in an organized way. I make sure to put the older items on top and the fresher items on the bottom. I also keep a basket in my freezer for things that I just need to use and probably won't if I don't have a plan. This might be the last bag of Frozen Breaded Squash Fries (page 298), with only a few fries in it, or a bag with two slices of Frozen Breaded Green Tomatoes (page 283). Neither of these are enough for a meal, but both would be great for a "buffet" leftover dinner night.

The most important thing about managing your freezer is to not toss items in it and forget about them. The second most important thing: freeze only what you'll use in a year. Don't freeze 50 bags of green beans if your family doesn't like frozen green beans or if 20 bags is all you need for the year.

Freezer-Safe Containers

In order to safely freeze food, you need freezer-safe containers, which are especially important for long-term storage. The containers need to be moisture-resistant, leakproof, durable and easy to seal. Some good choices are Mason jars, plastic freezer bags, vacuum-sealed bags and freezer paper.

Mason jars, such as the wide-mouth pint-size (500-ml) jars that have straight sides are ideal for using in the freezer. You can also use Mason jars that have shoulders, but you'll need to leave more headspace. I especially love using the 4-ounce (125-ml) and half-pint (250-ml) Mason jars for things like pesto, dipping sauces and hot pepper paste.

To safely freeze in glass, be sure to leave at least 1 inch (2.5 cm) of headspace; if you're using a jar with a shoulder, fill it only three-quarters of the way up. Put the filled jar in the refrigerator overnight to cool. In the morning, loosen the lid and put the jar in the freezer. I like to just barely have the lid on the jars until the contents are frozen. When the contents are frozen, put the lid on properly. I've had very few broken jars using this method.

Plastic freezer bags are an inexpensive way to freeze vegetables. A good thing about using freezer bags is that you can open them and get out just what you want and leave the rest in the bag. Just be aware that opening the bag over and over will cause ice crystals to form on the food. Because of this, I like to use smaller bags for things that I'm not going to use all at once, such as Frozen Hash Brown Patties (page 234). It's fine to open the bags once or twice, but not a dozen times.

When you use zippered bags, it's important to get as much air out of the bag as possible. To get almost all the air out, insert a straw into the bag and zip the bag closed around the straw. Suck the air out of the bag through the straw and then, very quickly, remove the straw and close the last bit of the bag.

I also have a vacuum sealer that I like to use for foods that aren't liquid. One of the great things about these bags is that you can buy the plastic on a roll and make your own size bags. This allows you to freeze in amounts that are good serving sizes for your family, instead of feeling like you need to fill bags full. The plastic on a roll is more expensive than the regular freezer bags, so I only use it for long-term storage.

I like to freeze some things overnight on a baking sheet that's lined with parchment paper, then transfer these items to freezer bags or vacuum-sealed bags. This allows the items to freeze more quickly than if they were stacked in bags, and it keeps the items from sticking to each other inside the bag. If I don't think we'll be using those items within a month, I put them in vacuum-sealed bags. This is just a personal preference, but I think the vacuum-sealed bags keep the food fresher than zippered freezer bags do.

Freezer paper is another option, a good one for those trying to reduce their plastic usage. Freezer paper is great for meats, but is a little trickier for vegetables, because it's hard to get all the air out that is trapped between the vegetable pieces. You'll need to wrap the paper snuggly around the vegetables and try not to leave any air pockets. If you use freezer paper, you also need to use freezer tape, which looks like masking tape but isn't. Freezer tape is formulated to adhere at colder temperatures; if you use masking tape, you run the risk of the seal failing.

Everything that goes into your freezer needs to be labeled with what it is, how much is in the container and the date it was frozen. I promise you, it will all start to look the same once it's frozen. You can use freezer tape and a marker, or buy labels that are specifically made for labeling freezer items.

Other equipment you might need includes basic kitchen items, such as sharp knives, cutting boards, a blender and a food processor.

To Blanch or Not to Blanch?

Blanching is needed to prepare most vegetables for freezing. However, I don't blanch every vegetable for which it is recommended. This is a personal choice based on my experience of freezing the vegetable blanched and unblanched, then using it in a meal. If my family prefers the blanched version, then I continue to blanch that vegetable before freezing it. If they can't tell the difference or prefer the unblanched version, then I will probably stop blanching the vegetable.

The purpose of blanching is to inactivate enzymes that can cause loss of flavor, color and texture; the loss can occur in as little as 4 weeks. If you decide not to blanch a vegetable, make sure you test it after it has been in the freezer for at least 4 weeks. At that point, how you feel about the quality of the vegetable when you eat it should make your final decision about not blanching that vegetable in the future.

To blanch: Boil the vegetables for the recommended time.

Using a large slotted spoon, transfer the vegetables from the boiling water to the ice bath.

Patting the vegetables dry will help keep ice crystals from forming.

Before blanching vegetables, you'll want to wash, peel and chop them, if needed. Fill a stockpot about halfway with water and, if you wish, add ¼ teaspoon of citric acid to prevent the vegetables from discoloring. As a guideline, you need 1 gallon (4 L) of water per pound (453 g) of prepared vegetables. If you're blanching more than 1 pound (453 g) of vegetables, you'll need to do it in batches. You can reuse the water.

Fill a large bowl about halfway with ice and add some water to prepare the ice bath you will use to stop the cooking process.

Bring the water in the stockpot to a rolling boil. If your stockpot has a blanching basket, put the vegetables in the basket and then lower it into the boiling water. If you don't have a blanching basket, just put the vegetables in the boiling water and use a large slotted spoon to remove them when they're done blanching.

When you put the vegetables into the water, the temperature will drop and the boiling will slow down; it should return to a full rolling boil within 1 minute of putting the vegetables in the water. If it doesn't, you used too many vegetables for the amount of water in the pot. Once the water starts boiling again, put the lid on the pot and set a timer for the recommended blanching time for that vegetable.

When the time is up, remove the vegetables from the boiling water, and put them in the bowl of ice water to stop the cooking process. The water needs to stay cool, about 60°F (16°C) or less. The vegetables should cool off in about the same amount of time as their blanching time.

If you want to retain more nutrients, you can use a steam blancher. If you don't own one, make a mock steam blancher by setting a colander inside a deep pot. You need enough room to have about 2 inches (5 cm) of water in the pot that is not touching the colander. Steam blanching takes about 50 percent longer than water blanching and you'll need to use smaller amounts per batch. As a general rule, multiply the blanching time by 1.5 to calculate a time for steam blanching. For these reasons, I recommend water blanching.

Blanching Times for Vegetables for the Freezer

Here is a list of vegetables and their blanching time for freezing. There are a few vegetables that don't need to be blanched before freezing and a few that need to be fully cooked before freezing. The vegetables that don't need to be blanched are cucumbers, diced or sliced onions, peppers and tomatoes. The vegetables that need to be fully cooked are beets, winter squash and sweet potatoes.

It's super important to blanch vegetables for the full recommended time. Under-blanched vegetables will be tougher than vegetables not blanched at all. It's better to over-blanch than under-blanch, so if you forget to set a timer, estimate the time left on the high side, or just start timing from the beginning.

Vegetable	Size	Blanching Time (minutes)*
Asparagus	Small Stalk	2
	Medium Stalk	3
	Large Stalk	4
Beans: Snap, Green or Wax	—	3
Beans: Fresh Lima, Butter or Pinto	Small	2
	Medium	3
	Large	4
Beets	—	Cook
Broccoli	Florets (1½ inches [3.8 cm] across)	3
Brussels Sprouts	Small Heads	3
	Medium Heads	4
	Large Heads	5
Cabbage or Chinese Cabbage (shredded)	—	1½
Carrots	Small	5
	Diced, Sliced or Lengthwise Strips	2
Cauliflower	Florets (1 inch [2.5 cm] across)	3
Corn	Corn-on-the-cob: Small Ears (ears blanched before cutting corn from cob)	7
	Corn-on-the-cob: Medium Ears (ears blanched before cutting corn from cob)	9

Vegetable	Size	Blanching Time (minutes)*
Corn (continued)	Corn-on-the-cob: Large Ears (ears blanched before cutting corn from cob)	11
	Whole Kernel or Cream Style	4
Cucumbers	—	None
Greens	Collards	3
	All Other	2
Onions	Small (whole: blanch until center is heated, page 188)	3
	Medium (whole: blanch until center is heated, page 188)	5
	Large (whole: blanch until center is heated, page 188)	7
	Rings	10–15 seconds
	Diced or Thinly Sliced	None
Peas: Edible Pod	—	1½–3
Peas: Field (fresh blackeye)	—	2
Peas: Green	—	1½
Peppers: Hot	—	None
Peppers: Sweet (optional)	Halves	3
	Strips or Rings	2
Potatoes: Irish (new)	—	3–5
Radish (thin slices)	—	2–3
Squash: Summer	—	3
Squash: Winter (including pumpkin)	—	Cook
Sweet Potatoes	—	Cook
Tomato	—	None

*At 5,000 feet (1,524 m) elevation or higher, heat 1 minute longer than the blanching times given, which are for sea level.

Preventing Spoilage

There are two main reasons that food goes bad in the freezer. One is because the enzymes continue to be active, even while the food is frozen, and they can cause an "off" color and flavor. Blanching inactivates the enzymes to take care of this issue. The second reason for spoilage is improper packaging that can lead to freezer burn, the formation of ice crystals and oxidation. All of these issues can be addressed by leaving only the amount of headspace needed for expansion when using glass jars, removing all the air from freezer bags and making sure that, if you're using freezer paper, the paper is snug up against the food.

How to Thaw Frozen Vegetables

When you thaw frozen vegetables, thaw only what you need for that day. Frozen and then thawed vegetables will spoil faster than freshly cooked vegetables, so plan on not having any leftovers. You can thaw vegetables in the refrigerator, at room temperature, in cold water or in the microwave.

To thaw vegetables in the refrigerator, transfer the frozen vegetables to the refrigerator and put a plate or bowl under them. The plate or bowl will catch any liquid if the bag happens to have a small hole.

Frozen vegetables can be left out at room temperature for up to 2 hours to thaw. Put a plate or bowl under the vegetables to catch any liquid or condensation. If you're not ready to use the vegetables when the 2 hours are up, put them in the refrigerator until they're needed.

Putting frozen food in a sink or bowl of cold water is another acceptable way to thaw food. The water needs to be cold, not hot, for this to be a safe method. I usually use this method only for glass containers. Sometimes freezer bags will get small holes in them in the freezer and you won't notice until the bag starts filling up with water.

If you have a microwave, you can use the defrost mode to thaw frozen vegetables. It's important to use the defrost mode and not just hit minute plus, especially if you are thawing out something in a glass container. I've never had a glass container break in the microwave, but if it gets hot too fast, the glass can break.

Frozen vegetables can also be added to casseroles or soups, or even just a skillet with some oil in it, and they will thaw while cooking, just like store-bought frozen vegetables do.

Freezer Recipes

- Frozen Bacon-Wrapped Asparagus Spears (page 64)
- Frozen Roasted Chipotle–Asparagus Pesto (page 67)
- Frozen Beet and Horseradish Sauce (page 76)
- Frozen Creamy Broccoli Dip (page 89)
- Frozen Cabbage Rolls (page 103)
- Frozen Carrot Top Pesto (page 115)
- Frozen Ginger Cauliflower Rice (page 127)
- Frozen Creamed Corn (page 141)
- Frozen Cucumber Tzatziki (page 158)
- Frozen Summer Garden Mix (page 170)
- Frozen Snap Beans and Tomatoes (page 171)
- Frozen Creamy Spinach Rice (page 181)
- Frozen Spicy Fajita Veggie Mix (page 194)
- Frozen Pea Pod Soup Concentrate (page 205)
- Frozen Harissa Paste (page 215)
- Frozen Hash Brown Patties (page 234)
- Frozen Winter Squash Butter (page 243)
- Frozen Spaghetti Squash with Pesto (page 245)
- Frozen Radish Top Pesto (page 253)
- Frozen Sweet Potato Balls (page 265)
- Frozen Breaded Green Tomatoes (page 283)
- Frozen Roasted Tomatoes and Herb Sauce (page 287)
- Frozen Breaded Squash Fries (page 298)
- Frozen Summer Squash Soup (page 301)

dehydrating vegetables for long-term storage

Long before refrigeration—or even canning—was a thing, people preserved food by dehydrating it. Those before us knew that if they could get all the moisture out of the vegetables, they could be stored much longer. There was no special equipment needed, just a large piece of cloth on which to lay the cut vegetables, and the sun.

For dehydrated food to be shelf-stable, it needs to have 80 to 90 percent of its moisture removed. This will inhibit bacteria from growing. This can still be done by laying food out in sun, or you can use more modern equipment, such as an oven, electric dehydrator or solar dehydrator.

Pros and Cons of Dehydrating Vegetables

Over the years, dehydrating food has lost some of its popularity to canning and freezing, but it's making a comeback as people realize the benefits of preserving food by dehydration. Dehydrating is a great way for a gardener to preserve a lot of produce in a little bit of space. It's also a great way for hikers, bikers and campers to carry lightweight, nutrient-dense food with them. And it's an easy way for the home cook to not waste bits and pieces of leftovers.

There are many reasons I choose to dehydrate vegetables instead of preserving them by canning, fermenting or freezing. But the main reason is that I like to have a variety of shelf-stable vegetables available and some vegetables turn to mush when canned: *Zucchini, I'm looking at you.*

Dehydrated food retains more of its nutrients than canned or frozen food does, even if the vegetable needs to be blanched before dehydrating.

Dehydrated food also takes up much less space than hydrated food. It's amazing to me that 20 pounds (9.1 kg) of fresh summer squash can be stored in just a couple of Mason jars, since it dehydrates down to about 2 pounds (907 g).

Dehydrated vegetables can be added directly to soups and will rehydrate while cooking. But they can also be rehydrated in water and then cooked just like you would cook fresh vegetables. A fun way to use dehydrated vegetables is to grind them into a powder, using a blender, and add the powder to other dishes you're making, such as eggs, rice, casseroles and even smoothies.

You can also make shelf-stable snacks in the dehydrator. You can make zucchini chips, like the Dried Squash Fruit Chews (page 295), and carrot ribbons (page 118) for a healthier alternative than potato chips to serve with dip. Pumpkin puree can be dehydrated into a fruit leather (page 242) that you can pack in your family's lunches or backpacks. Seasoned green beans (page 172) and snap peas (page 201) can be dehydrated and eaten as a guilt-free "I-have-the-munchies" snack.

Types of Dehydrators

Using the Sun

If you live in a climate that isn't humid, you might just choose to dehydrate your vegetables outside in the sun. To keep critters out of your food, I suggest building a structure that is enclosed but allows the sun and wind to penetrate. Sometimes, if I have a lot of greens to dehydrate, I'll spread a couple of sheets on the trampoline and lay out the leaves for several hours to let them dry. This works great for things that dehydrate quickly, such as leaves and herbs.

Dehydrating in the Oven

To dehydrate in an oven, you'll want to keep the oven on its lowest setting, preferably no higher than 140°F (60°C). You might need to keep the door ajar if your oven won't go that low. If you have a gas oven with a pilot light that always keeps the oven warm, you might not even need to turn on the oven.

Electric Dehydrators

The easiest way to dehydrate food is with an electric dehydrator. Because electric dehydrators are equipped with a fan, you'll get more consistent results using them than you will using an oven or the sun.

Electric dehydrators come in two basic forms: round with stackable trays and a square box with removable trays. Both are good, and each has its benefits and challenges.

The round dehydrators with stackable trays are less expensive. You can usually find a new one with a temperature dial for about $80. The ones without a temperature dial usually sell for about $40. I have both, and I find that I really like to be able to adjust the temperature, especially when dehydrating herbs (page 307).

A dehydrator, which can come in various shapes, sizes and prices, is the only specialty equipment needed for dehydrating.

Lower temperatures, 95°F (35°C), are used for foods such as aromatic herbs and spices, so they don't lose their flavor. Most fruits are dried at 110 to 115°F (43 to 46°C), which allows them to dehydrate slowly. Fruits dehydrated at higher temperatures can experience "case hardening," which is when the outside of the fruit is too dry for the interior moisture to evaporate. Most vegetables are dehydrated at 125 to 135°F (52 to 57°C), since they are usually sliced thin and don't have a high moisture content.

Another benefit of round dehydrators is that you can add or remove trays, depending on how many you need. If you buy one with only four trays, you can later order additional trays if you find you use more than four trays at a time.

Because the fan and heat are coming from either the base or the top, you may have to rotate your full trays so that the food dehydrates evenly. The food on the trays closest to the fan and heat will dehydrate faster than the food on the trays farther away from the fan.

Because the trays are round, you might not be able to get as much produce on them as fits on square trays. Also, things like fruit leather will have to be cut in a trapezoid shape instead of in rectangles.

The square box dehydrators are considered top-of-the-line, and that is reflected in the price ($150–500). I have a nine-tray Excalibur that is one of the more inexpensive models and it does everything I need it to do. There's a power switch and a temperature gauge.

One neat thing about the square dehydrator is that it's in a box and the trays are removable. That means if you're dehydrating something bulky, like curly kale, you can remove a tray to make more room. You can use this dehydrator for other kitchen tasks that require a consistent low temperature, such as making yogurt or raising bread dough.

The square trays have more surface area than the round trays, so you'll be able to put more food on each tray. And you'll be able to cut fruit leather into rectangles instead of trapezoids.

Since the square dehydrators are in a box, you must use the whole box even if you're dehydrating one or two trays. This also means that there is no space-saving way to store it. It won't get any smaller or any bigger. If you decide you need more trays, you'll need to get another dehydrator, as there's no way to add more trays to this type.

If you're just starting out with dehydrating, I suggest you look at thrift stores and garage sales and buy a used one first. You'll probably be able to find a round dehydrator for $10 or so. It's best if it has a temperature dial, so you can adjust the temperature, but even if it doesn't, you'll be able to dehydrate food in it. Then, if you find that you are using the dehydrator a lot and need a larger one, you can confidently invest in one of the more expensive square dehydrators.

A dehydrator is really the only specialty item needed to dehydrate food. You probably have in your home all the other items you'll use, such as sharp knives, cutting boards, peelers, a colander and a medium stockpot for blanching vegetables that need it. You might also want a mandoline to cut vegetables into uniform slices.

To Blanch or Not to Blanch?

I don't always follow blanching recommendations when I'm freezing vegetables. However, I do follow blanching recommendations when I'm dehydrating. Blanching vegetables stops enzyme actions that can cause flavor and color loss. Blanching also softens the vegetable and helps keep the texture of the dried vegetables from being tough and woody.

Blanching vegetables for freezing and dehydrating is done exactly the same. You can find complete blanching instructions, along with a handy blanching chart, in the freezing section (page 32).

How to Dehydrate Vegetables

To dehydrate vegetables, you simply need to prepare them by washing, peeling and chopping the vegetables. If the vegetable needs to be blanched, go ahead and blanch it (page 34).

I like to lay the vegetable pieces out on a clean dish towel and pat them dry before I put them in the dehydrator. This helps reduce drying time.

If you're dehydrating something that browns, such as potatoes, you can dip them in a lemon juice and water solution, but don't towel dry them before you put them in the dehydrator. To make the solution, use 2 cups (474 ml) of lemon juice per quart (1 L) of water. If you don't have lemon juice, you can use 2 teaspoons (8 g) of citric acid dissolved in 1 quart (1 L) of water.

The vegetable slices should be laid close to each other but not touching.

There are other dips you can use to add flavor and spice to the vegetable. You can use oil, honey, maple syrup, spices and vinegar, to name a few. I'll share some of our favorite seasonings in the vegetable sections.

Place the prepared vegetable pieces on the dehydrator trays, and put the trays back in the dehydrator. Plug the dehydrator in, and set the temperature. Let the vegetables dehydrate for the time indicated for that vegetable. Check the dehydrator every couple of hours to make sure the pieces are dehydrating evenly. It's better to over-dry than to under-dry.

To be shelf-stable, at least 80 to 90 percent of the moisture needs to be removed from the vegetable. Once the vegetables have been in the dehydrator for the recommended time, let them fully cool and then test them. Fully dehydrated vegetables should be either leathery or brittle, depending on the vegetable.

Leathery vegetables will have sharp edges, but instead of breaking in two will spring back after being bent. Brittle vegetables will crumble when bent or shatter when hit with a hammer. Vegetable-specific guidelines are in each vegetable's section.

If the vegetables still seem moist after dehydrating for the recommended time, go ahead and dehydrate them longer, checking them every 30 minutes. You should be able to easily snap fully dehydrated vegetables in half. If the vegetable is too small to snap in half, such as corn, it should shatter when it's hit with a hammer. If you aren't sure if a vegetable is fully dehydrated, you should condition it using the instructions below before storing it.

Once the vegetable pieces are fully dehydrated, it's time to store them.

Storing Dehydrated Vegetables

Before you store dehydrated vegetables for the long term, it's a good idea to condition them. If the vegetables are "bone dry" and shatter easily, this step is not necessary. However, since it's relatively easy, I still do it.

Conditioning simply means to put the cooled, dried vegetable pieces in a jar and put on a tight-fitting lid. Put the jar on the counter out of direct sunlight. Every day for the next 7 to 10 days, check the jar for condensation. I like to gently shake it each day to mix it up a bit.

When food is dehydrated, it never all dries at the same rate, so you'll end up with some pieces that are drier than others. In the sealed environment of the jar, the moisture will equalize from the moister pieces to the drier pieces. If, at any time, you see haze or condensation in the jar, you'll need to put the contents back in the dehydrator for several hours to remove the excess moisture. When they're done, you'll need to condition them again for another 7 to 10 days.

If, after 7 to 10 days, there's no haze or condensation in the jar, you can safely store the vegetables for long term. You can leave them in the jar or use vacuum-sealed or freezer-weight plastic bags.

The National Center for Home Food Preservation recommends conditioning for 7 to 10 days. I condition dehydrated food for the whole 10 days to be on the safe side.

If you live in a humid climate or it just happens to be humid when you store your dehydrated vegetables, it will not affect what's inside the jar if the lid fits tightly. Any moisture from the air that gets into the jar when you fill it will equalize into the drier vegetable pieces.

If you are going to store your dried vegetables in jars, you can use oxygen-absorber or silica-gel packets to help maintain freshness. The oxygen-absorber packets will vacuum-seal the jar, but silica-gel packets will not.

It is important to note that when using the sealing methods (either the vacuum-sealed bags or oxygen absorbers), you need to be sure the vegetables are completely dried to inhibit the growth of *Clostridium botulinum*, the bacteria that causes botulism. *C. botulinum* needs three conditions to grow: an oxygen-free environment, low acidity and adequate moisture. If your vacuum-sealed jars or bags are bulging, or the foods look or smell funny when you open the jars or bags, discard the foods immediately without tasting them.

Some experts recommend boiling dried vegetables that have been vacuum-sealed for 10 minutes before eating them to be sure *C. botulinum* is not present. I prefer to just not vacuum-seal my dried vegetables.

If possible, pack the dried vegetables in smaller containers, as each time the container is opened, it is exposed to moisture. If you don't want to have a lot of small jars or bags taking up space, you can put most of the dried vegetables in a larger jar and then use that to refill smaller jars. I do this with our Dried Superfood Green Powder (page 179). I keep a gallon (4-L) jar in the back of the pantry and then a pint (500-ml) jar in the front. I use the powder just about every day in smoothies, eggs, rice, etc., so the pint jar gets opened almost daily, but the gallon jar doesn't and the green vegetable powder stays fresh longer.

How to Rehydrate Dehydrated Vegetables

Vegetables dehydrated for long-term storage need to be rehydrated when we use them. How you do this will depend on how you're using the vegetable.

If you're making soup with them, you can just toss the dehydrated vegetables right into the soup pot with broth and they will rehydrate as the soup cooks.

If you're using them for something else, you can use the hot-soak or cold-soak method.

My usual preference is the hot-soak method, because it's faster. Put the dehydrated vegetables in a glass or stainless-steel bowl and pour boiling water over them, just enough to cover them. Let them sit until they're soft, anywhere from 15 minutes to a couple of hours. Pour off the water, saving it to use in soups or rice if you'd like, and use the vegetables. Vegetables that were dehydrated in large pieces or that were dehydrated with their skin will take longer to rehydrate than smaller pieces and those that were peeled.

The cold-soak method is the same procedure, but with cold water. You'll need to move the bowl to the refrigerator if the vegetables need to soak overnight. This method can take several hours to a full day.

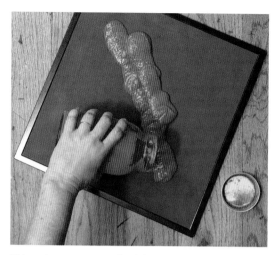

Using silicone mats on the dehydrator tray makes making "fruit" leather super easy.

Fruit Leather

Fruit leather, or fruit roll ups, are so very easy to make at home and preserve with vegetables in the mix. There are several recipes in this book that can inspire you to mix and match flavors to create your own fruit leathers, using what you have on hand.

The basic guidelines for making fruit leather are that you need about 2 cups (474 ml) of blended fruit and vegetables to fill a tray and the consistency of the mixture needs to be similar to applesauce. It can be as simple as using applesauce as a base and adding cinnamon and Dried Beet Powder Food Coloring (page 81) to make apple-spiced fruit leather. Or, try a more involved recipe, like the Dried Carrot Fruit Leather (page 116).

Hopefully, your dehydrator came with a fruit leather tray. If not, you can use parchment paper as a liner for a regular tray. You'll just need to cut it to size. Once the fruit leather mixture is made, pour it onto the prepared tray and spread it to a thickness of about ¼ inch (6 mm). Then, put the tray in the dehydrator and dehydrate at 125°F (52°C) for the recommended time.

Fruit leather dries from the outside edge toward the center. There are several ways to check for dryness. Dark spots visible on the top of the leather are a sure sign that the fruit is not completely dry. Another way to check is to press the leather with your finger. If no indentation is visible, the leather is dry. Or, test by trying to pull the leather from the parchment paper or the dehydrator trays. If the leather peels easily, comes off in one piece and holds its shape, it is dry. The leather should be pliable. It's important for the fruit leather to be completely dry, or it will mold during storage. But, if the leather becomes too dry, it will crack and crumble and won't roll. However, it is still edible and good to eat, so err on the side of over-drying, not under-drying.

Sometimes the outer edges will get overdried while the center is still not quite dry. One thing I try to do to avoid this is to spread the fruit leather mixture a little thicker toward the edges than in the center. I've also been known to just cut off the dried parts and put the part that's still damp back into the dehydrator.

Fruit leather goes quickly in my house, so I don't worry about it sticking to itself when I roll it up. However, if you don't want your fruit leather to stick, use plastic wrap or parchment paper to prevent it.

Place a length of plastic wrap or parchment paper on the counter or table and lay the uncut leather on top of it. Cut the leather and the plastic wrap or parchment together into long slices. Then, roll the fruit leather and plastic or paper onto itself, just like a commercial fruit roll up.

The rolled fruit leather can be stored in a food-grade plastic bag or a clean, dry, insect-proof container, such as a glass jar or a metal tin with a lid. The leather may be stored in a cupboard for 4 months to 1 year. The cooler the storage area, the longer the shelf life of the leather. For instance, in the refrigerator or freezer, the product will keep for more than 1 year.

Dehydrating Recipes

- Dried Asparagus Crisps (page 61)
- Dried Beet Powder Food Coloring (page 81)
- Dried Asian Broccoli Crisps (page 90)
- Dried Broccoli and Ranch Florets (page 92)
- Dried Carrot Fruit Leather (page 116)
- Dried Carrot Chai Ribbons (page 118)
- Dried Cheesy Cauliflower Crisps (page 125)
- Dried Chili-Lime Corn Snacks (page 145)
- Dried Cucumber-Dill Chips (page 155)
- Dried Parmesan Bean Crisps (page 172)
- Dried Superfood Green Powder (page 179)

- Dried Seasoned Onion Crisps (page 193)
- Dried Asian Snap Pea Chips (page 201)
- Dried Spiced Pea Crisps (page 208)
- Dried Chili Powder (page 222)
- Dried Scalloped Potatoes (page 232)
- Dried Pumpkin Pie Roll Ups (page 242)
- Dried Spiced Winter Squash Chips (page 247)
- Dried Spiced Maple Radish Chips (page 254)
- Dried Sweet Potato and Apple Roll Ups (page 263)
- Dried Cheesy Tomato Crisps (page 281)
- Sun-Dried Tomato Pesto (page 289)
- Dried Squash Fruit Chews (page 295)

fermenting vegetables to be good to your gut

More than any of the other preservation methods, fermentation is both a science and an art. The science is that, with the right amount of salt, and maybe some additional water, vegetables can not only be preserved, but also made more nutritious. As long as all the solids stay below the liquid, the fermented food is perfectly safe and healthy to eat.

The art is in the length of time allowed to ferment and in the combination of flavors and spices. Unlike canning, where it might be unsafe to mix and match vegetables, or dehydrating, where you're limited on texture because 80 to 90 percent of the moisture must be removed for safety reasons, fermenting is a creative person's playground.

This means that, instead of the exact times and amounts you find in the other preserving recipes, the fermenting recipes will be more general. Some people love vegetables that have been fermented for weeks and would never dream of opening a ferment after only 5 days to try it. Other people prefer the flavor of shorter ferments and rarely ferment vegetables for more than 7 days. While there may be other reasons for having a longer or shorter fermenting time, there's not a safety reason. Therefore, feel free to sample and test and figure out what length of time and flavor combinations are best for you.

Pros and Cons of Fermenting Vegetables

Fermentation is the only food preservation method that actually increases the nutritional value of the food being preserved, specifically vitamins B and C. For that reason alone, fermented foods have a place in my home-preserved pantry. But there are other benefits as well.

Fermented food is full of probiotics that help keep the gut healthy. I believe the gut is the health center of the body and, when it's not working properly, you'll feel the effects in the rest of your body. Fermented foods also support the immune system and make the nutrients easier for your body to digest.

A practical reason for fermenting food is that it doesn't take a lot of fancy equipment and is probably the cheapest way to preserve food, not including solar dehydration.

Equipment Needed for Fermentation

To successfully ferment food, you need a container, something to keep the solids under the brine and a cover. This is a pretty basic list, but within this list there are a lot of options.

The first thing you need to decide on is a **container** in which to ferment your vegetables. There are **special fermentation crocks** that you can purchase. Stoneware crocks are beautiful and are the original fermentation containers. Fermenting crocks have a water gutter around the lid that allows air to escape as the pressure builds, but doesn't allow air to enter the crock. You can easily find new ones online; just be sure to get one that comes with a lid and a follower, which we'll talk about on the next page. If you decide to buy an older used crock, you'll want to have it tested for lead just to be on the safe side.

Fermenting supplies clockwise: mandoline, digital scale, kraut pounder, guard for mandoline, wide-mouth Mason jar, fermentation weight and lid.

The downside to crocks is that they are expensive. If you want to do several different ferments at the same time, you'll need to purchase several crocks. On the other hand, once the ferment is complete, it can be transferred to another container for storage, so you have the crock available for another ferment.

If you're making large amounts of sauerkraut and pickles, then you might consider using **5-gallon (19-L) food-grade buckets**. We get these buckets for free from our local bakery; we just have to wash out the leftover frosting that was in them. I don't use these buckets for fermenting, but I've heard from those who have that there is sometimes a subtle taste difference between vegetables fermented in plastic and those fermented in crocks or glass. However, once the vegetable is fully fermented, it can be stored in plastic buckets without a change in the flavor.

Glass jars are a good choice for fermenting containers because they are cheap, you can watch what's happening and you can easily make small batches. Using jars allows you to experiment with flavors and vegetable combinations without committing to a large amount. It also allows you to ferment various combinations at the same time. Lastly, the ferment can be stored in the container in which it was fermented.

There are several downsides to using jars. The first is that ferments need to be kept out of direct sunlight for the good bacteria to thrive, and glass allows sunlight in. An easy fix is to cover the jars with a clean kitchen towel. Another issue with jars is that, if you use cheesecloth or a loose-fitting Mason jar lid as the cover, it is harder to keep everything weighted under the brine and all the brine in the jar. When the vegetables are actively fermenting, they will swell, push the brine out of the jar and create air pockets around the vegetables. Often during the active fermentation stage, small pieces of solids will be pushed up over the weight and will float on the brine. Since the brine is an anaerobic environment and is what keeps the ferment from molding, anything floating on top can cause mold. You can push down on the weight several times a day to get the brine back down between the vegetables, get rid of the air pockets and skim off any floating solids. However, an even easier fix is to use an **airlock lid**, which will create an anaerobic environment in the jar by allowing the air bubbles to escape without allowing oxygen to get back into the jar. I use an airlock system for all of my ferments.

A **primary follower** goes right on top of the ferment and acts as a barrier to keep small vegetable pieces from floating on top. Usually, it's a cabbage leaf, but could also be grape or horseradish leaves. If you don't have leaves or don't want to use them, you can make reusable followers out of a food-grade silicone mat. You'll just need to cut it to size to fit the fermentation container. A fermentation weight can be used as a primary follower if the ferment does not have small pieces.

A **secondary follower** adds weight to the ferment to help keep everything under the brine. For most crocks, a small plate will work just fine. For jars, you can get glass weights that fit inside the jars.

When the fermentation begins, the lactic-acid bacteria can produce enough carbon dioxide that it can lift the follower right off the crock. The more weight you can add, the more likely that all the brine will stay in the crock or jar. There are many weight options, ranging from sterilized rocks to freezer bags filled with water to purchased glass weights. If you use rocks, make sure they don't have a high lime content or the acid will dissolve them. If you use freezer bags with water, use the heavy-duty freezer bags and check for leaks. I prefer to use glass weights.

A **cover** is just what is sounds like, something to cover the crock or jar to keep bugs and dust out while letting carbon dioxide escape. A flour sack towel works well as a cover. If you are using an airlock lid, this will be the cover.

While I would love to be the kind of fermenter who has time to check on her ferments several times a day to make sure everything stays under the brine, the reality is that I don't.

In order for me to successfully ferment food, I have to have a super simple system. If you're just starting out or find that you can't tend to your ferments the way they need to be tended to, I suggest you follow this simple system until you have more confidence or time.

Use wide-mouth Mason jars for the fermenting container. These come in four sizes: pint (500 ml), quart (1 L), half gallon (2 L) and gallon (4 L), which are plenty of sizes for fermenting whatever your family needs. If you decide later that you want to make large-batch ferments, you can invest in a large crock.

Make followers out of silicone mats that will fit in each size jar you use. You might not need a follower for every ferment, but you'll want to have a couple for each size jar just in case.

Use store-bought glass weights for most ferments. I've found that, unless I'm using a half-gallon (2-L) or gallon (4-L) jar, glass weights work just fine. For the larger jars, I use freezer zipper bags filled with water.

Use an airlock lid. I've used several different airlock lids, and they've all worked well. However, there's a fairly new lid, The Easy Fermenter, that has made fermenting foolproof for me. This lid doesn't require an airlock filled with water and has a dial for noting the day that the ferment is ready to be checked. You need only a few lids; once the ferment is done, you'll replace the fermenting lid with a regular storage lid.

For the purposes of this book, the fermenting instructions and recipes are written with this system in mind. If you use a crock or a jar without an airlock lid, you'll need to adjust the instructions to accommodate your equipment.

Most of the other equipment you need to ferment vegetables are things commonly found in a well-stocked kitchen: cutting board, sharp knives and a box grater. A food processor and mandoline are nice to have, especially if you're cutting a lot of vegetables or making large batches.

The only specialty item—a kraut pounder or tamper—isn't necessary but comes in handy. This wooden tool packs down the ferment into the jar since it can be hard to get your hand down into small jars. This tool can also be used to bruise shredded and salted vegetables to help them release more of their juices.

Simplifying Salt

Salt is what makes foods preserved by fermentation different from just plain old rotten food that has been left out too long. The salt draws out the juices from the vegetables to create the brine that lactic acid bacteria needs to survive. Lactic acid needs an anaerobic environment, while most other bacteria needs oxygen. This is why it's so important to keep all the solids in a ferment under the brine.

Lactic acid can thrive in a correct saline environment, where other bacteria, including *C. botulinum,* can't. This is what the World Health Organization has to say about botulism:

"C. botulinum will not grow in acidic conditions (pH less than 4.6), and therefore the toxin will not be formed in acidic foods (however, a low pH will not degrade any pre-formed toxin). Combinations of low storage temperature and salt contents and/or pH are also used to prevent the growth of the bacteria or the formation of the toxin." [3]

But don't make the mistake of thinking that if a little salt is good, more is better. Too much salt will inhibit the lactic acid and no fermentation will occur.

As a general rule, most vegetables will ferment just fine in a 2 percent brine solution. That means that, for every 100 grams of vegetables, you'll use 2 grams of salt. Cucumbers and peppers need a little stronger solution of 3 percent. And kimchi uses a stronger brine of 5 percent. As with most guidelines, there's some wiggle room, so feel free to experiment. That being said, I don't use less than a 2 percent solution for any vegetable.

There are many salt options. You'll want to choose unrefined salt with no additives or anti-caking agents, which means iodized salt is not used for fermenting. I prefer to use Redmond Real® Salt, a fine sea salt I use for all of our food, including preserved food,

[3]   https://www.who.int/news-room/fact-sheets/detail/botulism

because having just one salt simplifies my kitchen. Another good choice is pickling salt. Whatever salt you use, just read the label and make sure there's only salt in the container.

Different salts have different weights, so you'll need a digital scale to make sure you have the right amount of salt in the ferment. A tablespoon of coarse salt will weigh less than a tablespoon of fine salt, which is why you'll need to weigh the salt instead of measuring it. We'll discuss how to do this in the next section.

How to Ferment Vegetables

There are two basic ways to ferment vegetables. I call them *sauerkraut style* and *pickle style.* Sauerkraut style uses grated or shredded vegetables that are brined in their own juices. Pickle style uses chopped, sliced or whole vegetables that have a saltwater brine poured over them.

To make sauerkraut-style ferments, rinse the vegetables and remove any stems or tough outer leaves. Grate or shred the vegetables. Using a metric kitchen scale and a large bowl, weigh the shredded vegetables. Calculate how much salt you need by multiplying the weight of the vegetable in grams by 2 percent. This will tell you how many grams of salt you need. Weigh the salt and sprinkle it over the shredded vegetables.

Use your clean hands to massage the salt into the vegetables; you'll notice they release a lot of liquid. That's exactly what's supposed to happen. After 5 to 10 minutes, the vegetable mixture and juice can go into a clean wide-mouth jar. Tightly pack the vegetables into the jar, using a kraut pounder or tamper if necessary. Leave at least 2 inches (5 cm) of headspace for expansion.

Put a weight in the jar to keep everything under the brine. If you notice pieces floating above the weight, you will need to remove the weight, add a primary

After adding salt to the shredded vegetables, they will release their juices to create a brine.

Use a kruat pounder, or tamper, to pack the shredded vegetables into the jar.

follower to keep everything under the brine, then put the weight back in the jar. Screw on a fermentation lid and set the jar in a cool place, out of direct sunlight.

To make pickle-style ferments, rinse the vegetables and remove any stems. Cut the vegetables and put them in a clean wide-mouth Mason jar, leaving at least 1 inch (2.5 cm) of headspace for expansion. In another jar, mix the saltwater brine solution and then pour it over the vegetables. Add a primary follower, if needed, and a weight, then screw on the fermentation lid.

You can use the following as a rough guide for making the brine. However, you'll get more exact results if you weigh the salt and water yourself. A gallon of water weighs 3.8 kilograms, which means you need 76 grams salt for 2 percent brine; 114 grams for 3 percent brine and 190 grams for 5 percent brine.

- 2% brine = ½ cup (76 g) salt per 1 gallon (4 L) of water
- 3% brine = ¾ cup (114 g) salt per 1 gallon (4 L) of water
- 5% brine = 1 cup (190 g) salt per 1 gallon (4 L) of water

For convenience, the fermenting recipes in this book have a measured amount of salt listed in the ingredients. This amount is based on using Redmond Real® Salt. It should be very close to any other salt that has a similar texture to Redmond fine salt, which is like table salt. However, if you use a finely ground salt or a coarse salt, the measurement will be off.

I suggest that you put the jar on a kitchen scale and zero out the scale. Then put the vegetables, spices and water in the jar and weigh them in grams. Calculate how much salt you need to make the brine by multiplying the weight in grams by either 2 percent, 3 percent or 5 percent. Add the salt to the jar and stir the mixture; a chopstick makes a perfect stirrer for this.

When making the saltwater brine, it's important to use filtered, non-chlorinated water. If you have city water, you can dechlorinate the water by boiling it for 20 minutes. Alternatively, use spring water or distilled water. If you boil the water, cool it to room temperature before you pour it into the ferment. If you buy spring water, make sure it's not chlorinated. If you have well water, the minerals in it might interfere with the fermentation process and produce soft or slimy ferments. If you notice this, use spring or distilled water.

How Long to Ferment

There are many variables that come into play when deciding how long to ferment vegetables. Vegetables with high sugar content will ferment more quickly than vegetables with less sugar content. Also, vegetables will ferment faster in warm conditions than they will in cold conditions, and small batches will ferment faster than large batches.

Recipes will give you a general time frame for fermenting, but you'll also want to keep an eye on the ferment and look for signs of readiness.

A practical sign of readiness is when the acidity level reaches 4.6 pH. You can buy pH strips to test the acidity level of ferments if you need something definitive to gauge the readiness of your ferments.

If you don't want to use pH strips, then look for other signs, such as the lack of bubbles escaping the jar, vegetables that look translucent, cloudy brine, soft texture and a sour smell and taste. The sour smell and taste should be pleasant, not putrid.

I like to taste the ferments when I start noticing that there are fewer bubbles in the jars. If I like the flavor, it's done. If I don't like the flavor or texture, I'll let it ferment longer.

So, how long do you let vegetables ferment? It depends.

This is the artistic part of fermenting.

Using Whey

There are many fermenters who use whey from yogurt, cheese or kefir to inoculate the vegetable ferment with lactic acid. This will speed up the fermentation process.

However, the natural bacteria on the vegetables and the saline environment will produce all the lactic acid the ferment needs. I've found that the results are less predictable when I use whey in vegetable ferments. I've had them end up with a "cheesy" undertone and slimy texture. However, I do realize this isn't everyone's experience and that a good ferment can be made by adding whey.

For me, using whey complicates the ferment and adds one more level of things that can go wrong. Therefore, none of the recipes in this book have whey added to them.

Storing Fermented Vegetables

Once a jar of fermented vegetables is done, it will need to be stored in a cool place. A root cellar is an ideal place to store ferments; however, most of us don't have root cellars.

Thankfully, a refrigerator is also a great place to store ferments, and most of us have one. We have an old refrigerator in the garage that we use to store extra produce and ferments, so we don't clutter up our kitchen refrigerator.

If you live in a cold climate and have a basement that you don't heat or a cold corner in your home, those may be good places to store your ferments. The fermentation action continues even while in cold storage; it slows down, but it doesn't stop. If the environment is warm, the fermentation action won't slow down and the ferment will become very sour and mushy in a short amount of time.

To store the ferment, change out the fermenting lid for a plastic storage lid. **Don't use metal canning lids, as the acid in the ferments can corrode the lids.** If you've made several batches of the same thing, you can put them together in a larger jar or bucket so you have fewer jars in storage. If you used a crock, you'll probably want to transfer the ferment into another container for storage, so your crock is available when you want to use it again.

While they are in storage, the brine of the sauerkraut-style ferments may need to be topped off every once in a while, so everything stays under the brine. If the vegetables aren't kept below the brine, they can mold. To top off the ferments, make a small batch of the appropriate brine and pour it into the jar.

Some ferments may develop a white film on them; this is most likely kahm yeast and is harmless. However, if there's mold, slime or a foul smell, the ferment should be discarded. I know there are fermenters who just scoop off mold and eat the ferment, but that's not what I recommend.

Most fermented vegetables can be fermented for up to a year, as long as there's no sign of spoilage.

Fermenting Recipes

- Fermented Garlicky Asparagus (page 70)
- Fermented Beets and Onions (page 80)
- Fermented East-Meets-West Sauerkraut (page 100)
- Fermented Red Cabbage with Apple and Ginger (page 102)
- Fermented Mexican Carrots (page 119)
- Fermented Cauliflower with Curry (page 130)
- Fermented Corn Salsa (page 144)
- Fermented Cucumber Relish (page 153)
- Fermented German Mustard Pickles (page 154)
- Fermented Thai Green Beans (page 166)
- Fermented Snow Peas (page 206)
- Fermented Green Hot Sauce (page 221)
- Fermented Winter Squash Chutney (page 246)
- Fermented Radish Slices with Dill (page 257)
- Fermented Sweet Potatoes with Ginger (page 266)
- Fermented Green Tomato Relish (page 284)
- Fermented Cherry Tomatoes (page 286)
- Fermented Squash Relish (page 302)

PART 2

preserving seasonal vegetables and herbs to enjoy all year

In this section, you'll find an A to Z guide to the most popular garden vegetables, with some tips on growing the vegetable, harvesting and preserving it using the four main methods covered in this book (canning or pickling, freezing, fermenting and dehydrating). I then share my family's favorite recipes, including some for each preservation method. You'll find lots of tips on what to serve these preserves with, so I truly hope these recipes are an inspiration to you.

One of my goals is to not have to buy any vegetables that I grow. Other than onions, tomatoes and potatoes, I can usually meet that goal when I take the time to preserve our garden abundance. But some years we don't grow all the vegetables we need, so I rely on the farmers' market or a local U-Pick farm to supplement.

Here are my tips for making full use of your local resources: Make friends with your local farmers and ask them lots of questions. Just as preserving food isn't a competition, neither is gardening. Many farmers at the farmers' market will gladly share growing, cooking and preserving tips with you. If you decide to try to "get a deal" from a local farmer, it needs to be a good deal for both of you. Farmers will often donate their excess to local charities and would rather do that than haggle with customers who can pay fair prices but don't want to.

If you're looking for something specific, like fully ripe peppers or large quantities of something for preserving, contact the farmers' market ahead of time and see if any of the farmers can accommodate your request. Most are happy to set aside certain things to help market day go faster. Also know that in order to prepare for the market, the vegetables will need to be picked a day or two before. Don't expect them to be as fresh as vegetables from your own garden.

asparagus
Preserving the Comeback Vegetable

Every spring, asparagus shows up in the produce department, displayed on ice and sporting a hefty price tag. For years, I would purchase the spring treat several times before the season was over, then we'd wait for the next spring, when it would be available again. Then we started growing it.

You get the biggest bang for your buck in gardening when you can plant something and get a harvest year after year—we call these perennials. There aren't many perennial vegetables, but asparagus is one of them, and it deserves a place in the garden.

Growing

Once asparagus is planted, it needs to stay put, so think carefully about where to plant it. Many people like to plant it on the side of the garden as a border instead of in the middle of the garden.

To grow asparagus, you can start with crowns or seeds. Crowns are more expensive, but you'll get a harvest sooner. Even when starting with crowns, it will be 2 to 3 years before you can harvest the asparagus. If you start with seeds, it will be 4 to 5 years before you get a harvest.

To plant the crowns, dig a trench 8 to 10 inches (20.3 to 25.4 cm) deep. Set the crowns in the trench with the roots fanned out and fill the trench with loose, well-draining, fertile soil. You can fill the trench just halfway until the spears emerge, then fill the rest later in the summer as the spears grow.

If you have clay soil, you will need to dig the trench deeper and then fill it with sandy soil before you put the crowns in the trench. This will keep the roots from rotting.

Asparagus is a heavy feeder and needs rich compost added to it each year. Traditionally, asparagus has been grown in manure; if you have access to well-composted manure, the asparagus bed is a great place to use it. Asparagus does not compete well with weeds, so keep the bed free of weeds.

In cold climates, the asparagus ferns will die back during the winter and go dormant. If you live in a warm climate, this might not happen and you'll need to cut the ferns back to create dormancy.

After the ferns die back, add old hay or leaves to protect them from the cold. In the early spring, pull back the mulch, add a layer of compost to the bed and watch for the spears to pop up.

Harvesting

I tell my children that the asparagus needs to be at least the diameter of a pencil before it can get harvested. When spears come up that are smaller than a pencil, just leave them to grow into ferns.

If fat spears happen to come up the first 2 years, resist the urge to harvest them. It will be hard to resist, but it will be better for the asparagus in the long run. Asparagus is a long-term game; if well-tended and allowed to get established, it can produce year after year for 15 to 20 years!

If you have planted asparagus crowns, you can start harvesting the asparagus in year three. Each crown will send up multiple spears, beginning in early spring. We harvest about half the spears that eventually come up. Ideally, we try to harvest spears with tightly closed top buds that are about 5 inches (12.7 cm) long and at least ½ inch (12 mm) thick. But asparagus is tricky and can go from just sprouting to 2 feet (61 cm) tall seemingly overnight. If we miss spears and they start to fern out, we just let them grow.

To harvest asparagus, cut the spear at, or just below, the soil line. I usually just snap them off, but you can use a knife or clippers. Asparagus is susceptible to fusarium, a fungus that can spread from plant to plant on a knife, which is why many people just snap the asparagus. There are asparagus varieties that are resistant to fusarium, so plant one of those if fusarium is an issue in your area.

Asparagus should be treated like flowers; once they're harvested, they should be put in water. If it's going to be longer than an hour or two before you're going to use them, put them in the refrigerator.

Asparagus Varieties to Try

Asparagus plants are either male or female and, while all varieties have both male and female plants, some varieties produce more of one than the other.

Since female asparagus spends a lot of energy producing seeds, they produce fewer and smaller spears than male plants do.

Asparagus varieties with the name *Jersey* produce mostly male plants and are resistant to many asparagus diseases, including crown rot and fusarium wilt. Jersey Knight, Jersey Giant and Jersey Supreme will produce three times more spears than open pollinated varieties. You also will not have to worry about a lot of volunteers popping up, since there are few female plants. A volunteer plant is one that grows on its own without being deliberately planted, usually from seeds that the plant dropped the previous season. The volunteer could also be from bird droppings or the wind carrying and then dropping the seeds.

Purple Passion produces sweet, purple spears that fade to green when cooked. It's a great novelty choice; just be aware that this variety produces both male and female plants.

If growing heirloom vegetables is important to you, then Mary Washington is a great choice. It's been grown in North America for over 100 years and produces long, deep green spears with purple tips. Be aware that this variety produces a higher percentage of female plants than Jersey varieties do.

White asparagus isn't a different variety; it's just grown by blocking the sunlight so the spears don't produce chlorophyll and turn green. You can block the sunlight by mounding up soil around the plant or covering it with a tub or light-blocking item.

Buying

Unless you have a large, mature asparagus patch, you'll probably need or want to buy asparagus when it's in season to preserve it for later. Just be aware that asparagus will lose its sugar content soon after harvesting if it's left at room temperature.

When buying asparagus, try to find a supplier who keeps the asparagus in water and refrigerated. If you're buying at a farmers' market, look for a farmer who keeps the asparagus in an ice chest with water and ice. If you're buying from a grocery store, choose one that stores asparagus on ice or in water. The asparagus should be crisp and not limp.

Once you bring asparagus home, either preserve it right away or clip the ends and put it in a glass of water in the refrigerator.

Preserving

Most people only eat the top 5 to 6 inches (12.7 to 15.2 cm)—the most tender part—of asparagus and toss the rest of the spear to the chickens or into the compost pile. They are missing out! The tough bottom stalk is filled with tender flesh that just needs to be uncovered.

Asparagus is expensive and the season is short. I make the most of the asparagus I have by peeling the thick stems and preserving those, too. To peel asparagus, insert the blade of a sharp paring knife under the thick skin at the base and work toward the thinner end, being careful to just peel off the tough skin and not the tender flesh.

I usually use the pieces of tender flesh to make Frozen Roasted Chipotle–Asparagus Pesto (page 67) or Dried Asparagus Crisps (page 61); they can also be used to fill spaces in the jars of canned and fermented asparagus recipes.

Canning

Asparagus is usually canned in a pickling brine using a water bath canner. But it can also be canned plain if you use a pressure canner. It just depends on how you want to use it after it's canned.

When you can asparagus spears, measure one spear in the jar and use that one spear as a guide to cut the other spears to the correct length. The asparagus spears need to be low enough in the jar to leave ¼ inch (6 mm) of headspace when you fill it with liquid. If you cut them too short, the spears will float up after being canned. It's not the end of the world if they float, but it's nice to can as much of the spear as possible.

It takes an average of 16 pounds (7.25 kg) of asparagus to fill nine pint (500-ml) jars and 25 pounds (11.34 kg) of asparagus to fill seven quart (1-L) jars. You need to process the equivalent of two quart (1-L) jars to properly use a pressure canner.

To can plain asparagus, you can use whole spears or chop them into smaller pieces. Season the asparagus with ¼ teaspoon of salt per pint (500 ml) or ½ teaspoon of salt per quart (1 L). The asparagus can be packed using the raw-pack or hot-pack method (page 24) and canned in the pressure canner.

When the jars are filled, use the bubble remover tool to remove the air bubbles and make sure the jars have 1 inch (2.5 cm) of headspace. Wipe the rim of each jar and put a lid and band on the jar. Process the jars, according to the manufacturer's instructions, at 10 psi (69 kPa) for 30 minutes for pints (500 ml) and 40 minutes for quarts (1 L). Adjust for altitude (page 25), if necessary.

To use canned asparagus, drain the water and sauté the spears or pieces by themselves or with other vegetables. You can also add them to soups or casseroles.

Asparagus can also be canned in a water bath canner by pickling the spears (page 60). Asparagus spears add an elegant touch to relish trays and can be wrapped in deli meat for a heftier appetizer. I like to add chopped pickled asparagus to salads—green salads, tuna salad, macaroni salad. You get the picture.

The asparagus will shrink up some during the canning process, so it's good to pack the jars tightly. For asparagus spears, I think the raw-pack method works best. I can arrange raw spears in the jar, gently shake the jar and then add more spears without worrying about handling hot spears. For cut asparagus, the hot-pack method works well because you don't have to worry about touching the asparagus with your hands.

Freezing

If you don't have a pressure canner, freezing asparagus is a good way to have plain asparagus for sautéing. The texture of frozen asparagus will not be as firm as fresh asparagus, but it shouldn't be mushy. Asparagus can be frozen in spears or pieces, depending on how you're going to use it later.

In order to freeze asparagus properly, it needs to be blanched for 3 minutes first; thicker spears need 4 minutes (page 34). This will help it retain its color and flavor. Some people don't blanch asparagus and find that they are happy with the results. If you're interested in cutting this corner, I suggest freezing some spears without blanching and then cook them, a few at a time, over a few months' time to see if you like the results before making a definite decision.

To freeze asparagus as spears, you first need to decide what you're going to freeze them in and cut the spears to fit that container. Then blanch the spears, unless you've decided against blanching. After the spears have been blanched and cooled, lay them on a clean dish towel and pat them dry. This will help keep ice crystals from forming on them when they freeze.

To keep the spears from freezing in a clump, lay them out on a baking sheet lined with parchment paper and place the baking sheet in the freezer for 2 to 3 hours. Transfer the frozen spears to a freezer-safe container and label and date the container.

For freezing pieces, chop the asparagus into 1-inch (2.5-cm) pieces and then blanch them for 2 minutes. Once they've cooled, lay them out on a clean dish towel to dry. I like to freeze asparagus pieces overnight on a baking sheet lined with parchment paper. The next day, I transfer them to a freezer-safe container. Remember to label and date the container.

If you freeze asparagus in small portions, know you're going to use it all at once and do not mind if the asparagus spears or pieces stick together, you can forgo freezing them on a baking sheet first. Just put them in the freezer-safe container after you dry them off from being blanched and call it good.

Asparagus will last in the freezer for up to 12 months.

Dehydrating

If you have a bumper crop of asparagus and want to preserve it without taking up a lot of room in your pantry or freezer, then dehydrating it is the way to go. One pound (453 g) of dehydrated asparagus can fit into a 1-cup (237-ml) Mason jar.

Blanching asparagus for 2 to 4 minutes before dehydrating it is recommended. Unlike when freezing asparagus, I do notice a difference in the quality of dried asparagus when I blanch it as opposed to when I don't blanch it.

To dehydrate asparagus, chop the asparagus spears into 1-inch (2.5-cm) pieces and peel the tough skin off any pieces that need it. Blanch the asparagus for 2 to 4 minutes (page 34) and then put it in an ice bath (page 33) to stop the cooking process. When the asparagus pieces have cooled, lay them on a clean kitchen towel and pat them dry.

If you're going to season them, now is the time. But most people dehydrate asparagus plain to use in cooking. Lay the asparagus pieces on the dehydrator tray and dehydrate at 135°F (57°C) for 6 to 10 hours. The crisps should snap in half when they're done.

To rehydrate dried asparagus, soak it in cool water for 30 to 60 minutes. If you're adding them to a soup, you can add them without rehydrating; they will absorb the water in the soup.

For snacking, I like to use the peeled end pieces to make Dried Asparagus Crisps (page 61). You can use this same idea with different seasonings to make quick snacks or crisps for adding to soups or salads. The possibilities are endless.

Fermenting

Because it's hard to get large harvests of asparagus at one time and because asparagus loses its sugar content so quickly, fermenting is a great way to preserve this vegetable. Fermenting asparagus is another way to pickle it. You can use whatever pickling spices you like for your pickles: dill, garlic, onions, mustard seed and peppercorns, to name a few.

The beauty of fermenting asparagus is that you can make one jar at a time using just 20 or so spears. I like to use the 1½-pint (750-ml) wide-mouth Mason jars for fermenting asparagus. These jars are tall, so you can use long spears, but are smaller around, so you don't need as many spears.

To make fermented asparagus, put rinsed asparagus, either whole or in slices, in a Mason jar and cover them with a 2 percent brine (page 51). You can add onions, garlic and spices, such as dill, bay leaves, peppercorns, mustard seed, red pepper flakes and ginger, to the jar before adding the brine. Add a weight and an airlock fermenting lid.

Put the jar of fermenting asparagus on a plate or small cookie sheet to catch any overflow and store it, out of direct sunlight, for 5 to 8 days. After 5 days, test the asparagus each day until they are as sour as you like, being sure to replace the weight and fermenting lid each time you test. When the asparagus is ready, remove the weight and fermenting lid. Seal the jar with a plastic storage lid and store it in the refrigerator for up to 1 year.

Preserving Asparagus Cheat Sheet

	Water Bath Canning	Pressure Canning	Freezing	Dehydrating	Fermenting 2% brine
How to prepare	Whole or pieces	Whole or pieces	2–4-minute blanching recommended; whole or pieces	2–4-minute blanching required; in pieces	Whole
Flavors	Pickled; seasoned with herbs	Plain or as a soup base	Plain, seasoned or bacon-wrapped	Plain or seasoned	Seasoned with herbs
Length of processing	10 minutes	Pints (500 ml): 30 minutes Quarts (1 L): 40 minutes	—	6–10 hours	8–14 days
Storage life	12 months	12 months	8–12 months	12 months for plain; 1 month for seasoned	6–12 months

Dried Asparagus Crisps

This is a recipe that's good for using the leftover peeled stems from canned or fermented asparagus, although tender asparagus spears can also be used.

Makes 1 pint (500 ml)

½ lb (226 g) asparagus, cut into 1-inch (2.5-cm) pieces

1 tbsp (15 ml) apple cider vinegar

1 tbsp (15 ml) lemon juice

1 tsp olive oil

2 tbsp (5 g) chopped chives

Pinch of salt

Pinch of ground black pepper

Blanch the asparagus pieces by filling a medium stockpot about halfway with water and bringing it to a boil over high heat. Put the asparagus into the boiling water and let it come back up to a boil. Cover the pot and cook the asparagus for 2 to 4 minutes. While the asparagus is in the boiling water, prepare a bowl of ice water. Using a slotted spoon, take the asparagus pieces out of the boiling water and immediately put them into the bowl of ice water to stop the cooking.

Mix the vinegar, lemon juice, olive oil, chives, salt and pepper together in a medium bowl.

Drain the water from the asparagus, put the asparagus pieces on a clean kitchen towel and pat them dry. Carefully add the asparagus to the bowl, then combine the asparagus and the vinegar mixture, tossing to coat all the pieces.

Lay the seasoned asparagus pieces on a dehydrator tray. You can put the pieces close together, as they will shrink considerably. Dehydrate the pieces at 125°F (52°C) for 10 to 12 hours, or until brittle. The chips should easily snap in half when bent.

When the asparagus are fully dry, remove the tray from the dehydrator and let the crisps cool. Put the dried asparagus in a glass jar with a tight-fitting lid, and use the asparagus chips within 1 month.

Asparagus crisps are best eaten within a few days. If they lose their crispness, they can be put into the dehydrator on high for 15 to 30 minutes to crisp them.

Serving Suggestions: Enjoy asparagus chips as a crunchy snack or use to add crunchiness to salads, sandwiches or soups.

Canned Asparagus Soup

One of my favorite things about canning is when I can take a plain recipe, like a jar of canned asparagus, add a few seasonings and turn it into a main dish. This creamy soup paired with crusty bread makes for a simple, cozy meal.

Makes 8 pint (500-ml) jars

For the Soup

4 cups (948 ml) water

2 cups (474 ml) vegetable or chicken broth

4 tbsp (59 ml) lemon juice

2 tsp (12 g) salt

1 tsp ground black pepper

6 lbs (2.75 kg) asparagus, cut into 1-inch (2.5-cm) pieces

2 cups (300 g) chopped onions

For Serving

½ tsp garlic powder per jar of soup

¼ cup (59 ml) heavy cream or milk per jar of soup

¼ cup (25 g) grated Parmesan cheese per jar of soup

Chopped chives, croutons, Dried Asparagus Crisps (page 61) or Frozen Bacon-Wrapped Asparagus Spears (page 64)

For the soup, to prepare the pressure canner, rinse it and its rack, place the bottom rack inside, and fill the canner with a few inches of water, according to the manufacturer's instructions. Put the pressure canner on the stove over low heat while you prepare the jars. This is a raw-pack recipe, so the water in the pressure canner needs to be no higher than 140°F (60°C) before you put the jars into the canner.

Wash eight pint (500-ml) jars in hot, soapy water and check them for any nicks or cracks in the jars. Rinse the jars in clean water and set them aside. Wash the lids in hot, soapy water, rinse them and set them aside.

Mix the water, broth, lemon juice, salt and pepper in a large pot and bring it to a boil over high heat. Add the asparagus and onions to the broth mixture and bring the mixture back to a boil. Turn the heat off and divide the asparagus, onions and broth among the jars, leaving a generous 1 inch (2.5 cm) of headspace. Use a bubble remover tool or a chopstick to remove the air bubbles, and recheck the headspace. If you run out of the broth and water mixture before each jar is filled properly, top off the jars with boiling water.

Process the jars, according to the manufacturer's instructions, at 10 psi (69 kPa) for 30 minutes for pints (500 ml), adjusting for altitude (page 25), if necessary. Let the pressure canner depressurize naturally (page 25). Arrange a folded towel on the counter or table. Open the canner and remove the jars, using a jar lifter, and place the jars on the towel. Cool the jars for at least 12 hours. Remove the bands, check the seals and store the jars for up to 1 year. If any jars failed to seal, put them in the refrigerator to use first.

For serving, empty a jar of the soup into a medium stockpot, bring the soup to a boil, then reduce the heat to a simmer. Stir in the garlic powder, cream and Parmesan. Add more salt and pepper, if needed. This soup can be blended with an immersion blender to create a creamy, smooth soup. If you do this, you might need to add a thickener, such as arrowroot powder or dried potato powder (page 227). Garnish the soup with the chives.

Frozen Bacon-Wrapped Asparagus Spears

Bacon makes good things better, doesn't it? Roasted asparagus spears are a treat all by themselves. When they're wrapped in bacon and baked to a crunchy crisp, we've gone from a treat to a celebration. I always make a large batch of these, serve a portion for dinner and then freeze the rest for later.

Makes 32 pieces

16 slices thin-cut bacon (approximately 1 lb [453 g])

32 asparagus spears with tough outer skin peeled, if needed

Preheat the oven to 350°F (177°C).

Cut each bacon slice in half lengthwise so you have 32 thin strips of bacon. Wrap each asparagus spear with one of the strips of bacon and arrange the spears on a baking sheet.

Bake the spears for 15 to 18 minutes. About halfway through the cooking time, use a silicone basting brush to brush the asparagus with the bacon grease from the baking sheet. The spears are done when the bacon is cooked, but not crispy, and the asparagus is tender, but not mushy. Brush the asparagus spears one more time with the bacon grease. Let them cool completely before you put them in a freezer-safe container for storage. I like to use the vacuum sealer and plastic bags for freezing these, but regular freezer bags work. Use the spears within 6 months.

To reheat the asparagus spears, preheat the oven to 350°F (177°C). Place the spears on a baking sheet and bake them for 10 to 12 minutes, or until the bacon is crispy and the asparagus is cooked all the way through. You can cover the asparagus tips with foil to prevent them from browning too much.

Serving Suggestions: *Use as a unique garnish on bowls of soup or plated food. Cut the baked asparagus spears in half or in thirds and serve on an appetizer tray.*

Frozen Roasted Chipotle–Asparagus Pesto

"THAT is amazing!" will be the words you hear when you serve this creamy pesto. Roasted Chipotle–Asparagus Pesto is a great substitute for mayonnaise or other spreads on a sandwich or as a dip for crackers. You can also serve it over pasta. This recipe was created when I wanted to make something special from large peeled asparagus stems.

Makes 2½ cups (592 ml)

2 small (60 g total) jalapeños

¼ cup (59 ml) olive oil

1 lb (453 g) asparagus, cut into 2–3-inch (5–7.6-cm) pieces

2 cloves garlic

2 tsp (10 ml) lime juice

½ tsp salt

½ cup (50 g) grated Parmesan cheese

Preheat the oven to 400°F (204°C). Put the jalapeños in a small baking pan and roast them for 5 minutes, or until the skins blister. Remove them from the oven, let them cool and then remove the stem and seeds if you want a milder pesto. See the note for another way to cook the peppers.

In a large skillet, heat the oil over medium heat and sauté the asparagus pieces for 5 to 7 minutes, or until they're soft but not mushy.

Transfer the asparagus, along with any oil from the pan, to a blender. Add the jalapeños, garlic, lime juice, salt and Parmesan, and blend for 1 to 2 minutes, or until smooth. You may need to add more olive oil to get the pesto to blend well.

Transfer the pesto into freezer-safe containers, such as 4-ounce (125-ml) Mason jars or plastic freezer bags. If you're using glass jars, be sure to leave ½ inch (12 mm) of headspace for expansion. Put the pesto into the refrigerator to cool overnight, then transfer it to the freezer. Pesto can be stored in the freezer for up to a year.

Note: *If you want to roast the peppers over an open flame, use your gas grill, wood-burning grill or a campfire. Using a long pair of tongs, hold each pepper over the fire until the skin bubbles, turning the pepper until all the sides are done. When each pepper is done, put it in a bowl to cool.*

Canned Dilly Asparagus

Dilly asparagus will have you pulling out the water bath canner in early spring when your pickle supply is probably running low. Use thicker asparagus spears to get crunchy "pickles" every time.

Makes 2 quart (1-L) jars

55–60 asparagus spears

3½ cups (829 ml) white wine vinegar

1½ cups (355 ml) water

1 tbsp (18 g) sea salt

½ cup (100 g) sugar

1 tsp celery seed

4 tsp (8 g) mustard seed

4 tsp (1 g) dill weed

4 cloves garlic, divided

Serving Suggestions: *Enjoy right out of the jar or as part of a relish tray. Pickled asparagus can be added to any recipe that calls for pickles or relish, such as potato or pasta salad.*

Prepare the water bath canner by filling it halfway with water and putting it on the stove to simmer. Check two quart (1-L) jars for any nicks or cracks, wash them in hot soapy water and rinse them in hot water. Keep the jars hot until it's time to use them. Wash the lids in hot soapy water, rinse them and set them aside.

Rinse and cut the asparagus spears so that they can stand up in the jars and still leave ½ inch (12 mm) of headspace.

Combine the vinegar, water, salt, sugar, celery seed, mustard seed and dill in a stainless-steel or nonreactive pot and bring the mixture to a boil, stirring occasionally.

Put 2 cloves of garlic in the bottom of each jar and pack the asparagus spears tightly into the jars. Using a ladle, pour the vinegar brine into the jars, leaving ½ inch (12 mm) of headspace. Remove the air bubbles with a bubble remover tool or chopstick and recheck the headspace; add more brine if necessary. Wipe the rims with a clean cloth, put the lids on the jars and screw on the bands. Place the jars in the prepared hot water bath canner, making sure that the jars are covered by at least an inch (2.5 cm) of water.

Bring the water to a full rolling boil, and put the lid on the canner. Process the jars for 10 minutes, adjusting for altitude (page 17), if necessary. Arrange a folded towel on the counter or table. Remove the jars, using a jar lifter, and place them on the towel. Let the jars cool for at least 12 hours.

When the jars are cooled, remove the bands and check the seals. If any jars failed to seal, put them in the refrigerator to use first. Wipe the jars with a clean cloth and store them for up to a year.

*In the photo, the dilly asparagus is shown in the jar on the right.

Fermented Garlicky Asparagus

Sometimes when you pick asparagus at its prime, there's too much to cook for dinner but not enough for a full canner for canned asparagus. That's when I make this garlicky ferment, since I can make just one jar at a time. Fermented asparagus is a nice treat after months of eating cold weather crops, such as cabbage, kale and swiss chard.

Makes 1 quart (1 L)

¾ lb (340 g) asparagus (approximately 25–30 spears)

½ tsp mustard seed

1 bay leaf

½ tsp dill seed or 1 head fresh dill seed

2 cloves garlic

20 black peppercorns

1½ tbsp (27 g) sea salt

2 cups (474 ml) filtered water

Rinse the asparagus, peeling any thick stems so they can also be used. Cut the asparagus so that it can stand up in a wide-mouth quart (1-L) Mason jar and still leave 2 inches (5 cm) of headspace. Pack the asparagus into the jar. Add the mustard seed, bay leaf, dill seed, garlic and peppercorns to the jar.

Mix the salt into the water to make the brine. Pour the brine over the asparagus and spices, making sure to cover the asparagus but leaving enough room for a weight and expansion. Put a weight into the jar to keep everything under the brine. Top the jar with a fermentation lid. Put the jar on a plate or small cookie sheet to catch any overflow.

Set the jar in a cool place, out of direct sunlight for 8 to 14 days. You can start tasting the ferment any time after 8 days. If the asparagus need to ferment longer, replace the weight and fermentation lid and ferment for a few more days. When the asparagus is to your liking, replace the weight and fermentation lid with a plastic storage lid. The fermented asparagus can be stored in the refrigerator for up to 9 months.

*See photo on page 69 (this recipe is shown in the jar on the left).

Serving Suggestions: *Enjoy straight from the jar or on a relish tray. Fermented asparagus can also be added to recipes, such as potato or pasta salad, that call for pickles or relish.*

beets

Adding Color to Your Cooking

When it comes to novelty vegetables, the beet family takes the top prize for beauty, ease of growing and taste. Beets are a cool-weather crop with edible greens and an edible bulb that's usually red, although it can also be golden or red-and-white striped. Beets are usually grown for their bulbs, but the greens are also a powerhouse of nutrition.

Beets are related to Swiss chard, and their greens can be eaten just like you would any other green (page 174). I like to use the small, tender beet greens in salads and add larger ones to my Dried Superfood Green Powder (page 179).

Growing

Beets thrive in temperatures from 50 to 85°F (10 to 29°C). Beets can tolerate temperatures as low as 20°F (-7°C) with only damage to the leaves and not the root. As long as the ground is still workable, they will be fine. They are also fairly heat tolerant and can survive temperatures well into the 90s Fahrenheit (30s Celsius).

Beet seeds are actually clusters of 2 to 4 seeds, not a single seed, which means when it germinates, you'll have 2 to 4 beet plants in a cluster. In order for the roots to grow, you'll need to remove all but the best-looking beet plant in each cluster; this is called *thinning*. Beets like loose, well-drained soil and regular watering; they have a high moisture content and do well with about an inch (2.5 cm) of rain a week. If you don't get that much rain during the week, you'll need to water the beets.

If you live in a mild winter climate that doesn't see prolonged freezes, you can plant beets in the fall and grow them unprotected all winter. If you live in an area with real winters, you can plant beets in early spring and grow them into summer. If you have mild summers, you can grow beets all through the summer and fall.

Unlike other root crops, beets do fine when started early and then transplanted to the garden, since their root is a bulb rather than a long taproot. They can be transplanted as soon as the ground is workable, even if the danger of frost has not passed.

Beets don't compete well with weeds, so try to keep the garden bed as free of weeds as possible. It's best to hand-pull weeds around beets, so you don't run the risk of accidently hitting the beetroot with a hoe and cause it to bleed.

I've found growing beets to be fairly problem free. Most issues arise from watering the leaves instead of the soil or from having poor soil. Beets should grow well if you build the soil by adding compost and nutrients, practice crop rotation and water the soil instead of the leaves.

Harvesting

Beet greens can be harvested at any time, although the younger leaves will be more tender than older leaves. When you thin the beet plants, keep the best-looking plant in the cluster and gently pull the rest. You can thin them a few at a time and use the leaves for dinner, or thin the entire bed at once and preserve the leaves just like you would kale or Swiss chard (page 176).

I like to harvest the bulbs when they are 1½ to 2 inches (3.8 to 5 cm) in diameter. I think these are the best for eating fresh and roasting. If you let them grow too large, they will be woody and tough. It's better to harvest beets before they get too big and store them in the refrigerator until you can preserve them.

If you have loose soil, you should be able to gently pull the beet by its leaves and the root will come out of the soil. If your soil is harder, then use a spade and gently loosen the soil around the beet before pulling it out. Be careful with the spade. Beetroots have a very thin skin and are full of water, so any small cut will result in the beet bleeding.

When you cut the greens off, don't cut close to the root. Leave 2 to 3 inches (5 to 7.6 cm) of leaf stalks attached to the root to keep the beetroot from bleeding out. And be gentle with beets; they seem hard like carrots, but they really aren't.

Beetroots will store well in the refrigerator for a few weeks; just cut the greens off a couple of inches from the bulb and put them in an open container without washing them, as washed beets tend to turn to mush.

Beet Varieties to Try

All beets prefer mild weather, not too hot and not too cold, and mature within 45 to 75 days. Choose varieties based on how you want to use them, how much you like the "earthy" flavor of beets and how long it takes them to mature.

A good all-around beet variety is Detroit Dark Red, which is an heirloom variety. The roots are deep reddish purple throughout, making it a great choice for Dried Beet Powder Food Coloring (page 81). Detroit Dark Red beets also have a lower amount of geosmin, which is the compound that makes beets taste earthy. If you have room for only one beet variety, Detroit Dark Red is a great choice.

If it's the color of beets that is keeping your family from enjoying this highly nutritious food, then try growing Touchstone Gold beets, which have a yellowish orange root. Touchstone Gold beets have a sweet flavor and are less earthy than most red varieties. This is a later-maturing variety, so start it early indoors and transplant it outside when the conditions allow.

For a fun, fresh variety, try Chioggia beets, which are candy cane–striped, with alternating circles of red and white in the root. Chioggia beets are sweet and mature in 60 days, making it a good variety for a second planting.

While we normally think of round beetroots, they also come in a cylinder shape, similar to a carrot. The Cylindra beet variety is really great for achieving uniform beetroot slices. Because of the elongated root, it also gives you more root than other varieties, making it a good choice for those who have limited garden space. The texture of Cylindra beets is smooth. In fact, some call them "butter slicer" beets. Cylindra matures quickly at 55 to 60 days.

Buying

You can find beets year-round at most grocery stores, but you will pay a premium for them. At the farmers' market, you'll find them anytime that's not blazing hot or snowing. Toward the end of the season, beets should be less costly than at the beginning of the season, so keep that in mind if you want to preserve them.

The most important thing to look for when buying beets is whether the greens were cut off properly. It's fine if they haven't been cut off, but if they have been, are there still 2 to 3 inches (5 to 7.6 cm) of stems attached to the root? Are the bottom roots still attached, or have they been removed close to the bulb?

If the beets don't have some stems and roots attached, pass them by, as they have probably lost a lot of juice. Also, pass by any beets that are pale in color, soft or with dented or bruised flesh, as they have probably lost a lot of juice.

If the beets still have the greens attached, the greens should be fresh and crisp, not limp. If you're going to eat the leaves fresh, they should be shorter than 8 inches (20.3 cm).

Preserving

The most popular way to preserve beets is to pickle them, a great option for those who love pickled foods. But there are so many other ways to preserve beets.

When you peel and slice beets, be mindful of their juice. I like to peel and slice beets on a glass plate instead of a wooden cutting board, so I can save the juice that bleeds out. Beet juice can stain your hands and clothes, but will usually wash out if treated quickly.

Canning

Beets can be water bath canned (page 16) by pickling or using them in a jam, jelly or marmalade. They can also be grated and added to relishes to add color—just don't change the total amount of low-acid food in the recipe.

Plain beets can be canned whole, sliced or cubed by using a pressure canner (page 22). It is not recommended that plain mashed beets be canned. Small beets that are under 2 inches (5 cm) in diameter can be canned whole; larger beets can be sliced or cubed.

It takes approximately 14 pounds (6.4 kg) of beetroots to fill nine pint (500-ml) jars and 21 pounds (9.5 kg) of beetroots to fill seven quart (1-L) jars. You need the equivalent of two quart-sized (1-L) jars to properly use the pressure canner.

The hot-pack method (page 24) is recommended for canning beets. You'll want to handle the beets carefully, so they don't bleed out before they're canned. You will naturally lose some juice, but you don't want to lose it all. Remove the greens by cutting an inch or two (5 to 7.6 cm) away from the crowns; leave the small roots attached. Scrub the beets well, but be careful not to cut the skin.

Put a teakettle or medium stockpot full of water on to boil; this is the water you'll use to fill the jars.

Boil water in a large stockpot and add the cleaned beets to it. Gently boil the beets for 15 to 20 minutes, or until the skins can be easily peeled away. Remove the beets from the boiling water and let them cool just enough to handle. Remove the skins, the stems and roots from the beets. If you're going to slice or cube the beets, go ahead and do that now, so you handle each beet only once. The beets won't be fully cooked; they'll finish cooking while they're in the pressure canner.

The beets need to stay hot until they go into the jars, so I like to fill one jar at a time with hot beets and then pour fresh boiling water over them before moving on to the next jar.

When the jars are filled, use the bubble remover tool or a chopstick to remove the air bubbles and make sure the jars have 1 inch (2.5 cm) of headspace. Wipe the rims of each jar and put a lid and band on the jar. Process the jars, according to the manufacturer's instructions, at 10 psi (69 kPa) for 30 minutes for pints (500 ml) and 40 minutes for quarts (1 L). Adjust for altitude (page 25), if necessary.

Beets can be pickled and processed in a water bath canner for 30 minutes, but they have to be boiled until tender before processing.

Freezing

Beets need to be fully cooked, not just blanched, to be frozen. You'll want to leave the skin on, the roots intact and 1 to 2 inches (5 to 7.6 cm) of the stems attached to reduce bleeding. You can also add 1 to 2 tablespoons (15 to 30 ml) of lemon juice or vinegar to the boiling water to reduce bleeding.

To cook the beets, put them in a pot of boiling water for 45 minutes to an hour. Or, roast them. Put them in a roasting pan with a couple of inches (5 cm) of water, cover the pan with aluminum foil, and bake the beets at 350°F (177°C) for the same amount of time. Set up an ice bath. To test for doneness, insert a knife into the beet; it should go through the beet easily and smoothly. Don't cook them so long that they turn to mush.

Once the beets are cooked, put them into the bowl of ice water to stop the cooking process. When the beets are cool enough to handle, remove the skin, roots and stems. Slice or cube the beets. If you don't mind them freezing into one lump, put the beets in a freezer-safe container, label the container and put it in the freezer. If you don't want them in a frozen lump, freeze them on a baking sheet lined with parchment paper first, then transfer the beets to a freezer-safe container. Store in the freezer for up to a year.

Frozen beets can be added to smoothies and salads or tossed with olive oil and seasonings and roasted or sautéed with other vegetables.

Dehydrating

Just like when freezing, beets need to be fully cooked before dehydrating. You can cook them in the oven or on the stovetop, following the instructions in the freezing beets section above.

After the beets are cooked, cooled and peeled, cut them into ⅛-inch (4-mm) slices. I like to cut the beets in half and then slice them. If the beets are large, I'll cut the slices in half again so that they're a quarter of a circle instead of a half circle. Lay the beet slices on the dehydrator trays and dehydrate them at 125°F (51°C) for 10 to 12 hours. The beets should be hard when completely dried.

The dried beets can be rehydrated by soaking 1 cup (60 g) of dried beets in 2 cups (474 ml) of warm water for 30 to 60 minutes. The consistency of rehydrated beets should be the same as that of freshly cooked beets, and you can use them just as you would cooked beets.

The dried beets can be powdered and added to smoothies, or to anything to which you want to give a deep red color, such as tomato paste, fruit leather (page 44) and Dried Squash Fruit Chews (page 295). Dried beets can also be used to make a natural red food dye, the Dried Beet Powder Food Coloring (page 81). But don't powder it all at once; I've found that beet powder tends to lose its bright red color and turn brownish over time. The slices don't lose color, so I leave them whole and make the powder a little at a time as I need it.

Fermenting

Beets can be tricky to ferment because their high sugar content can turn to alcohol easily. And since beets are root vegetables, they need time to soften up in a ferment. It's a fine balance to give them enough fermentation time to soften up, but not so much that they become an adult beverage.

One way to get around the trickiness is to use very thin pieces of beets—paper thin–slices, spiralized pieces, thin matchsticks or coarsely grated beets. This gives more surface area for the brine to do what it does.

To make fermented beets, wash the beets, cut off the stems and root and slice them thinly. Put the beets in a wide-mouth Mason jar and cover them with 2 percent brine (page 51). You can add onions, garlic and spices, such as dill, bay leaves, peppercorns, mustard seed, red pepper flakes and ginger, to the jar before adding the brine. Add a weight and an airlock fermenting lid.

Put the jar on a plate or small cookie sheet to catch any overflow, and store the jar out of direct sunlight for 4 to 5 days. After 4 days, test the beets each day until they are to your liking, being sure to replace the weight and fermenting lid each time, until they are done. When the beets are done, remove the weight and fermenting lid, add a regular plastic storage lid and store them in the refrigerator for up to 1 year.

Lastly, you can add beets to other vegetables. Grated beets make a fun addition to any fermented sauerkraut or relish (page 50). You can add a few ribbons of beets to sliced onions or relishes, such as the Fermented Onion Bulbs (page 191), for a festive pink color.

Preserving Beets Cheat Sheet

	Water Bath Canning	Pressure Canning	Freezing	Dehydrating	Fermenting 2% brine
How to prepare	Must be boiled first; whole if under 2 inches (5 cm), slices	Must be boiled first; whole if under 2 inches (5 cm), slices	Fully cooked before freezing; slices, chunks, pureed	Fully cooked before dehydrating; slices	Slices
Flavors	Pickled	Plain	Plain or seasoned	Plain	Savory
Length of processing	30 minutes	Pints (500 ml): 30 minutes Quarts (1 L): 35 minutes	45-minute boiling before freezing	45-minute boiling before dehydrating for 10–12 hours	4–5 days
Storage life	12 months	12 months	8–12 months	12 months	6–9 months

Frozen Beet and Horseradish Sauce

This beet and horseradish sauce is very similar to chrain, which is a traditional Jewish recipe, usually served at Passover. I'm not Jewish, but I love this sauce. It pairs perfectly with fish. And I like it smeared on meat sandwiches or eaten straight out of the jar with saltines.

If you have access to fresh horseradish, use it; but if you don't, prepared horseradish will do just fine.

Makes 5 (4-ounce [125-ml]) jars

1 lb (453 g) beets, roasted (page 74), peeled and chopped

4 tbsp (4 g) grated horseradish or 2 tbsp (30 ml) prepared horseradish

3 tbsp (45 ml) white wine vinegar

2 tbsp (30 ml) lemon juice

2 tbsp (30 g) sugar

2 tsp (12 g) salt

Put the beets, horseradish, vinegar, lemon juice, sugar and salt in a blender, and blend for 2 to 3 minutes, or until the mixture is smooth.

Transfer the sauce to freezer-safe containers and label them. You will want to freeze this in small quantities; I like to use 4-ounce (125-ml) Mason jars for freezing this sauce, but you can use plastic freezer bags or even ice cube trays (when the cubes of sauce are frozen, transfer them to plastic freezer bags).

Put the filled containers in the refrigerator to cool overnight, then move them to the freezer. Use the sauce within 12 months.

Serving Suggestions: *Use on roast beef or turkey sandwiches instead of mayonnaise or mustard. This also makes a great dip for crackers or seafood.*

Canned Beet and Orange Marmalade

Whenever I serve this marmalade to friends, they always comment about how festive and tasty it is. They're always surprised to find out it's made from beets, because they thought they didn't like beets.

Makes 6 half-pint (250-ml) jars

2½ cups (420 g) cooked, peeled and chopped beets

1 cup (237 ml) lemon juice

2 small oranges (approximately 300 g total), thinly sliced then chopped with the peel

5 tbsp (45 g) pectin

4 cups (800 g) sugar

Prepare the water bath canner by filling it halfway with water and putting it on the stove to simmer. Check six half-pint (250-ml) jars for any nicks or cracks, wash them in hot soapy water and rinse with hot water. Keep the jars hot until it's time to use them. Wash the lids in hot soapy water and rinse them.

In a medium stockpot, combine the beets, lemon juice, oranges and pectin and bring the mixture to a boil. Add the sugar and boil for 1 minute. Remove the pot from the heat. Ladle the marmalade into the hot jars, leaving ¼ inch (6 mm) of headspace.

Wipe the rims with a clean cloth, put on the lids and screw on the bands. Place the jars in the prepared hot water bath canner and process them for 15 minutes, adjusting for altitude (page 17) if necessary. Arrange a folded towel on the counter or table. Remove the jars, using a jar lifter, and place them on the folded towel. Let the jars cool for at least 12 hours.

When the jars are cooled, remove the bands and check the seals. If any jars failed to seal, put them in the refrigerator to use first. Wipe the jars with a clean cloth, label them and store the marmalade for up to a year.

Serving Suggestions: *This marmalade is fantastic served with cream cheese and crackers. It also makes a fun topping for biscuits, and it can be used as a marinade for meat.*

Fermented Beets and Onions

Jazz up a salad bar staple by adding onions and spices. These sweet, tangy, melt-in-your-mouth beets will surely please the pickled beet lover in your life.

Makes 1 quart (1 L)

1 or 2 medium (120 g total) beets, sliced

1 medium (120 g) sweet onion, sliced

2 whole cloves

2 tsp (10 ml) honey

1 tbsp (18 g) salt

2 cups (474 ml) filtered water

Put the beet and onion slices, along with the cloves and honey, in a wide-mouth quart (1-L) Mason jar.

Mix the salt and water together to make a brine, then pour it into the jar to cover the vegetables. Put a weight in the jar to keep everything under the brine, and top the jar with a fermentation lid. Put the jar on a plate or small cookie sheet to catch any overflow.

Set the jar in a cool place, out of direct sunlight, for 5 to 7 days. You can taste the beets and onions any time after 5 days. If they need to ferment longer, replace the weight and fermentation lid and ferment for a few more days. When the ferment is to your liking, replace the weight and fermentation lid with a plastic storage lid. Store the beets and onions in the refrigerator for up to 9 months.

Serving Suggestions: *These beets are a fun addition to salads and tasty as a cold side dish. The brine can be used with a little oil to make a fantastic salad dressing or marinade for meats.*

Dried Beet Powder Food Coloring

There are a couple of ways to make beetroot food coloring. One way is to grind dehydrated beetroot into a powder and sprinkle that into whatever needs coloring. But that may not be the best for things that require a smooth texture, like frosting. In that case, you'll want to use this liquid beetroot food coloring.

Makes ¼ cup (59 ml)

1 tbsp (5 g) dehydrated beetroot slices

3 tbsp (45 ml) glycerin

Break the dehydrated beetroot into smaller pieces by hand, if possible, or with a mortar and pestle. You don't want them powdered, because it will make straining the solids out harder. But you do want more surface area than large round slices will give you.

Put the beetroot pieces into a small jar and pour the glycerin over them. Put a tight-fitting lid on them and set them out of direct sunlight for 2 weeks. Every day or two, shake the jar to mix the contents.

Remove the beetroot pieces from the glycerin by pouring the mixture through a fine-mesh strainer into a bowl. Put the strained liquid back in the jar, and return the lid to the jar. Label the jar and store the food coloring in the pantry for up to 1 year.

It's important to use fully dehydrated beetroot in this recipe for it to be shelf-stable for a year. The moisture in fresh beetroot can cause mold. If you decide to make this with fresh beetroot, it will need to be stored in the refrigerator.

Serving Suggestions: *Use to color cake batter, cookie dough, frosting and icing by adding a few drops at time, until you have the color you want. The earthy flavor of the beets is not noticeable in the dye. This dye can also be used to add color to smoothies or tomato products.*

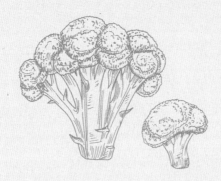

broccoli

There's More than Just Florets

While broccoli is a mainstream vegetable today and can be found in almost any grocery store year-round, that wasn't always the case. Broccoli didn't appear in the US on a widespread basis until the 1920s, when Southern Italian immigrants brought seeds in and began growing it. It was developed in Italy through selective breeding of wild cabbage, and it has been grown there for hundreds of years.

Broccoli is one of my family's most anticipated cool-weather crops—it tastes great and, unlike cabbage or cauliflower, will give us more than one harvest per plant. Broccoli is highly nutritious, as are all the plants in the *Brassica* genus.

All above-ground parts of the broccoli plant are edible, although most people just eat the head, which is also called the *crown*. What we call the broccoli crown is, in fact, the seed stalk of the plant. If it's left on the plant, each of those little buds will become yellow flowers that are also edible.

Our family eats all parts of the broccoli—the leaves, stem, head and flowers—but we preserve only the leaves, stem and heads. I do not preserve a lot of broccoli because it grows over the winter in my climate, and I don't need a lot of preserved broccoli during the summer growing season.

Growing

Broccoli is a cool-weather crop. If you live in a climate with cold winters, you can plant broccoli in the very early spring and grow it until the summer heat sets in. You might also be able to get a fall crop if you plant broccoli early and choose early-maturing varieties.

If you live in a climate that has very mild winters, you can plant broccoli in the fall and grow it through the winter and early spring.

Broccoli transplants well, so it's a good candidate for starting indoors and then moving outdoors. Because it's cold hardy, broccoli can be transplanted outdoors a few weeks before your average last frost date.

You'll want to plant broccoli in fertile, well-draining soil and water it regularly. If you're growing broccoli over the winter, it can be hard to remember to water. My rule of thumb is: if we don't get an inch (2.5 cm) of rain during the week, I need to water.

The seeds are small, which is another reason starting them indoors is a good idea. I don't have an indoor seed-starting setup, so I sow a bunch of seeds directly in the garden when we're expecting a few days of rain. When the new plants have several true leaves, I thin them and transplant the plants I thinned to other beds.

Cabbage loopers are little caterpillars that love broccoli and can really wreak havoc on young plants. You can use row covers to protect the broccoli. Row covers work great because broccoli doesn't need any kind of pollination to produce. Just make sure to put the row covers on early, before the little white butterflies lay their eggs.

Bacillus thuringienis (Bt) is an organic pesticide that targets caterpillars and is non-toxic for humans. I spray once when I first see caterpillar damage. That will usually control them for the whole growing season. I don't mind some caterpillar damage on larger plants, but the cabbage loopers can do so much damage to a young plant that it won't grow.

Harvesting

We start harvesting broccoli leaves when the plants have five or six large leaves. We're conservative when harvesting leaves and harvest only a few leaves per plant each week.

Once the broccoli forms a head, we let it grow until the little green buds start plumping up. Don't wait too long, or you'll end up with a head full of flowers instead of buds. Cut the stalk about 5 to 6 inches (12.7 to 15.2 cm) down from the head.

We peel and use the stalk just like we do with asparagus (page 58). Inside the stalk is pale, tender flesh that tastes mildly like broccoli.

Let the plant continue to grow and it will produce small side shoots, like broccoli florets, all season long. Some varieties produce more than others, but every variety I've ever planted has produced some. Cut the little florets off once you notice the green buds are getting plump.

If some of the buds open and produce a little yellow flower, the broccoli is still edible and tasty. I wouldn't want a large head full of flowers, so we harvest before that happens. The little florets that have flowers make fun, edible garnishes. Also, bees love broccoli flowers, so leave some flowers for them if you can.

Broccoli Varieties to Try

Broccoli varieties come in many shapes and sizes. Some have really large heads and then produce just a few side shoots. Others have smaller main heads and will produce many side shoots. Some are more heat tolerant than others, but all taste better when harvested in cool weather. Broccoli also comes in various shades of green, from bright green to blueish green, and even in purple.

My favorite varieties are those that produce a lot of side shoots. This allows me to get a more consistent harvest out of the plants. If you want to preserve large amounts of broccoli, you probably want to plant a variety that produces large heads.

Di Cicco is an Italian heirloom broccoli variety dating back to 1890, when it was first introduced in Italy. It makes a modest size main head that is about 4 inches (10 cm) across. Then it goes into prolific side-shoot production. You can start harvesting Di Cicco as early as 45 days, which makes this a good variety for fall planting and for spring planting in climates with a very short spring.

Another variety that has good side-shoot production is Calabrese. It matures a little slower than Di Cicco, but it's more cold hardy, which also makes it a good fall planting variety.

Waltham 29 is a large-head variety that is also drought tolerant and holds its head longer than other varieties. Waltham 29 produces side shoots for 6 to 8 weeks after the main head is harvested.

For color, try Purple Sprouting broccoli, which is an heirloom variety that produces many small purple florets instead of one large head. Bred for overwintering in mild climates, this variety will mature in about 70 days. Like purple beans, purple broccoli will turn green when cooked.

Buying

Broccoli can be purchased fresh year-round in almost any grocery store. But that doesn't mean it's truly fresh. Look for broccoli that has been kept cool, either on ice or in refrigerated cases.

Properly stored broccoli should have closely bunched florets and firm stems. Avoid woody stalks with open cores at the base; these will be tough and hollow, which means you won't be able to use them. (And, of course, you want to use them.)

While I happily harvest broccoli from my garden that has a few flowers opening on it, I wouldn't spend money on it. When I have broccoli with flowers in the garden, that means it's the end of the winter/ spring garden and pickings are slim. I'll use what I have and cook it with other vegetables so it isn't so strongly flavored and odoriferous. If I'm going to spend money, I want produce that is not overly mature.

Pass by limp, tired-looking heads. These haven't been stored properly and have lost their texture and can't be revived.

Preserving

Before using broccoli, it's a good idea to immerse the head in a bowl of warm saltwater to flush out any bugs hiding in the florets. To make the salted water, mix 4 teaspoons (24 g) of salt per gallon (4 L) of water. Let the florets soak for 20 minutes, then rinse them with fresh water and drain them.

The head will need to be chopped into smaller florets; I like to make them no bigger than 1½ inches (3.8 cm) across. They'll preserve better if they're all about the same size. The stem can be peeled and sliced into matchsticks, rounds, cubes or grated.

Canning broccoli is not recommended, although I know some people do it. The end result is often mushy and very strong flavored—kind of like what overcooked broccoli smells like the day after. Since there are no recommended times for processing broccoli, we won't be covering pressure canning broccoli in this book. Remember, our goal is to preserve food in such a way that our families will eat it, not just to have jars of food in the pantry.

That being said, I have successfully canned pickled broccoli stems using a recipe for pickled cauliflower and Brussels sprouts from the National Center for Home Food Preservation and will share that (Canned Asian-Style Pickled Broccoli Stems, page 87).

Freezing

Freezing broccoli is, by far, the most popular method for preserving it. Broccoli needs to be blanched for 3 minutes (page 34) before freezing it. If you're using a steam blancher, blanch for 5 minutes. If you're freezing broccoli stems that are cut in matchsticks, rounds or cubes, blanch for 3 minutes. If you're freezing grated broccoli, there's no need to blanch it first.

When the time is up, put the broccoli pieces in ice water to stop the cooking process. After they have completely cooled off, put the pieces on a clean kitchen towel and let them dry. This will help keep ice crystals from forming on the broccoli.

To freeze the broccoli pieces, lay them on a baking sheet covered with parchment paper and put them in the freezer for 3 to 4 hours. Once they are frozen, transfer the pieces to freezer-safe containers and put them back into the freezer. Broccoli can be frozen for up to a year.

Because I like to have prepared food stored and not just ingredients, I also make Frozen Creamy Broccoli Dip (page 89). This dip can be made with any part of the broccoli, but is especially good when the tender core of the stem is used.

Dehydrating

Since canning broccoli isn't recommended, dehydrating broccoli is the only way to have shelf-stable broccoli. Broccoli is a little bulky, even dehydrated, so be aware that for every 2 cups (140 g) of fresh broccoli you dehydrate, you'll end up with 1 cup (35 g) of dried broccoli.

Before dehydrating broccoli, blanch it for 3 minutes (page 34). After the 3 minutes is up, but the broccoli pieces in ice water to stop the cooking process. Lay the cooled broccoli pieces on a clean kitchen towel to dry a bit. This keeps my dehydrator cleaner, and, if I'm seasoning the broccoli, it helps the seasonings stick better.

Put the broccoli pieces on dehydrator trays and dehydrate at 135°F (57°C) for 12 to 15 hours, or until they are crisp and brittle.

A pound (453 g) of fresh broccoli that has been dehydrated will fit into a 1-quart (1-L) Mason jar. The broccoli can be used in soup or reconstituted for stir-frying or sautéing for a side dish. If you crush dried broccoli or put it in a blender, you will get a powder that can be used to make cream of broccoli soup.

The leaves can be dehydrated just like kale (page 177) and added to the Dried Superfood Green Powder (page 179).

Broccoli florets, stems and leaves can also be seasoned and dehydrated for snacking. I like to dehydrate the stems as I do the asparagus stems (page 59) and dehydrate the florets with ranch-style seasonings (Dried Broccoli and Ranch Florets, page 92) or Asian-style seasonings.

Fermenting

Fermented broccoli can be delicious or disastrous. In my opinion, the key to making delicious fermented broccoli is to start with broccoli that has small buds that are showing no signs of opening. The older broccoli with plump buds and maybe even a bit of yellow peeking out will probably produce a very strong-smelling and strong-flavored ferment.

To ferment broccoli, slice the florets and stalks lengthwise. The broccoli will ferment more evenly if the slices are approximately the same size. If you find that you like the fermented stalks better than the florets, you can use just the stalks for fermenting and the florets for freezing and dehydrating.

Once the broccoli is sliced, put it in a bowl and sprinkle it with 1¾ teaspoons (10 g) salt for every pound (453 g) of broccoli. Mix the broccoli and salt well, and let it sit for about 15 minutes. The salt will help the broccoli release its moisture. After 15 minutes, put the broccoli in a clean quart (1-L) wide-mouth Mason jar and push it down. This will help the broccoli release even more moisture. Once the broccoli is in the jar good and tight, pour enough filtered, non-chlorinated water over it to ensure all the broccoli is submerged. Add the fermentation weight and lid, and let the broccoli ferment for 7 days. After 7 days, taste the broccoli. If it's still salty, replace the weight and the fermentation lid and let the broccoli ferment for another day or two to mellow. When the broccoli is fermented to your liking, remove the weight and fermentation lid and replace them with a plastic storage lid. Store the fermented broccoli in the refrigerator for up to 3 months.

If you want to add spices to the broccoli while it's fermenting, try onions, bay leaf, garlic, peppercorns, fennel seeds or rosemary. You can add them to the jar before you put the broccoli in it.

I suggest you make a very small amount of fermented broccoli the first few times you make it and take good notes on it. Then if you find a combination you really like, you can make larger batches.

Preserving Broccoli Cheat Sheet

	Water Bath Canning	Pressure Canning (Not recommended)	Freezing	Dehydrating	Fermenting
How to prepare	Peeled stems only	N/A	3-minute blanching recommended; florets or pieces	3-minute blanching recommended; florets or pieces	Sauerkraut style; small florets and sliced stems
Flavors	Pickled with herbs	N/A	Plain or in a dip	Plain or seasoned	Savory with herbs
Length of processing	15 minutes	N/A	3-minute blanching recommended	8–12 hours	7 days
Storage life	12 months	N/A	8–12 months	12 months for plain; 1 month for seasoned	3–6 months

Canned Asian-Style Pickled Broccoli Stems

These pickled broccoli stems remind me of an Asian-style salad, you know the one that some people put crushed ramen noodles on? I like to eat these straight out of the jar or poured over shredded green and red cabbage with a sprinkle of toasted sesame seed oil for a quick side dish.

Makes 2 pint (500-ml) jars

1 tsp coriander seed

2 tsp (8 g) mustard seed

12 black peppercorns

½ tsp salt

1 tsp dill seed

2 cups (474 ml) unseasoned rice vinegar (5% acidity)

½ cup (100 g) sugar

⅔ lb (302 g) broccoli stems, cut into matchsticks

2 Thai chili peppers, divided

2 cloves garlic, divided

Prepare the water bath canner by filling it halfway with water and putting it on the stove to simmer. Check two pint (500-ml) jars for any nicks or cracks, wash them in hot soapy water and rinse them in hot water. Keep the jars hot until it's time to use them. Wash the lids in hot soapy water, rinse them and set them aside.

Combine the coriander seed, mustard seed, peppercorns, salt, dill seed, vinegar and sugar in a large stockpot and bring the mixture to a boil, stirring occasionally. Once it's boiling, add the broccoli and simmer it for 3 minutes.

Put 1 Thai pepper and 1 clove of garlic in each jar. Add the broccoli and pickling mixture to the jars, leaving ½ inch (12 mm) of headspace. Remove the air bubbles with a bubble remover tool or chopstick and recheck the headspace; add more brine or vinegar if necessary. Wipe the rims with a clean cloth, put the lids on the jars and screw on the bands. Place the jars in the prepared hot water bath canner, making sure that the jars are covered by at least an inch (2.5 cm) of water.

Bring the water to a full rolling boil, and put the lid on the canner. Process the jars for 15 minutes, adjusting for altitude (page 17), if necessary. Arrange a folded towel on the counter or table. Remove the jars, using a jar lifter, and place them on the towel. Let the jars cool for at least 12 hours.

Once the jars are cooled, remove the bands and check the seals. If any jars failed to seal, put them in the refrigerator to use first. Wipe the jars with a clean cloth and store them for up to a year. This recipe will have the best flavor if you wait at least 3 weeks before cracking open a jar.

Serving Suggestions: *These pickled broccoli stems can be chopped and added to anything that calls for relish: deviled eggs, potato or pasta salad, even tuna salad.*

Frozen Creamy Broccoli Dip

This dip is a great way to use the tender inside of the broccoli stem, but it can also be made with a combination of peeled stems and florets. When you cook fresh broccoli for dinner, take a few minutes and make this dip for the freezer. The next time you need dip for a veggie or cracker tray, you can just pull it out of the freezer.

Makes 2 cups (474 ml)

2 cups (182 g) chopped broccoli florets or peeled stems

2 cloves garlic

¼ cup (30 g) chopped onion

8 oz (225 g) cream cheese

¼ tsp salt

Steam the broccoli for 3 to 5 minutes, until it is fork tender and still vibrant green. Put the garlic in a food processor and pulse a few times to chop it. Add the broccoli, onion, cream cheese and salt to the food processor and process until the mixture is smooth.

Transfer the dip into freezer-safe containers, such as 4-ounce (125-ml) Mason jars or plastic freezer bags, and label the containers. If you're using glass jars, be sure to leave ½ inch (12 mm) of headspace for expansion. Put the filled containers into the refrigerator to cool overnight, then transfer them to the freezer. The dip can be frozen for up to a year.

Serving Suggestions: *This dip is a great addition to a vegetable tray or deli platter. The dip can be thinned with milk to make a dip for potato chips or Dried Asian Snap Pea Chips (page 201). It also makes a fantastic spread for flatbread wraps.*

Dried Asian Broccoli Crisps

Use just the florets for this recipe and you'll have a crisp, airy snack that your family will devour. Of course, you can use the stems too, but don't be surprised if your family eats the florets first and leaves the stems for "someone else."

Makes 1 quart (1 L)

1 lb (453 g) broccoli florets, cut into small, uniform pieces, and/ or stems, peeled and sliced

2 tbsp (30 ml) tamari or low-sodium soy sauce

2 tbsp (16 g) grated Parmesan cheese

¼ cup (33 g) sunflower seeds, sesame seeds or hemp seeds

½ cup (118 ml) chicken, beef or vegetable broth

1 tsp onion powder

1 clove garlic

Fill a medium stockpot about halfway with water and bring it to a boil over high heat. Put the broccoli into the boiling water and let it come back up to a boil. Cover the pot and blanch the broccoli for 3 minutes. While the broccoli is in the boiling water, prepare a bowl of ice water. Using a slotted spoon, immediately transfer the broccoli from the boiling water to the bowl of ice water to stop the cooking.

While the broccoli is cooling, put the tamari, Parmesan, seeds, broth, onion powder and garlic into a blender, and blend to chop up the seeds and garlic.

Drain the water from the broccoli pieces, put them onto a clean kitchen towel and pat them dry. Put the broccoli into a bowl with room for mixing and pour the seasoning mixture over them. Mix to coat all the pieces.

Lay the seasoned broccoli pieces on a dehydrator tray. You can put the pieces close together, as they will shrink considerably. Dehydrate at 135°F (57°C) for 8 to 12 hours, or until the pieces are brittle. The crisps should easily crumble when pinched.

Remove the tray from the dehydrator and let the florets cool. Put the cooled florets in a glass jar with a tight-fitting lid and label the jar. Use the dried broccoli florets within 1 month.

These are best eaten within a few days. If they lose their crispiness, they can be put into the dehydrator on high for 15 to 30 minutes to crisp them.

Serving Suggestions: *Use as a crunchy snack right out of the jar. These can also be roughly crushed and added to salads or soups to add a nice crunch.*

Dried Broccoli and Ranch Florets

Dipping mini trees, aka broccoli florets, into ranch dressing has won over many children who thought they didn't like broccoli. This recipe was created for children who need ranch dressing to enjoy broccoli and can now eat mini trees without the mess of dipping them in dressing.

Makes 1 quart (1 L)

¾ lb (340 g) broccoli florets, cut into small, uniform pieces, and/or stems, peeled and sliced

2 tbsp (30 ml) vegetable broth

1 tbsp (9 g) buttermilk powder

½ tsp garlic powder

½ tsp onion powder

¼ tsp dried dill weed

¼ tsp salt

⅛ tsp ground black pepper

Fill a medium stockpot about halfway with water and bring it to a boil over high heat. Put the broccoli in the boiling water, and let it come back up to a boil. Cover the pot, and blanch the broccoli for 3 minutes. While the broccoli is in the boiling water, prepare a bowl of ice water. Using a slotted spoon, immediately transfer the broccoli pieces from the pot into the bowl of ice water to stop the cooking.

While the broccoli is cooling, mix the broth, buttermilk powder, garlic powder, onion powder, dill weed, salt and pepper in a large bowl.

Drain the water from the broccoli pieces, put them onto a clean kitchen towel and pat them dry. Carefully add the broccoli to the bowl with the seasoning mixture. Mix to coat all the pieces.

Lay the seasoned broccoli pieces on a dehydrator tray. You can put the pieces close together, as they will shrink considerably. Dehydrate at 135°F (57°C) for 8 to 12 hours or until they are brittle. The crisps should easily crumble when pinched.

Remove the tray from the dehydrator and let the broccoli cool. Put the cooled broccoli in a glass jar with a tight-fitting lid and label the jar. Use the dried broccoli florets within 1 month.

These are best eaten within a few days. If they lose their crispiness, they can be put into the dehydrator on high for 15 to 30 minutes to crisp them.

Serving Suggestions: *Dried ranch–flavored broccoli makes a nice crouton substitute for salads or soups. They can also be enjoyed as a crunchy snack.*

cabbage
A Winter Vegetable Staple

Cabbage is a member of the *Brassica* family, along with broccoli, Brussels sprouts, cauliflower and kale. I think cabbage is the more tender member of the family, with the mild flavor of its inner leaves. Most of us are familiar with coleslaw, the shredded green cabbage tossed with way too much mayonnaise, or the flecks of red cabbage in bagged salad, but those are just the beginning of what cabbage offers.

Along with green storage cabbage and red head cabbage, there are also the delicate savoy cabbage of France and Belgium, the long celery cabbage of China and the spicy mustard cabbage, called *pak choi* or *bok choy*, of India and China.

All of these cabbages taste wonderful, but are often avoided because of their strong flavor and odor. It's the overcooking of cabbage that's the culprit, not the cabbage itself. Cabbage tastes great when it's raw or barely cooked but not when it's overcooked and mushy.

Growing

Cabbage is a cool-weather crop and one of the crops my family looks most forward to each winter. Unlike broccoli, each cabbage plant will give you just one harvest. You can pick the outer leaves to prolong the harvest a bit, but after you cut the cabbage head off the plant, the plant is finished producing.

Because of this, I like to stagger the cabbage plantings, so we have cabbage maturing at different times throughout the season. Cabbage seeds can be started indoors, and the transplants can be planted outside before the average last frost date. Cabbage is cold hardy. Light frosts won't harm it; indeed, it will probably make it sweeter.

When you plant the cabbage transplants outside, sow seeds directly in the garden for the next crop. This should give you about 3 weeks between harvesting the first cabbages and the second crop. If you want to have fresh cabbage all season long, continue sowing new seeds every 2 to 3 weeks during the growing season.

Cabbage is a heavy feeder and needs rich soil that has had compost worked into it. Cabbage also does well with a midseason top dressing of compost. Cabbage likes loose, well-draining soil. It also needs to be watered regularly, even if it's growing over the winter months. If it hasn't rained at least an inch (2.5 cm) that week, the cabbage needs to be watered.

The biggest problem with growing cabbage is cabbage loopers and cabbage worms. These are little caterpillars that feast on cabbage and other members of the *Brassica* family. One solution is to grow cabbage under row covers since it doesn't need pollination. Another solution is to spray them with *Bacillus thuringiensis (Bt),* which is a naturally occurring bacteria that affects only caterpillars. I've found that if I spray cabbage plants when I first notice the damage, I need to spray only once. I don't mind some pest damage. As long as the plants are still strong enough to grow and produce, I won't spray again.

Harvesting

The outer cabbage leaves can be harvested at any time. These leaves are tougher than the inner leaves and are great for adding to long-simmered soups. Head cabbage can be harvested whenever the head is firm and fully formed. Chinese cabbage is harvested when the head is still compact and firm, before a seed stalk is formed.

Most cabbage varieties will mature in anywhere from 50 to 100 days. A good way of knowing when to harvest cabbage is to count the days to maturity on the calendar and make a note of it.

Cabbages that are harvested before they are fully mature will still taste good, the head just won't be as dense as a fully mature head. Cabbages that are harvested late will also taste just fine, as long as the temperatures have remained cool—consistent temperatures above 80°F (27°C) will cause cabbage to get bitter.

To harvest cabbage, cut the stalk at ground level. Many people cut off just the head of the cabbage and leave the outer leaves because they are tougher than the inner leaves. I harvest the whole cabbage. As I mentioned before, the outer leaves are good in dishes that are cooked using a slow and gentle method, such as braising or in a soup.

Once harvested, cabbage can be stored in the vegetable compartment of the refrigerator until you are ready to use it. However, since it will slowly lose moisture as it is stored; it's best to use cabbage soon after picking.

Cabbage Varieties to Try

There are many varieties of cabbage. The colors range from light green, almost white, to deep green and even purple. While most of us think of head cabbage when we think of cabbage, there are also varieties of leaf cabbage.

Cabbage varieties have a huge range of maturity dates, from 55 days to over 100 days. I like to use the maturity dates as the primary factor for choosing the cabbage varieties I grow.

Early-season cabbage varieties mature in less than 70 days and include Copenhagen Market, Savoy Express, Gonzalez and Red Acre. All of these produce fairly small heads. Savoy Express has fun crinkly leaves and Red Acre is a red variety.

Specialty cabbages, such as Pak Choi and Napa, are also early cabbage varieties.

Midseason cabbage varieties mature in 70 to 90 days and include varieties such as Primero, which is green, and Mammoth Red Rock, a red variety. Both of these produce round heads. Savoy Perfection is a savoy midseason variety.

Late-season cabbage takes over 90 days to mature and are usually very large plants. Late varieties also tend to store better than early or midseason varieties. Some late-season varieties are Late Flat Dutch and Danish Ballhead, which are green. Another late variety, January King, takes over 120 days to mature and has beautiful red outer leaves. It is extremely cold hardy, reportedly surviving temperatures as low as 5°F (-15°C).

Buying

When buying cabbage, look for firm heads with crisp leaves. If the outer leaves are wilted, the cabbage is either old or has not been stored properly.

If you're buying cabbage directly from a farmer and the cabbage has no sign of pest damage, ask about the sprays he uses. I'm comfortable with *Bt* being used on my food, but not some of the other pesticides. I'm also comfortable with there being some bug damage on the cabbage that I buy, as long as it doesn't look like Swiss cheese.

Regardless of where you buy the cabbage, the leaves should look fresh and brightly colored. The cabbage head should be firm and heavy.

Preserving

Because cabbage holds a lot of water in its leaves, it's a wonderful storage vegetable and can keep for months if given the proper environment. However, cabbage is not as versatile as other vegetables when it comes to preserving.

When preserving cabbage, you'll want to start with the freshest cabbage you can find. If the outer leaves are wilted, you can feed them to the chickens or put them in the compost pile.

Before preserving cabbage, you want to remove the outer leaves, wash the cabbage head and slice or shred it. If the cabbage is fresh from the garden or farmers' market and you're concerned that there might be pests still in it, you can soak it in a tub of water for 30 to 60 minutes before cutting it.

Canning

It is not recommended to can cabbage by itself in a pressure canner because it usually discolors and has a strong flavor. What is recommended is that naturally fermented sauerkraut be canned to make cabbage shelf-stable. Cabbage can also be pickled with other vegetables to make slaw, relish and chutney.

If you can ferment sauerkraut to make it shelf-stable, the canning process will kill the probiotics in the sauerkraut. Since I make fermented sauerkraut specifically for those probiotics, I do not can our sauerkraut. I store it in the refrigerator.

However, you can combine cabbage with other vegetables and a vinegar brine and water bath can them. Most people call this relish, but I call it slaw. We grow cabbage over the winter months, and I like to make Canned Sweet and Tangy Slaw (page 99) so we can have coleslaw available for summer meals.

Freezing

One of our favorite quick meals is something we call *hash*; it's really more like the inside filling of an eggroll than what most people refer to as hash. And shredded cabbage is the star of this one-skillet dish, along with pan sausage, chopped onions and grated carrots. It's one of those meals that uses what you have in whatever quantities you have.

I keep several bags of shredded cabbage in the freezer so we can have this meal even when cabbage isn't growing in our garden. Frozen cabbage is also great for adding to soups and casseroles.

Shredded cabbage can be frozen without blanching it first, but you'll want to use it within a few months. If you want to freeze it for longer than a few months, you'll need to blanch it for 1½ minutes (page 34). Cabbage leaves and wedges can also be frozen after being blanched for 1½ minutes.

After blanching, put the cabbage in ice water to stop the cooking process. Once cooled, drain the cabbage and pat it dry with a clean kitchen towel. Put the cabbage in freezer-safe containers, label them and put them in the freezer.

Even with patting it dry, cabbage will freeze into a big clump. Therefore, I like to freeze cabbage in portions that I'm going to need for making hash or adding to soups and casseroles. Frozen shredded cabbage looks a lot like frozen shredded zucchini, so be sure to label it with the name and amount.

To thaw frozen cabbage, put it on a plate in the refrigerator for a few hours. Or add it directly to recipes, if it doesn't matter that it's in a clump. It will loosen as it's cooked.

I like to make a bunch of Frozen Cabbage Rolls (page 103) when cabbage is in season. If I have a lot of cabbage that needs to be harvested but not enough time to make cabbage rolls, I'll blanch the outer leaves and freeze them for making cabbage rolls later. Then I shred the interior leaves that are too small for cabbage rolls and either freeze or dehydrate them.

To freeze large cabbage leaves, blanch and cool the leaves first. Then stack them in sets of five and roll them up. Put the rolled leaves into labeled freezer bags, and store them in the freezer for up to a year.

Dehydrating

Dehydrating cabbage is a great way to preserve it, especially if you don't have a lot of freezer space and don't care for pickled products. Even though I have a very large freezer, I still dehydrate cabbage to have some in storage that is shelf-stable. I use dehydrated cabbage to add to soups and smoothies.

It is recommended that cabbage be blanched before dehydrating, but I've found that we prefer the texture of the reconstituted cabbage when it hasn't been blanched first. I suggest you try a small amount each way to see if it's worth the extra effort of blanching for your family.

To dehydrate cabbage, cut it in quarters and then slice into ⅛-inch (4-mm) slices; blanch them if desired. Then lay the pieces out on the dehydrator trays and dehydrate them at 135°F (57°C) for 8 to 11 hours, or until they are crisp. Turn off the dehydrator and let the cabbage cool. Then store the pieces in a glass jar with a tight-fitting lid for up to a year.

The dehydrated cabbage can be added directly to soups and smoothies; just remember that it will soak up moisture and make the soup or smoothie thicker. To rehydrate the dehydrated cabbage, put it in a bowl and pour boiling water over it. Let the cabbage soak for 10 to 15 minutes; it should be fully rehydrated.

Fermenting

Fermented cabbage, aka sauerkraut, is probably the most recognized fermented vegetable. Many people ferment cabbage by the gallons and store it in the refrigerator or cold root cellar to be used all year long. There's little that can go wrong when making sauerkraut, so it's great for beginner fermenters.

Because cabbage has high water content, it will make its own brine when salted. To make fermented cabbage, shred the cabbage and weigh it before you put it in a large bowl. Sprinkle salt on the cabbage at the rate of 1 tablespoon (18 g) for every 1¾ pounds (793 g) of shredded cabbage. Massage the salt into the cabbage for several minutes. You'll notice that the cabbage is releasing its juice as you massage it, making its own brine.

After a few minutes of massaging, put the shredded cabbage and its juices in a clean jar or other fermenting container. As you pack it down, you'll notice that more juice is coming out. That's a good thing. Leave at least 2 inches (5 cm) of headspace, because the contents will expand as they ferment and you don't want all the juice bubbling out of the jar.

Add a fermentation weight to keep the cabbage under the brine. If there's not enough brine to completely cover the cabbage, you can add enough 2 percent brine (page 51) to cover it. Put the fermentation lid on the jar and label the jar. Put the jar on a plate or small cookie sheet to catch any overflow. Sauerkraut is usually fermented for at least 14 days. After 14 days, remove the lid and weight, and taste the sauerkraut. If you think it needs more fermenting, replace the weight and lid and let it ferment longer. Check it every 2 or 3 days, until you like the taste.

When the sauerkraut is done fermenting, remove the fermentation lid and weight and replace them with a plastic storage lid. Store the sauerkraut in the refrigerator for up to a year.

While traditional sauerkraut is made with just cabbage and salt, you can mix in other shredded vegetables, such as beets, carrots, onions and radishes. And you can add spices, such as peppers, garlic, mustard seed, caraway seed, coriander and celery seed. My Fermented East-Meets-West Sauerkraut (page 100) combines traditional sauerkraut vegetables with Asian flavors for a new twist on a classic dish.

Preserving Cabbage Cheat Sheet

	Water Bath Canning	Pressure Canning (Not recommended)	Freezing	Dehydrating	Fermenting
How to prepare	Shredded	N/A	Blanching recommended for whole leaves and wedges; not necessary for shredded	Blanching recommended	Sauerkraut style; shredded
Flavors	Pickled; seasoned with herbs	N/A	Plain or filled cabbage rolls	Plain	Seasoned with herbs
Length of processing	15 minutes	N/A	—	8–11 hours	14–21 days
Storage life	12 months	N/A	8–12 months	12 months	12 months

Canned Sweet and Tangy Slaw

Coleslaw is a summer staple, but cabbage is often grown over winter or early spring, not in the summer. Fortunately, you can make a canned sweet and tangy slaw to get your fill of coleslaw all summer long.

Makes 8 pint (500-ml) jars

3 lbs (1.4 kg) green cabbage, shredded

1½ lbs (679 g) red cabbage, shredded

2 carrots, grated

1 onion, cut into thin shreds

¼ cup (65 g) salt

¼ cup (48 g) mustard seed

¼ cup (27 g) celery seed

2 cups (200 g) sugar

3 cups (711 ml) apple cider vinegar

1 cup (237 ml) white vinegar

Note: *To safely water bath can this recipe, the prepared vegetables need to total no more than 6 pounds (2.7 kg) before salting.*

Serving Suggestions: *This coleslaw is great as a side dish as is, or you can drain most of the brine and stir in some mayonnaise for a creamy coleslaw. Coleslaw can also be used as a topping for sandwiches, burgers and tacos.*

First, weigh the shredded cabbage. Then add the carrots and onion to the scale. Stop adding them when you get to 6 pounds (2.7 kg). If you don't get to 6 pounds (2.7 kg), you can add more shredded vegetables, or just leave it short and have extra brine.

Sprinkle the salt over the vegetables, mix them well and let them sit for an hour.

Prepare the water bath canner by filling it halfway with water and putting it on the stove to simmer. Check eight pint (500-ml) jars for any nicks or cracks, wash them in hot soapy water and rinse them in hot water. Keep the jars hot until it's time to use them. Wash the lids in hot soapy water, rinse them and set them aside.

Make the brine by combining the mustard seed, celery seed, sugar, apple cider vinegar and white vinegar in a large stockpot. Bring the brine to a boil over medium-high heat.

After the vegetables have been salted for an hour, drain them in a colander and rinse them with cold water. Put the rinsed vegetables into the brine and turn off the heat. Stir the vegetables and then pack them into the prepared jars, leaving ½ inch (12 mm) of headspace.

Remove the air bubbles with a bubble remover tool or chopstick and recheck the headspace; add more brine if necessary. Wipe the rims with a clean cloth, put the lids on the jars and screw on the bands. Place the jars in the prepared hot water bath canner, making sure that the jars are covered by at least an inch (2.5 cm) of water.

Bring the water to a full rolling boil, and put the lid on the canner. Process the jars for 10 minutes, adjusting for altitude (page 17), if necessary. Arrange a folded towel on the counter or table. Remove the jars, using a jar lifter, and place them on the towel. Let them cool for at least 12 hours.

Once the jars are cooled, remove the bands and check the seals. If any jars failed to seal, put them in the refrigerator to use first. Wipe the jars with a clean cloth and store the coleslaw for up to a year.

Fermented East-Meets-West Sauerkraut

This sauerkraut is my nod to kimchi, which is super spicy and made with Napa cabbage. I prefer a less spicy ferment, and I use whatever cabbage variety happens to be in the garden. Don't be afraid to add fish sauce; it smells terrible but tastes delicious in small quantities.

Makes 1 quart (1 L)

2 lbs (907 g) green cabbage, shredded

2 grated (165 g) carrots

½ cup (75 g) chopped onion

1 large (24 g) grated radish

2–3 cloves garlic, minced

1 tsp red pepper flakes (optional)

1 tbsp (15 ml) fish sauce

4 tsp (24 g) salt

In a large bowl, combine the cabbage, carrots, onion, radish, garlic, red pepper flakes, if desired, and fish sauce. Sprinkle the cabbage mixture with the salt and mix it well. Use your hands or a kraut pounder to massage the cabbage and help it release its juices to make its own brine. After 5 to 10 minutes, the cabbage mixture and juice can go into a clean wide-mouth jar. Continue pushing the cabbage mixture down until it's all in the jar but be sure to leave at least 2 inches (5 cm) of headspace.

Put a weight in the jar to keep everything under the brine, and top the jar with a fermentation lid. Put the jar on a plate or small cookie sheet to catch any overflow. Set the jar in a cool place, out of direct sunlight, for 14 to 21 days. You can taste the sauerkraut any time after 14 days. If it needs to ferment longer, replace the weight and fermentation lid and ferment for a few more days.

When the sauerkraut is fermented to your liking, replace the weight and fermentation lid with a storage lid, label the jar and store it in the refrigerator for up to 12 months.

*In the photo, the sauerkraut is shown in the jar on the right side.

Serving Suggestions: *Serve as a cold side dish or use this ferment to top tacos, sandwiches or burgers.*

Fermented Red Cabbage with Apple and Ginger

Red cabbage deserves a place at the table, and I'm not talking about the small shreds in a green salad. This recipe reminds me of German–style red cabbage with the addition of apples and a savory fermented brine. The difference is you don't have to cook it. You can get your German cabbage fix by eating it right out of the jar.

Makes 1 pint (500 ml)

3 cups, approximately 10 oz, (300 g) shredded red cabbage

½ cup (65 g) chopped apple (I like it with the peel.)

2 tsp (5 g) diced ginger

1½ tsp (9 g) salt

In a large bowl, combine the cabbage, apple and ginger. Sprinkle the cabbage mixture with the salt and mix it in well. Use your hands or a kraut pounder to massage the cabbage and help it release its juices to make its own brine. After 5 to 10 minutes, the cabbage mixture and juice can go into a clean wide-mouth jar. Continue pushing the cabbage mixture down until it's all in the jar, but be sure to leave at least 2 inches (5 cm) of headspace.

Put a weight in the jar to keep everything under the brine and top the jar with a fermentation lid. Put the jar on a plate or small cookie sheet to catch any overflow. Set the jar in a cool place, out of direct sunlight, for 14 to 21 days. You can taste the ferment any time after 14 days. If it needs to ferment longer, replace the weight and fermentation lid and ferment for a few more days.

When it's fermented to your liking, replace the weight and fermentation lid with a storage lid, label the jar and store it in the refrigerator for up to 12 months.

*See photo on page 101 (this recipe is shown in the jar on the left).

Serving Suggestions: *Serve as a topping for hot dogs, sandwiches and burgers. This can also be served as a cold side dish and is especially good with sausage.*

Frozen Cabbage Rolls

Cabbage rolls are a treat that my family loves. Fortunately, they freeze well, so we can make a bunch and have them even when it's not cabbage season. I try to make these when my kids are home to help; you never know what conversations you'll have as everyone sits around the table stuffing and rolling cabbage. It's a bonding experience, for sure.

Makes 12–16 rolls

For the Cabbage Rolls

1 large head of green cabbage

1 lb (453 g) ground beef

1 small onion, chopped

1 cup (237 ml) tomato sauce

1 tbsp (1.5 g) dried parsley

½ tsp salt

⅛ tsp cayenne powder

1 cup (200 g) cooked rice

For Serving

1 pint (500 ml) Canned Tomato-Basil Soup (page 282) or other canned tomato soup

For the cabbage rolls, fill a large stockpot with water and bring it to a boil over medium-high heat. While the water is heating, rinse the cabbage and remove any tough outer leaves and the center core. Those leaves can be dehydrated and added to your jar of Dried Superfood Green Powder (page 179).

When the water begins to boil, put the entire head of cabbage in the water. After about 3 minutes, remove the outer leaf with a pair of tongs and put it on a platter to cool. Continue removing leaves as they become soft enough to remove. It should take about 15 minutes to remove all the leaves that will work; the leaves need to be about the size of your hand. When the leaves get smaller than that, just remove the rest of the head from the pot. I like to let it cool, then shred it for the freezer or dehydrator.

To make the filling, cook the ground beef and onion in a large skillet over medium-high heat for 10 minutes, or until the meat is browned and the onions are translucent. Transfer the meat mixture to a large bowl, then add the tomato sauce, parsley, salt, cayenne and rice; mix well.

Line a baking sheet with parchment paper. This will make freezing a lot of cabbage rolls a snap.

Put one of the cabbage leaves in the palm of your hand with the rib side near your wrist and add a scoop of filling. Fold the two sides in and then fold the rib side down and roll it into the opposite side, just like you roll a burrito.

(Continued)

Frozen Cabbage Rolls (continued)

Lay the finished cabbage roll on the prepared baking sheet. Continue making cabbage rolls until you run out of either filling or leaves that are big enough. Hopefully, you'll run out of both at about the same time.

If you have leftover filling, you can put it in a freezer-safe container and freeze it for later use. If you have leftover cabbage leaves, stack them with the ribs on top of each other and roll them up. Put them in a freezer-safe container, like a zippered plastic bag, remove the air and freeze them for later.

When all the cabbage rolls are made, put the baking sheet in the freezer overnight. In the morning, remove the baking sheet from the freezer and put the cabbage rolls in freezer-safe containers. I like to use the vacuum sealer and bags for this, so I can make my own size bags and put the amount of cabbage rolls we need for a meal in a bag.

Label the bags, put them in the freezer and use the cabbage rolls within 9 months.

For serving, cook the frozen cabbage rolls in the oven or a slow cooker. Pour some tomato soup on the bottom of a baking dish or into the slow cooker. Add the frozen cabbage rolls and pour the rest of the canned soup over them.

If you are using the oven, cover the baking dish with foil or a lid and bake the cabbage rolls at 350°F (177°C) for 45 to 60 minutes, until the centers of the cabbage rolls are hot.

If you are using a slow cooker, put the lid on and cook the cabbage rolls on low for 3 to 4 hours, until the centers of the cabbage rolls are hot. There is a lot of variance in temperature for slow cookers, so the first time you use one for this recipe, choose a time when you'll be home to keep an eye on it and adjust the temperature as needed. Be sure to make a note for next time about how long it takes the rolls to cook in your slow cooker.

carrots

Preserving the Rainbow

Freshly harvested carrots have a sweetness and crispness that store-bought carrots just can't compete with. To be sure, store-bought carrots are still tasty, just not quite as tasty as ones pulled from the ground just moments ago. We've even been known to pull carrots and just brush the soil off with our hands to have an impromptu snack in the garden.

Carrots are one of the most popular vegetables to buy and to grow. It's no wonder, as they taste great raw or cooked and are highly nutritious. Carrots are high in beta carotene, which gives them their orange color. The human body converts beta carotene to vitamin A, which is involved in immune function, vision, reproduction and cell growth.

Carrots come in a wide variety of colors, from almost white to deep purple. Although they all taste like carrots, some have stronger flavors than others and some are sweeter than others.

The entire carrot is edible, although most of us eat just the root. It's a shame, as the carrot tops are quite tasty and can be used to fill in gaps in harvesting greens between seasons.

About Carrot Tops

When we harvest carrots, we use all the carrot, including the greens. We use them to make Frozen Carrot Top Pesto (page 115), which fills the gap I have every year from when we use all of our basil pesto to when basil is ready again.

If we harvest only one or two carrots that day, I might sauté the tops with onion, garlic and grated carrots, and possibly other greens, for dinner. Or I might dehydrate them to add to our Dried Superfood Green Powder (page 179) jar.

Carrots are a biennial and will send up a flower stalk in their second year if they've been left in the ground that long. I reached out to a local county extension agent through their Ask An Expert website[4] to find out if the flowers were edible. Here is his reply: "All parts of the carrot plant are edible. There is no evidence of anyone becoming ill from ingesting any part of the Daucus carota var, sativa or domesticated carrot." If you have carrot flowers, you could use them as you would Queen Anne's Lace, which is a wild carrot, or leave them for the bees.

---

4   https://ask.extension.org/ask

Growing

The first year of growing, the carrot will send a taproot deep into the ground. Some varieties are short and have only a 3-inch (7.6-cm) taproot. Long varieties will have a 6- to 7-inch (15.2- to 17.8-cm) taproot.

Carrots need loose soil for the taproot to grow as it should. If you have clay soil, you should choose a short variety until you've built up enough loose soil to grow longer varieties. Trust me, there's nothing worse than having a beautiful, long carrot that's stuck in the clay and breaks in half while you're trying to pull it out.

The soil also needs to be clear of rocks or other things that can make the carrot root misshapen. Misshaped carrots are fun, especially if you have children, but they're a little harder to deal with, so try to keep the soil loose and clear.

The toughest part about growing carrots is the germination stage. Carrot seeds are tiny, and the ground needs to stay damp for them to germinate. You can sow seeds just before you're expected to have rain for a few days, which is what I do. Some gardeners will cover the seeds with burlap or even a piece of plywood until the seeds germinate.

Carrots don't transplant well, so don't try to start them inside. The good news is, carrots don't mind the cold, so you can sow seeds as soon as the soil is workable.

Carrot Varieties to Try

There are a lot more carrot varieties than what you can find in your local grocery store. Some are short and fat, some long and thin. Some are orange. There are also purple, yellow and red carrots.

Short carrot varieties are good for container gardens or those who have clay soil. Parisian is a short carrot with a bulb type root and looks like an orange beet. The Little Finger variety was developed in France for canning whole and only gets 3 inches (7.6 cm) long. Chantenay is a little longer, but still considered a short carrot and is very sweet.

Long carrot varieties are what most of us think of when we think of carrots. Nantes is a popular variety that grows 6 to 7 inches (15.2 to 17.8 cm) long, has a mild flavor and is not tapered. Danvers carrots are 6 to 8 inches (15.2 to 20.3 cm) long and tapered. They can handle heavy soils better than other long varieties, so if you are still working on getting your soil loose, try planting Danvers.

If you have soil that's loose and at least 12 inches (30.4 cm) deep, you might want to try the Imperator carrot variety. These carrots are slender and can grow up to 11 inches (27.9 cm) long.

If you're looking to plant various colored carrots in your garden, Black Nebula carrots are dark all the way through and have a purple core. Cosmic Purple carrots have a reddish-purple skin and an orange inside. Kyoto Red carrots are an orangish-red color throughout. Amarillo carrots are yellow, and Lunar White carrots are white throughout.

Harvesting

Carrots grow their taproot all the way down first, then start filling it out. One way of checking to see if carrots are ready is to dust the dirt off the top of the root and see how wide it is. This isn't a perfect method, and you still might pull a carrot that has completely developed the top of the root but has a super thin bottom root.

Some gardeners make a note in their gardening journal or calendar of when the seeds germinated, then count forward the number of days to maturity to get a good idea of when the carrots will be mature. This isn't a perfect method either, and you might still harvest some carrots that are not fully mature; but it will give you a good starting point.

Because carrot seeds are small, they are often sown close together and then thinned to the proper planting distance. When I thin carrots, we sauté them, greens and all, for dinner. When you thin carrots, thin every other one. It doesn't have to be done all at once either. You can thin a few at a time and toss them in with whatever vegetable you are cooking that night. Carrots go with pretty much any vegetable.

Carrots can stay in the ground until the first freeze in all climates and can overwinter in the ground with a thick layer of mulch in many climates. Therefore, there's no need to hurry the harvest. You can harvest a few carrots daily as you need them or a few pounds at a time to preserve them.

Toward the end of the season, you might come across carrots that are so big their core is a bit woody. No worries: just cut out the core and use the rest of the carrot. These are good carrots to use for Canned Carrot-Jalapeño Jam (page 111) or the Dried Carrot Fruit Leather (page 116), but could truly be used for any of the carrot recipes.

Buying Carrots

While carrots are easy to grow, they aren't in season year-round, so most of us will need to buy carrots at some point during the year. The best way to know if carrots are fresh is to buy carrots with the greens still attached. Carrots tend to dry out quickly once they're harvested, and being able to see the tops will give you an idea of how well the carrots have been taken care of since being harvested. Plus, you can eat the tops.

Avoid carrots that are super fat or hairy, as they may have woody cores and you'll need to cut them out. If you are buying carrots to preserve them, try to find a local farmer who will give you a deal on a case of them. Maybe he has some misshapen ones he can't sell to his regular customers, or it's nearing the end of the season and he still has a lot of carrots in the ground. This is a great opportunity for both of you.

Preserving

Stored properly, carrots can last for months in a root cellar or in the ground all winter in many climates. So why would we preserve carrots?

First, many of us don't have root cellars to store our produce. Secondly, in warmer climates, carrots grow from fall to spring, instead of from spring to fall, which means no carrots during the summer months.

If you are not going to preserve the carrots the day you get them, mist them with water and store them in the refrigerator. Carrots tend to wilt soon after being harvested, so keeping them in a cool, humid environment will help them stay crisp.

Before preserving carrots, you'll need to wash them and cut off the tops. Since carrots are a root vegetable, they need to be peeled before canning, but they don't necessarily need to be peeled for other preserving methods. If the skins are dark and rough, they can be bitter, so peeling is recommended for those carrots. There's no need to peel carrots with smooth, light skin unless they are being canned.

Canning

To properly can carrots, you need to use a pressure canner, add enough acid in the form of lemon juice or vinegar to safely water bath can them or make jam with them (Canned Carrot-Jalapeño Jam, page 111).

The most common way of canning carrots is to simply can them in slices with a little salt using a pressure canner (page 22). This will give you canned carrots that you can cook for a side dish or add to soups or potpies. It takes approximately 11 pounds (5 kg) of carrots without the tops to fill nine pint (500-ml) jars and about 18 pounds (8.2 kg) to fill seven quart (1-L) jars. Remember, you need a minimum of the equivalent of two quart-sized (1-L) jars to properly use a pressure canner.

Wash, peel and cut the carrots. The carrots can be sliced or diced, or you can cut them into sticks. Think about how you are going to use the canned carrots and let that be your guide.

You can either hot pack or raw pack the carrots (page 24) into the prepared jars. When the jars are filled, use the bubble remover tool to remove the air bubbles and make sure the jars have 1 inch (2.5 cm) of headspace. Wipe the rims of each jar, and put a lid and band on the jar. Process the jars, according to the manufacturer's instructions, at 10 psi (69 kPa) for 25 minutes for pints (500 ml) and 30 minutes for quarts (1 L). Adjust for altitude (page 25), if necessary.

Carrots can also be pickled and processed in a water bath canner. Most commonly, carrots are pickled with jalapeño and onions, a combination often served in Mexican restaurants. I prefer to ferment carrots for this style of recipe (Fermented Mexican Carrots, page 119) instead of canning them.

Freezing

Carrots can be frozen to use later in soups and baked goods. If you freeze them sliced, diced or as matchsticks, they will need to be blanched first for 2 minutes (page 34). However, if you grate them, they don't need to be blanched. Small, whole carrots need to be blanched for 5 minutes (page 34).

To freeze carrot slices, chunks or matchsticks, lay them out on a kitchen towel after blanching and pat them dry. This will help keep ice crystals from forming on them. If you want to make sure the carrots don't freeze in a big clump, then lay them out on a parchment-lined baking sheet and freeze them. Once they are frozen, you can transfer them to a labeled, freezer-safe container.

My favorite way to freeze carrots is to just grate them and put them in plastic freezer bags. Write the contents, dates and measurement on the bag. These are good for baking and adding to soups and casseroles.

I also make a lot of Frozen Carrot Top Pesto (page 115). Try as I might, I can never freeze enough basil pesto to make it through the year; the more I freeze, the more my family feasts on it. Carrot top pesto has become a welcome and tasty substitute for our Friday pizza night and midweek pasta dishes.

Dehydrating

Dehydrated carrot slices can be reconstituted and used in soups or stir-fries. They can also be powdered and used to add flavor and nutrition to smoothies, muffins, homemade pasta and other dishes.

Carrots need to be blanched for 2 minutes before being dehydrated. I think it's best to slice the carrots about ¼ inch (6 mm) thick; if you slice them thicker, you will need to blanch them longer.

After blanching the carrots for 2 minutes, put them in a bowl of ice water to stop the cooking process. When they're cooled, lay them out on a kitchen towel and pat them dry. Transfer the carrots to a dehydrator tray lined with the mesh insert. Dehydrate at 135°F (57°C) for 6 to 10 hours.

To reconstitute the carrots, put them in a bowl and cover them with warm water. Cover the bowl and let the carrots soak for 15 to 30 minutes. These will be similar in texture to raw carrots. To cook dehydrated carrots, cover the carrots with water in a saucepan and boil them for 10 minutes.

Dehydrated carrots can be added directly to soup while it's cooking; just be aware that the carrots will soak up a lot of the liquid and make the soup thicker.

I've struggled finding a dehydrated carrot chip that my family likes. The flavor is good, but the texture is often off. However, they do like Dried Carrot Fruit Leather (page 116).

Fermenting

Fermented carrots are a delightful snack or relish tray item. They can be fermented as slices or sticks or grated. Spices and peppers can be added.

If you're fermenting slices or sticks, fill the jar with the carrots and then pour a 2 percent brine (page 51) over them. You can add onions, garlic and spices, such as dill, bay leaves, peppercorns, mustard seed, red pepper flakes and ginger, to the jar before adding the brine. Add a weight and an airlock fermenting lid.

If you are fermenting grated carrots, you will add the salt directly to the grated carrots and massage the salt into the carrots. You'll need 2 grams of salt for every 100 grams of carrots. The carrots will release their juices and make their own brine, just like cabbage does. However, since carrots don't hold as much moisture as cabbage, you might need to add a little prepared 2 percent brine to the jar to make sure the grated carrots can be completely submerged under the brine.

Put the fermenting carrots on a plate or small cookie sheet to catch any overflow and store the jar, out of direct sunlight, for 7 to 14 days. After 7 days, test the carrots each day until they are as sour as you like, being sure to replace the weight and fermenting lid each time. When the carrots are ready, remove the weight and fermenting lid, put a storage lid on the jar and store it in the refrigerator for up to 1 year.

Preserving Carrots Cheat Sheet

	Water Bath Canning	Pressure Canning	Freezing	Dehydrating	Fermenting 2% brine
How to prepare	Small whole, spears, slices or grated	Sliced, diced or matchstick	Blanching recommended for whole, slices, diced or matchstick; blanching not needed for grated	Blanching required for slices for long-term storage; blanching not needed for paper-thin slices or fruit leather	Small whole, sliced, diced, matchstick or grated
Flavors	Pickled or as a jam	Plain or as a soup	Plain	Plain or seasoned	Savory with herbs
Length of processing	15 minutes	Pints (500 ml): 25 minutes Quarts (1 L): 30 minutes	—	6–10 hours	7–14 days
Storage life	12 months	12 months	8–12 months	12 months for plain carrot slices or fruit leather; 1 month for seasoned	12 months

Canned Carrot–Jalapeño Jam

Occasionally, my husband will suggest an addition to a recipe that makes me raise an eyebrow. That's exactly what happened the first time he tasted my carrot jam and said, "Jalapeños would be good in this." I made a small trial batch and added jalapeños just for him. The only problem was that he was at work and by the time he got home only a small spoonful was left!

This jam is mildly spicy and has a distinct jalapeño flavor to it. You can make it spicier by adding ½ teaspoon of ground cayenne.

Makes 6 half-pint (250-ml) jars

3½ cups (385 g) grated carrots

½ cup (45 g) chopped jalapeño, seeded if you prefer a milder flavor

½ cup (118 ml) apple cider vinegar

1½ cups (355 ml) lemon juice

1 tsp ground cinnamon

½ tsp ground cloves

½ tsp ground nutmeg

½ tsp ground allspice

5 tbsp (45 g) powdered pectin

½ tsp ground cayenne (optional)

4 cups (800 g) sugar

Prepare the water bath canner by filling it halfway with water and putting it on the stove to simmer. Check six half-pint (125-ml) jars for any nicks or cracks, wash them in hot soapy water and rinse them in hot water. Keep the jars hot until it's time to use them. Wash the lids in hot soapy water, rinse them and set them aside.

Combine the carrots, jalapeño, vinegar, lemon juice, cinnamon, cloves, nutmeg, allspice, pectin and cayenne, if desired, in a stockpot. Bring the mixture to a boil over medium-high heat, stirring often. After it begins to boil, add the sugar, then bring the mixture back to a rolling boil and boil it for 1 minute, while continually stirring.

Remove the pan from the heat and ladle the jam into the hot jars, leaving ¼ inch (6 mm) of headspace.

Wipe the rims with a clean cloth, put on the lids and screw on the bands. Place the jars in the prepared hot water bath canner and process them for 10 minutes, adjusting for altitude (page 17), if necessary. Arrange a folded towel on the counter or table. Remove the jars, using a jar lifter, and place them on the towel. Let the jars cool for at least 12 hours.

When the jars are cooled, remove the bands and check the seals. If any jars failed to seal, put them in the refrigerator to use first. Wipe the jars with a clean cloth, label them and store them for up to a year.

Serving Suggestions: *This mildly spicy jam is perfect for serving over a block of cream cheese with crackers. It can also be used as a glaze for meats. You can also blend it until it's almost smooth and use it as a dipping sauce for jalapeño poppers.*

Canned Spice Carrot Soup

This soup is a practical way to preserve carrots and have shelf-stable meals for hectic days. While it is normally not recommended to can pureed soups, this recipe has been adapted from a tested Ball® Blue Book® Guide to Preserving recipe, using guidelines from the National Center for Home Food Preservation website.

Makes 6 quart (1-L) or 12 pint (500-ml) jars

For the Soup

1 tbsp (15 ml) olive oil

2 cups (320 g) chopped onions

2 cloves garlic, chopped

4 lbs (1.8 kg) chopped carrots

6 cups (1.4 L) chicken or vegetable broth

6 cups (1.4 L) water

1 tsp ground coriander

1 tbsp (5 g) ground ginger

½ cup (100 g) sugar (optional)

2 tsp (12 g) salt

1 tsp ground black pepper

For Serving

¼ cup (59 ml) cream, half and half or milk per pint (500 ml) or ½ cup (118 ml) cream, half and half or milk per quart (1 L)

Cracked black pepper, chopped cilantro or chopped chives

Note: *If you don't have a pressure canner or prefer not to can a pureed soup, this recipe can be preserved by freezing.*

For the soup, prepare the pressure canner. Rinse it and its rack, place the bottom rack inside and fill the canner with a few inches of water, according to the manufacturer's instructions. Put the pressure canner on the stove over low heat while you prepare the jars. This is a raw-pack recipe, so the water in the pressure canner needs to be no higher than 140°F (60°C) before you put the jars into the canner.

Wash 6 quart (1-L) or 12 pint (500-ml) jars in hot, soapy water and check for any nicks or cracks in the jars. Rinse the jars in clean water and set them aside. Wash the lids in hot, soapy water, rinse them and set them aside.

In a large stockpot, heat the oil over medium heat and sauté the onions and garlic for 5 minutes, or until the onions are transparent. Add the carrots and broth to the stockpot and bring the mixture to a boil. Reduce the heat to low and simmer for 15 to 20 minutes, until the carrots are tender.

Working in batches, puree the vegetable mixture in a food processor or blender. Return the puree to the stockpot and add the water. Stir in the coriander, ginger, sugar (if desired), salt and pepper. Simmer the soup for 30 minutes. Turn the heat off and divide the carrot soup among the jars, leaving 1 inch (2.5 cm) of headspace. Remove the air bubbles and recheck the headspace.

Process the jars, according to the manufacturer's instructions, at 10 psi (69 kPa) for 40 minutes for pints (500 ml) and 50 minutes for quarts (1 L), adjusting for altitude (page 25), if necessary. Let the pressure canner depressurize naturally (page 25). Arrange a folded towel on the counter or table. Open the canner and remove the jars, using a jar lifter.

Place the jars on the towel and let them cool for at least 12 hours. Remove the bands, check the seals and store the jars for up to 1 year. If any jars failed to seal, put them in the refrigerator to use first.

For serving, empty a jar of soup into a medium stockpot and heat the soup over medium heat for 5 to 10 minutes, until it simmers. Stir in the cream. Garnish with the cracked pepper.

Frozen Carrot Top Pesto

I've never been able to keep up with the pesto needs of my family. The more I make, the more they eat. Fortunately, there's carrot top pesto to fill in when we run out of basil pesto. Carrot top pesto not only tastes great, but is easy to make and uses something that most of us would toss in the compost pile.

Makes 1 half-pint (250 ml)

1 cup (50 g) carrot tops, rinsed and patted dry

3–6 (10–20 g) cloves garlic

1 tbsp (7 g) grated fresh ginger

½ cup (40 g) pecans (about 15 pecan halves)

2 tsp (10 ml) lemon juice

¼ tsp salt

½–⅔ cup (118–158 ml) olive oil, divided

⅓ cup (35 g) grated Parmesan cheese

In a blender, blend the carrot tops, garlic, ginger, pecans, lemon juice, salt and ½ cup (118 ml) of the olive oil until smooth. Add the Parmesan and blend again, until the mixture reaches the consistency you like; some like pesto to be like tomato paste, others prefer the texture of mashed potatoes. If it's too thick, add more of the remaining 2 tablespoons plus 2 teaspoons (40 ml) of olive oil.

Put the pesto into freezer-safe containers, such as 4-ounce (125-ml) Mason jars or plastic freezer bags, and label the containers. If you're using glass jars, be sure to leave ½ inch (12 mm) of headspace for expansion. Put the containers into the refrigerator to cool overnight, then transfer them to the freezer. Pesto can be stored in the freezer for up to a year.

Serving Suggestions: *This pesto is fantastic on a toasted slice of baguette, topped with a tomato slice and Parmesan cheese. You can also toss it with pasta or slather it on pizza.*

Dried Carrot Fruit Leather

Fruit leather is a popular snack in my home. In fact, I can barely keep it in stock. This leather takes advantage of seasonal carrots and adds extra nutrition to the usual applesauce fruit leather.

Makes 1–2 dehydrator trays

1 lb (453 g) carrots, roughly chopped

1 lb (453 g) apples, cored and sliced

¼ tsp cinnamon

¼ cup (59 ml) lemon juice

Line 2 dehydrator trays with a silicone mat or parchment paper.

Put the carrots, apples, cinnamon and lemon juice in a medium stockpot with a lid. Keep the lid on the pot and cook the carrots over medium heat for about 30 to 45 minutes, or until the carrots are very soft and can be easily pierced with a fork.

Once the carrots are soft, put the mixture into a blender and blend it until smooth. If it's too thick, add a little filtered water. You want the consistency to be like applesauce.

Pour 2 cups (474 ml) of the carrot mixture on a dehydrator tray and spread the mixture so that it evenly covers the tray. It should be about ¼ inch (6 mm) thick. Repeat with the remaining carrot mixture.

Put the trays in the dehydrator and dehydrate at 135°F (57°C) for 10 to 12 hours, although it can take longer, depending on how thick the fruit leather is spread. After 10 hours, check the leather for doneness (page 44); if there are still moist spots, continue dehydrating the leather.

When the leather is completely dry but still pliable, cut it into strips, roll up the strips and store them in a jar with a tight-fitting lid. Leave the jar of fruit leather on the counter and condition it for a week (page 42) before you put it into storage. Once it's conditioned, you can store the fruit leather in the jar for 4 to 12 months.

*In the photo, the fruit leather is shown in the jar on the right side.

Serving Suggestions: *Snack on the fruit leather right out of the jar! You can also cut fruit leather into strips or designs to decorate or garnish cupcakes, cakes, pies, ice cream or cold drinks—you know, the kind with whipped cream on top.*

Dried Carrot Chai Ribbons

The maple syrup adds just a bit of extra sweetness to the natural sweetness of the carrots, making these Dried Carrot Chai Ribbons a perfect snack when you want something crispy and sweet.

Makes 1 pint (500 ml)

2 tbsp (30 ml) maple syrup

1 tbsp (15 ml) melted coconut oil

1 tsp cinnamon

½ tsp ground cloves

½ tsp ground cardamom

1 tsp ground ginger

1 lb (453 g) carrots, cut into 3-inch (7.6-cm)-long paper-thin strips (see Note)

½–¾ tsp salt

In a large bowl, mix the maple syrup, coconut oil, cinnamon, cloves, cardamom and ginger. Carefully add the carrots to the bowl and mix them well with the seasoning mixture. We usually end up using our hands for this because some of the carrot slices will stick together and will need to be unstuck.

Lay the carrot slices on the dehydrator trays, and sprinkle them with the salt. Dehydrate the carrots at 155°F (68°C) for 2 to 3 hours, or until the slices are brittle. They should easily snap in half when bent.

When the carrots are fully dry, remove the trays from the dehydrator and let the carrots cool. Put the dried carrots in a glass jar with a tight-fitting lid and label the jar. Use the carrot ribbons within 1 month.

These are best eaten within a few days. If they lose their crispiness, they can be put into the dehydrator on high for 15 to 30 minutes to crisp them.

*See photo on page 117 (this recipe is shown in the jar on the left).

Note: *Blanching is normally recommended for carrots before dehydrating them. I think that works great for plain carrots that are being stored to reconstitute later, but it doesn't work well for seasoned carrots that are meant for snacking. Instead of blanching the carrots for this recipe, use a mandoline to make paper–thin long strips.*

Serving Suggestions: *In addition to being eaten right out of the jar, these dried carrot ribbons can be crushed and added to oatmeal or yogurt or even sprinkled on ice cream.*

Fermented Mexican Carrots

Love the spicy carrots that are often served in Mexican restaurants? Those are usually pickled in vinegar and canned. They are good, but have a distinct vinegar flavor. This recipe uses fermentation to get a similar dish without the overwhelming vinegar flavor.

Makes 1 quart (1 L)

1 lb (453 g) sliced carrots

¼ medium (50 g) onion, sliced

1 jalapeño (15 g), sliced, seeds removed if you prefer milder flavor

2–3 Mexican oregano leaves

1 clove garlic

15 coriander seeds, crushed

1 tsp honey

1 tbsp (18 g) sea salt

2 cups (474 ml) filtered water

Put the carrots, onion, jalapeño, oregano, garlic, coriander and honey into a quart (1-L) jar. There should be 2 inches (5 cm) of headspace.

Mix the salt into the water to make brine. Pour the brine into the jar, making sure to cover the vegetables but leaving room for the weight and expansion. Put a weight in the jar to keep everything under the brine, and top the jar with a fermentation lid. Put the jar on a plate or small cookie sheet to catch any overflow.

Set the jar in a cool place, out of direct sunlight, for 8 to 14 days. You can taste them any time after 8 days. If they need to ferment longer, replace the weight and fermentation lid and ferment for a few more days. When the carrots are to your liking, replace the weight and fermentation lid with a plastic storage lid. Store the carrots in the refrigerator for up to 9 months.

Serving Suggestions: *Fermented Mexican Carrots make a great side dish for cold meals, but they are also great on tacos or grilled meats.*

cauliflower
Not Just in White

Cauliflower is another plant in the *Brassica* family, and it's closely related to broccoli. In fact, cauliflower and broccoli are interchangeable in many recipes and are often served together. Like broccoli, the cauliflower head, or *curd*, is the undeveloped flower buds of the plant. If they keep growing, they will produce yellow flowers. The flowers are edible but not very tasty.

White cauliflower is the most common cauliflower, but there's also purple, orange and green cauliflower. Various cauliflower varieties naturally have some amounts of anthocyanin, beta carotene and chlorophyll in them. Through selective breeding, these food pigments have resulted in the various colors of cauliflower. The flavor and texture of all of these cauliflower varieties are similar.

In addition to the edible cauliflower head, the leaves are edible. It takes quite a bit of time for the cauliflower head to develop, so harvesting a few leaves per plant will allow you to benefit from cauliflower before the head is ready without harming the plant.

Growing

Cauliflower is a cool-weather plant. It will have the best flavor and resist flowering when it's grown in cool weather. Cauliflower is also cold hardy to 26°F (-3°C), making it a good fall and early spring crop.

When grown from seed, cauliflower takes between 70 and 120 days to mature, depending on the variety. If you plant transplants, expect to be able to harvest in 55 to 80 days. If you plant cauliflower in the spring, start it indoors 6 to 8 weeks before your average last frost. Cauliflower transplants can be planted outdoors about 4 to 6 weeks before the average last spring frost—or whenever the ground is workable.

You don't want the cauliflower maturing in the heat of the summer; ideally, it would mature before the daily temperatures are consistently 80°F (27°C) or higher.

If you have a short spring, meaning that it goes from snowing to hot in just a few weeks, growing cauliflower in the spring might be frustrating. However, it will probably make a great fall crop for you. By planting cauliflower in the summer, about

8 to 10 weeks before your average first fall frost, and choosing a quick maturing variety, you can have a delicious fall crop of cauliflower that will not be damaged by light frosts.

Cauliflower is a heavy feeder that needs rich soil and a midseason layer of compost. It needs to be watered regularly. If it doesn't rain at least 1 inch (2.5 cm) in a week, the cauliflower needs to be watered. This is sometimes hard to remember when the temperatures are cool.

If you've planted white cauliflower and want to harvest white cauliflower, you'll need to keep the sun off the white head. This is called *blanching*. If you don't blanch the cauliflower, then the head will be more yellow than white when it's harvested.

An easy way to blanch growing cauliflower is to remove one of the cauliflower leaves from the bottom of the plant and lay it over the top of the cauliflower head. Then tie the leaves that are next to the head together near the top of the leaves. Do this when the head is about 2 inches (5 cm) across and let it grow in darkness.

If you choose not to blanch the cauliflower head, that's just fine. It won't be white, but it will still taste good and have a bit more vitamins.

Unlike broccoli, cauliflower produces only one head; once it's harvested, the plant is done. Because of this, don't plant all the cauliflower at the same time. Instead, plant 3 to 4 cauliflower plants every 2 to 3 weeks. This is called *succession planting* and keeps you from having 10 cauliflower heads ready at the same time.

If you don't want to worry about planting multiple crops of cauliflower, then plant several varieties that have a different number of days to harvest. You can plant one variety that takes 70 days, a second one that takes 85 days and a third one that takes 100 days and accomplish the same thing.

The pests that bother cauliflower are the same pests that bother broccoli, cabbage and kale, with the cabbage looper and aphids being the most prevalent in our garden. Cabbage loopers can be controlled by using row covers, since cauliflower doesn't need pollinators; just make sure to put them on early before the cabbage looper moth lays her eggs. They can also be controlled by spraying with *Bt*, the organic pesticide that targets caterpillars and is non-toxic for humans. I usually spray once when I first see caterpillar damage and that usually controls them for the whole growing season.

Harvesting

For the best flavor, cauliflower should be harvested while the head is still tight and compact; once florets start to sprout, the flavor of the cauliflower will get stronger. Most cauliflower heads are 8 to 12 inches (20.3 to 30.4 cm) across at maturity, so you can use that as a guide.

As the head reaches maturity, you'll want to check it daily, as it can go from "not quite ready" to beginning to sprout in just a few days. If I've blanched the cauliflower, I feel through the leaves to get an idea of how big the head has gotten before I go to the trouble of untying the leaves.

It's fine to harvest cauliflower heads that are small, but since the plant will produce only one head, it's best to let them mature.

To harvest cauliflower, cut it off at the soil with a sharp knife. Most people just cut the head off and leave the roots and leaves, but since the leaves are edible, I harvest the whole thing. If there are leaves that we won't eat, I remove those and toss them into the garden bed to mulch and feed the soil. The roots will also decompose and feed the soil.

Cauliflower Varieties to Try

Because cauliflower is a mutation of wild cabbage that dates to the 1500s, there are not nearly as many heirloom varieties as there are for other vegetables. However, there is a wide range of color, days to maturity and disease resistance among the varieties.

Snowball is a self-blanching heirloom variety with large leaves that will protect the 6- to 8-inch (15.2 to 20.3-cm) head from the sunlight. This variety matures in 65 to 75 days.

Purple of Sicily cauliflower is an Italian variety that is, of course, purple. Since the head is purple, there is no need to hide it from the sun. This variety is resistant to many insects. The purple head will turn green when cooked. Purple of Sicily needs 90 days to reach maturity.

Is Romanesco a cauliflower or broccoli? You can often find it listed as either one, but we'll put it in the cauliflower group. Romanesco is a very unique green cauliflower that has small spiraled heads. It needs 85 days to mature, and the head doesn't need protection from the sun.

Cheddar is a hybrid orange variety that needs 60 to 70 days to mature. The heads are on the small side at 4 to 7 inches (10 to 17.8 cm) and they don't need protection from the sun.

If you're trying to squeeze in a fall crop of cauliflower, consider one of these hybrids. Fioretto 60 grows a loose head that looks similar to a creamy white broccoli rabe. It matures in 30 to 60 days. If you want to grow a more traditional looking cauliflower, try White Corona, which matures in less than 35 days. This variety is super compact, with 3- to 5-inch (7.6- to 12.7-cm) heads and a plant that is about half the height of other varieties. This variety will need help with sun protection, if you want pure white heads.

Buying

I'm convinced that when people say they don't like cauliflower it's because they've never had fresh cauliflower. Old cauliflower has a very strong flavor and odor when it's cooked; fresh cauliflower does not. Because of this, it's best to buy cauliflower only when it's in season in your area.

When you buy cauliflower, look for heads that are crisp, white and fresh looking. The head should be compact. If the bud clusters have started to separate or if the head has a rough or loose texture, it's past its prime.

Skip any cauliflower that has heads that are turning dark, as this is a sign that the cauliflower is old. If you've already bought cauliflower and then it starts getting dark spots, you can just scrape them off and use the rest of the head. But don't buy heads with dark spots on them.

If the cauliflower head has leaves on it, the leaves should be firm and fresh looking, not dull and limp. If you buy cauliflower directly from the farmer, ask him to leave the leaves on the cauliflower for you.

When you get the cauliflower home, store it in the crisper of the refrigerator for up to 7 days. If the cauliflower has been wrapped in plastic, take the plastic off. Just remember that the cauliflower will get stronger the longer it's stored.

Preserving

We eat most of our cauliflower fresh or sautéed for dinner. However, the cauliflower heads are often too big for just one meal. Since they don't store well, I preserve the cauliflower we don't cook that day in a variety of ways to enjoy it when there is no more cauliflower growing in the garden.

The quicker that cauliflower is preserved after harvesting, the milder the flavor will be. Therefore, using the leftover cauliflower from the evening meal to make a jar of Fermented Cauliflower with Curry (page 130) is a convenient way to stock my pantry and not have leftover cauliflower.

Cauliflower can also be frozen, dehydrated and canned. I usually reserve these for when I'm forced to harvest a head or two of cauliflower because it's getting too mature in the garden.

Canning

Unlike broccoli, there is a recommended way to can cauliflower and that is to pickle it. Cauliflower can be pickled and processed in a water bath canner as the only ingredient or it can be pickled in a mix. However, there are no safety recommendations for pressure canning cauliflower.

Because the canning process can cause the cauliflower to have a strong flavor and odor, it's best to start with freshly picked cauliflower that has a compact head. This will reduce the likelihood of it having a strong odor.

The canning process can also cause cauliflower to discolor. Remember those pigments we talked about earlier that will produce purple, yellow, green and orange cauliflower? If the cauliflower was exposed to sunlight and has these pigments coming through, they might turn gray or bluish when canned.

When pickled, cauliflower will often take on the color of the vinegar or spices. If you want white pickled cauliflower, you need to use a white vinegar and not apple cider or red wine vinegar. Spices like turmeric will also discolor pickled cauliflower.

Freezing

Frozen cauliflower can be added to soups and casseroles, but it can also be used as a grain substitute. Many people on specialty diets use cauliflower "rice" instead of real rice or use cauliflower instead of wheat to make crackers or pizza crust.

It's recommended that cauliflower be blanched for 3 minutes (page 34) or steam blanched for 5 minutes before being frozen. However, I've found that cauliflower doesn't need to be blanched if you chop it very small, basically turning it into rice.

There are a couple of ways to grate, or rice, cauliflower. One way is to use a box grater with medium holes, like the one you grate cheese with. The other is to use a food processor with the grater blade. The goal is to have small, rice-sized pieces of cauliflower. Don't worry if the pieces are different sizes; that's just how it is with cauliflower rice.

After blanching, put the cauliflower pieces in ice water to stop the cooking process. When they have completely cooled off, put them on a clean kitchen towel and pat them dry. This will help keep ice crystals from forming on the cauliflower.

To freeze the cauliflower pieces, lay them on a baking sheet covered with parchment paper and put them in the freezer. Once they are frozen, after 3 to 4 hours, transfer them to freezer-safe containers and put them back into the freezer. If you package grated cauliflower in serving-sized portions, you can put it directly into freezer-safe containers and not worry if it sticks together.

Cauliflower can be stored in the freezer for up to a year.

Dehydrating

If you're short on freezer space or want to have shelf-stable cauliflower, you can dehydrate cauliflower. Before dehydrating, cauliflower needs to be blanched for 3 minutes (page 34). After the 3 minutes is up, put the cauliflower pieces in ice water to stop the cooking process.

Lay the cooled cauliflower pieces on a clean kitchen towel and pat them dry. This keeps the dehydrator cleaner and, if you're seasoning the cauliflower, it helps the seasonings stick better.

Put the cauliflower pieces on dehydrator trays and dehydrate them at 135°F (57°C) for 12 to 15 hours, or until they are crisp and brittle.

A pound (453 g) of fresh cauliflower that has been dehydrated will fit into a quart (1-L) Mason jar. The cauliflower can be reconstituted and used in soup or stir-fries, or just sautéed for a side dish. It can also be powdered and use to make cream of cauliflower soup.

The cauliflower leaves can be dehydrated just like kale (page 177) and added to your Dried Superfood Green Powder (page 179).

If you want to have seasoned dehydrated cauliflower for snacking on, the florets, stems and leaves can be seasoned and dehydrated.

Fermenting

Fermented cauliflower has a crisp texture and tangy flavor that can turn the cauliflower hater into a cauliflower lover. Just remember to use fresh cauliflower to ferment, as old cauliflower can have a strong odor. Cauliflower can be fermented in florets or grated.

To ferment cauliflower, chop or grate it, then pack it into a wide-mouth Mason jar and cover it with a 2 percent brine (page 51). You can add onions, garlic and spices, such as dill, bay leaves, peppercorns, mustard seed, red pepper flakes and ginger, to the jar before adding the brine. Add a weight and an airlock fermenting lid.

Put the fermenting cauliflower on a plate or small cookie sheet to catch any overflow and store it, out of direct sunlight, for 8 to 14 days. After 8 days, test the cauliflower each day until it is as sour as you like, being sure to replace the weight and fermenting lid each time you test. When the cauliflower is ready, remove the weight and fermenting lid, add a plastic storage lid to the jar and store it in the refrigerator for up to a year.

Preserving Cauliflower Cheat Sheet

	Water Bath Canning	Pressure Canning (Not recommended)	Freezing	Dehydrating	Fermenting 2% brine
How to prepare	Pieces	N/A	3-minute blanching recommended for pieces; not necessary for riced	3-minute blanching required for pieces; not necessary for riced	Florets or grated
Flavors	Savory, pickled with herbs	N/A	Plain or seasoned	Plain or seasoned	Savory with herbs
Length of processing	15 minutes	N/A	—	10–12 hours	8–14 days
Storage life	12 months	N/A	6–12 months	12 months for plain; 1 month for seasoned	6–12 months

Dried Cheesy Cauliflower Crisps

Cauliflower and cheese are always a winning combination! This cheesy sauce can be used on cauliflower florets or leaves to make a tasty snack or topping.

Makes 1 pint (500 ml)

1 lb (453 g) cauliflower florets

2 tbsp (30 ml) lemon juice

¼ tsp ground black pepper

½ tsp salt

1 tbsp (7 g) grated Parmesan cheese

Fill a medium stockpot about halfway with water and bring it to a boil over high heat. Put the florets into the boiling water and let it come back up to a boil. Cover the pot and blanch the cauliflower for 3 minutes (page 34). While the cauliflower is in the boiling water, prepare a bowl of ice water. Using a slotted spoon, take the cauliflower out of the boiling water and immediately put it into the bowl of ice water to stop the cooking.

While the cauliflower pieces are cooling, mix the lemon juice, pepper, salt and Parmesan in a large bowl.

Drain the water from the cauliflower and put the cauliflower onto a clean kitchen towel; pat the florets dry. Carefully add the cauliflower to the bowl with the seasoning mixture. Mix to coat all the pieces.

Lay the seasoned cauliflower pieces on a dehydrator tray. You can put the pieces close together, as they will shrink considerably. Dehydrate at 125°F (51°C) for 10 to 12 hours, or until the pieces are brittle.

When the cauliflower is fully dry, remove the tray from the dehydrator and let the cauliflower cool. Put the dried cauliflower in a glass jar with a tight-fitting lid and use it within 1 month.

These are best eaten within a few days. If the cauliflower florets lose their crispiness, put them back into the dehydrator on high for 15 to 30 minutes to crisp them.

Serving Suggestions: *Enjoy Dried Cheesy Cauliflower Crisps as a snack or crush it and use it to top salads and soups.*

Frozen Ginger Cauliflower Rice

Adding cauliflower rice to a meal is a great way to lighten up a heavy meal by eliminating the starch of real rice. This is a great side to serve with stir-fries, grilled chicken and baked fish. You can add other herbs and spices when you cook the rice, so it pairs with the flavors of what you're serving that night.

Makes 4 cups (478 g)

For the Rice

1 lb (453 g) cauliflower, grated (page 123)

4 tsp (12 g) grated fresh ginger

2 tsp (12 g) salt

1 tsp ground black pepper

For Serving

2 tbsp (30 ml) olive oil

1 tsp lemon juice

Dash of cumin

For the rice, combine the cauliflower and ginger in a large bowl. Sprinkle the salt and pepper over the cauliflower mixture and mix it well.

Put the cauliflower mixture into freezer-safe containers, such as plastic freezer bags or vacuum-sealed bags, and label the containers. The bags can go straight into the freezer and be stored for up to a year.

For serving, heat the olive oil in a medium skillet, then add the cauliflower rice. It can be thawed or frozen when you add it. The cauliflower will release liquid as it thaws. Add the lemon juice and cumin. Cook the cauliflower, uncovered, over medium heat for 10 minutes, or until all the liquid has evaporated.

Serving Suggestions: *Ginger cauliflower rice can be used as a quick side dish or for stuffing for peppers or Frozen Cabbage Rolls (page 103). Add it to casseroles, too.*

Canned Spicy Cauliflower with Turmeric

This spicy cauliflower uses red pepper flakes instead of fresh peppers, so you can easily make it spicier for those who prefer a lot of heat.

Makes 4 pint (500-ml) jars

1½ cups (355 ml) rice wine vinegar (5% acidity)

1½ cups (355 ml) apple cider vinegar

1 cup (200 g) sugar

1 tsp turmeric

1 tsp celery seed

2 tsp (8 g) mustard seed

1 tsp (4 g) black peppercorns

½ tsp red pepper flakes

6 cups (500 g) chopped cauliflower florets

1 cup (115 g) sliced onion

Prepare the water bath canner by filling it halfway with water and putting it on the stove to simmer. Check four pint (500-ml) jars for any nicks or cracks, wash them in hot soapy water and rinse them in hot water. Keep the jars hot until it's time to use them. Wash the lids in hot soapy water, rinse them and set them aside.

Combine the rice wine vinegar, cider vinegar, sugar, turmeric, celery seed, mustard seed, black peppercorns and red pepper flakes in a stockpot and bring the mixture to a boil, stirring occasionally. Add the cauliflower and onion, reduce the heat to a simmer and simmer the mixture for 5 minutes.

After 5 minutes, remove the pot from the heat and ladle the cauliflower into the hot jars, leaving ½ inch (12 mm) of headspace. Remove the air bubbles with a bubble remover tool or chopstick and recheck the headspace; add more brine if necessary. Wipe the rims with a clean cloth, put the lids on the jars and screw on the bands. Place the jars in the prepared hot water bath canner, making sure that the jars are covered by at least an inch (2.5 cm) of water.

Bring the water to a full rolling boil and put the lid on the canner. Process the jars for 15 minutes, adjusting for altitude (page 17), if necessary. Arrange a folded towel on the counter or table. Remove the jars, using a jar lifter, and place them on the folded towel. Let the jars cool for at least 12 hours.

Once the jars are cooled, remove the bands and check the seals. If any jars failed to seal, put them in the refrigerator to use first. Wipe the jars with a clean cloth and store them for up to a year.

*In the photo, the cauliflower is in the jar on the left.

Serving Suggestions: *Serve the spicy cauliflower on a relish tray or use it to spice up salads or add crunch to flatbread wraps.*

Fermented Cauliflower with Curry

Curry is one of my very favorite flavors, but it wasn't until my son recommended that I use curry paste instead of curry powder in this recipe that I realized what I had been missing. The red curry paste takes this ferment to a whole new level, but if all you have is curry powder, don't let that stop you from making this recipe.

Makes 1 quart (1 L)

2 cups (170 g) cauliflower florets

2–4 cloves garlic

½ tsp red curry paste

Pinch of red pepper flakes (optional)

1 tbsp (18 g) sea salt

3 cups (711 ml) filtered water

Fill a quart (1-L) jar with the cauliflower and garlic, then add the curry paste and red pepper flakes, if desired, to the jar.

Mix the salt into the water to make a brine and pour it over the cauliflower and spices, making sure to cover the cauliflower but leaving enough room for the weight and expansion. Put a weight in the jar to keep everything under the brine and top the jar with a fermentation lid. Put the jar on a plate or small cookie sheet to catch any overflow.

Set the jar in a cool place, out of direct sunlight, for 4 to 5 days. You can taste the florets any time after 4 days. If they need to ferment longer, replace the weight and fermentation lid and ferment for a few more days. When the florets are to your liking, replace the weight and fermentation lid with a plastic storage lid, and store the ferment in the refrigerator for up to 12 months.

*See photo on page 129 (this recipe is shown in the jar on the right).

Serving Suggestions: *Chopped curry–flavored fermented cauliflower is great in tuna or pasta salad or served on its own as a cold side dish.*

corn

The Flavor of Summer

After tomatoes, corn is probably the most popular fresh vegetable, and for good reasons. Of course, it tastes great! But it's also a great source of B vitamins. B vitamins help with protein, lipid and carbohydrate metabolism and with adrenal function. Corn originated in the Americas and was an important part of the life of many Native American tribes. It was used for eating fresh and stored. It was even used as a filler for sleep mats. There are several types of corn, each with its own uses.

Sweet corn is grown for eating fresh and comes in different varieties, some super sweet and others mildly sweet. All sweet varieties are harvested before they start to dry out.

Popcorn corn is allowed to fully mature and dry on the stalk before being cooked to make classic popcorn. It can also be ground into cornmeal and used for baking or breading.

Field corn, also called *dent corn*, is a storage corn from which cornmeal or corn flour is made. Field corn is allowed to dry on the stalk and is then stored to use for cornmeal or animal feed. The texture of field corn is mealy and somewhat gummy, so don't try to pick field corn early and eat it fresh. You'll be disappointed.

Growing

Unless you have a large piece of land, you will probably want to grow only one type of corn. Since corn is wind-pollinated, it needs at least 400 feet (121.9 m) between types to prevent cross-pollination. When corn cross-pollinates, you usually end up with corn that is muddled and not good for eating fresh or storing.

While each corn plant will produce one or two ears of corn, the plant itself is large, making corn a heavy feeder. Corn needs to be planted in rich, well-draining soil, with compost added in. Add a top dressing of compost or blood meal to the corn when it's about 6 inches (15.2 cm) tall and again when it's about knee high.

Corn is normally planted about the same time as the average last frost date and needs 60 to 100 days to mature. If you live in a climate that has mild winters, you might be able to grow a spring and a fall crop of corn, which means you can grow one type in the spring and another type in the fall. The fall crop will need to be started 12 to 14 weeks before the average first frost.

Each strand of corn silk will need to get pollinated in order to have a well-filled ear of corn. Because corn is wind-pollinated, it won't do well in one or two long rows. Instead, grow corn in shorter rows with at least four rows side by side; this is called *block planting*. Planting in blocks helps ensure that the pollen won't be blown away from the corn and improves the chances the pollen will land on the corn silk. The corn silk will turn brown after it's pollinated.

Even though corn plants are really tall, their roots are shallow and spread out. They don't compete well with weeds, so try to remove the weeds before planting. Then, pull weeds when they are small to keep their roots from getting entangled with the corn's roots.

Corn needs about an inch (2.5 cm) of water per week; this is especially important during pollination. When you water corn, try to water only the soil and avoid watering overhead, as you might wash the pollen from the tassels.

Cutworms, a type of moth caterpillar, can be a problem for young corn shoots. Sprinkle diatomaceous earth, crushed eggshells or coffee grounds around each plant to help deter cutworms. You can also make a cardboard collar for each plant out of empty toilet paper rolls or other cardboard to prevent the worms from getting to the soft shoots of the corn.

Probably the most common pest is corn earworms. The moths lay eggs on the silk; when the worms hatch, they crawl down into the ear and feast on the corn kernels. To prevent them from reaching the corn, you can draw the husks closed with a rubber band a few days after the silk emerges, or plant a variety that has tightly wrapped husks. You can also treat each ear with four to five drops of vegetable or mineral oil after the silks start to turn brown. The oil will suffocate the worms.

Corn smut is a fungus that can attack corn. It causes the corn kernels to turn gray, swell and eventually burst. It's also edible. It's called *huitlacoche* and appears in some Mexican soups and sauces and Native American foods. It's also becoming quite the delicacy in some upscale restaurants because of its smoky-sweet flavor.

Harvesting

If you've planted sweet corn, start checking the corn about 3 weeks after the silks appear. To check the corn, peel back the husks just a bit and push your thumbnail into one of the kernels. If a milky liquid spurts out, the corn is ready to be picked. If the corn is underripe, the liquid will be watery; if it's overripe, the kernels will be tough-skinned with doughy interiors.

If you've planted popcorn or field corn, let the corn stay on the plant until the plant is dead and the corn is dry.

To harvest corn, simply pull the ear down and break it off the plant. If you're worried about damaging a plant that still has an underripe ear of corn on it, then use garden shears to cut off the ripe ear.

The sugar in sweet corn turns to starch extremely fast, so either eat or preserve it as soon as possible. If it can't be eaten or preserved that day, then store the corn in the refrigerator, preferably in its husks, until you can get to it.

Corn Varieties to Try

Sweet corn with tightly wrapped husks is a great choice if you have trouble with earworms. One such variety, Golden Bantam, matures in 78 days and was one of the first yellow sweet corn varieties. It was introduced in the early 1900s.

Country Gentleman sweet corn also has tightly wrapped husks and white kernels that do not form in neat rows; instead, the kernels grow randomly on the cob. This variety matures in 90 to 100 days and is one of the best for creamed corn. Country Gentleman will usually produce three ears per plant.

For small-space gardening, try Yukon Chief corn, which is a compact plant that produces multiple ears and matures in 55 days. This variety is also more cold tolerant that most other varieties.

If you want to grow corn for grinding into flour, look for varieties that have "dent" in the name. Hickory King dent corn is good for drying and grinding and for roasting. It's similar to hominy in that the skins are easily removed when the kernels are soaked. It matures in 85 to 100 days.

Strawberry Popcorn produces ears that are about 3 inches (7.6 cm) long and are full of red kernels. Each plant will produce two to four ears in about 100 days. The popcorn makes a really fun gift from the garden.

Buying

If you're buying corn, look for corn that has a damp, pale green stalk, which means the corn has been picked within the day. Your best bet for freshly picked corn is to buy from a local farmer or the farmers' market. The next best corn to buy is corn that has been held on ice.

Corn that has an opaque, chalky stalk is several days old. Corn that has a brown stalk is even older. This corn won't be nearly as tasty for eating off the cob, but it might do fine as cut or Frozen Creamed Corn (page 141).

If you're buying from a grocery store, talk to the produce manager and ask when they get new shipments of corn. Our local grocery stores carry locally grown sweet corn in season at very reasonable prices and will gladly sell the corn by the case from the back storage.

Preserving

Since sweet corn begins to convert its sugars into starch soon after harvesting, the sooner you can preserve it the better. If you've planted popcorn or field corn, you don't have to worry about preserving it; it's already preserved in its dried state. You just need to store it.

To shuck fresh sweet corn, pull the outer leaves off, then grab some of the silk and leaves and pull down. When you get to the stem, break the stem off and the rest of the leaves should easily come off. Remove any remaining silks by picking them off or gently rubbing the corn with a vegetable brush.

If you are preserving just the kernels, they will need to be cut off. Websites and local feed or hardware stores that sell canning goods sell several tools designed to cut off corn kernels. A sharp knife works really great too. Start at the skinny end and cut through the kernels all the way to the stem.

The leaves can be dehydrated and used for crafts and making tamales. The silk can also be dehydrated and used to make an herbal tea.

Canning

Corn can be canned using a pressure canner or by pickling it as a relish (Canned Sweet and Zesty Corn Salad, page 138). Corn must be shucked, rinsed and have the kernels cut off before it's canned.

It takes approximately 20 pounds (9.1 kg) of corn still in its husks to fill nine pint (500-ml) jars and 31½ pounds (14.3 kg) of corn still in its husks to fill seven quart (1-L) jars.

Whole kernel corn can be canned in the pressure canner using the raw-pack or hot-pack method (page 24). The National Center for Home Food Preservation recommends that corn be blanched for 3 minutes prior to cutting it off the cob. At this time, neither the Ball® Corporation nor the booklet that came with my All-American® pressure canner has this recommendation. I believe the recommendation is because it's easier to cut the corn off the cob if it's been blanched, not for safety reasons.

To can whole-kernel corn, loosely pack the corn into the jars. If the corn is hot packed, add the cooking water to the jars instead of fresh water. When the jars are filled, use the bubble remover tool to remove the air bubbles and make sure the jars have 1 inch (2.5 cm) of headspace. Wipe the rims of each jar and put a lid and band on the jar. Process the jars, according to the manufacturer's instructions, at 10 psi (69 kPa) for 55 minutes for pints (500 ml) and 85 minutes for quarts (1 L). Adjust for altitude, (page 25), if necessary.

Cream-style corn can also be canned in a pressure canner, but it will need to be cooked for 3 minutes first and then hot packed. Because of creamed corn's density, it's recommended that creamed corn be canned only in pint (500-ml) jars, not quart (1-L) jars. Process the jars, according to the manufacturer's instructions, at 10 psi (69 kPa) for 85 minutes, adjusting for altitude (page 25), if necessary.

Corn can be pickled in a relish in pint (500-ml) or half-pint (250-ml) jars.

Freezing

Corn can be frozen on the cob or off the cob. It's recommended that corn be blanched before freezing.

You can freeze just-picked corn in the husks without blanching. I've done this for years, and my family likes the flavor and texture. This isn't for long-term storage, but it is a great way to quickly put up a lot of corn and lock in the sweetness. Corn frozen this way is best used within 6 months.

To freeze corn on the cob in the husks, cut off the tip and the stem; if you've had any pest problems, you should peek inside the husks at the tip to see if there any worms in there. You can remove a few outer leaves that are damaged, but it's not necessary. Put the corn in freezer bags, label them and put them in the freezer. To cook the corn, heat the oven to 350°F (177°C), put the frozen corn on the racks or in a baking dish and cook for 45 to 50 minutes, or until the kernels are tender when pierced with a paring knife. Remove them from the oven and let them get cool enough to handle, then remove the husks and the silks. The silks should come right off.

Most experts recommend blanching corn on the cob before freezing it, and, if I were going to store the corn for longer than 6 months, I would blanch the corn first. Shuck the corn and then blanch it using the recommended times: small ears (1¼ inches [3.1 cm] or less in diameter), 7 minutes; medium ears (1¼ to 1½ inches [3.1 to 3.8 cm] in diameter), 9 minutes; and large ears (over 1½ inches [3.8 cm] in diameter), 11 minutes (page 34). Immediately cool the ears in an ice bath. Once the corn is cooled, pat it dry and put it into labeled and dated freezer bags.

Before you put up large quantities of frozen corn on the cob, I suggest you try a few ears blanched and unblanched to find out if your family prefers the flavor and texture of one way over the other.

Corn off the cob can be frozen plain or as Frozen Creamed Corn (page 141). Plain corn or whole-kernel corn is the most versatile way to freeze corn. To freeze whole-kernel corn, blanch the corn on the cob for 4 minutes, and then put it in an ice bath to cool. Once the corn is cooled, pat it dry and then cut the kernels from the cob. Pack the corn into freezer-safe containers in meal-sized portions, label the containers and freeze them for up to 12 months.

Dehydrating

Dehydrating corn will turn 18 pounds (8.2 kg) of corn into 2½ pounds (1.1 kg) in less than a day, which is great if you want shelf-stable food and don't own a pressure canner or don't have much pantry or freezer space. Corn can be dehydrated plain and then rehydrated later to use in soups and casseroles.

To dehydrate corn, blanch it first for 4 minutes while it's still on the cob. After the blanching time, put the cobs into an ice bath to stop the cooking process. When the corn is cool, remove it from the ice bath, pat it dry and cut the kernels off the cob. Lay the corn kernels on a dehydrator tray and dehydrate them at 135°F (57°C) for 8 to 10 hours, or until the corn is crisp and brittle.

To reconstitute the corn, put it in a bowl and cover it with warm water. Cover the bowl and let the kernels soak for 30 to 60 minutes. Dehydrated corn can be added directly to soup while it's cooking; just be aware that the corn will soak up the liquid and make the soup thicker.

Fermenting

Because it has a high sugar content, which causes it to ferment quickly, corn needs just a few days of fermenting time.

To ferment corn, shuck it and cut the kernels off the cob. Put the corn kernels in a clean glass jar and add a 2 percent brine (page 51). Put a weight in the jar and a fermentation lid on the jar, then put the jar on a plate or small cookie sheet to catch any overflow. Set the jar, out of direct sunlight, for 3 to 5 days. You can start testing it after 4 days. When it's to your liking, store it in the refrigerator for up to 2 months.

Fermented corn doesn't store as long as other fermented vegetables, so don't make a bunch at once. However, you can use whole-kernel frozen corn to make additional batches throughout the year. If the frozen corn has been blanched, add a couple of tablespoons of the brine from the previous batch of fermented corn to the new batch that's being made with frozen corn.

Preserving Corn Cheat Sheet

	Water Bath Canning	Pressure Canning	Freezing	Dehydrating	Fermenting 2% brine
How to prepare	Off the cob or corn cob jelly	Off the cob, whole, kernel or creamed	Blanching recommended; on or off the cob	Blanching required; off the cob	On or off the cob
Flavors	Savory or sweet	Plain or as a soup base	Plain or creamed	Plain or seasoned	Plain or seasoned with herbs
Length of processing	15 minutes	Whole kernel Pints (500 ml): 55 minutes Quarts (1 L): 85 minutes Creamed: 85 minutes; pints (500 ml) only	—	8–10 hours	3–5 days
Storage life	12 months	12 months	6–12 months	12 months for plain; 1 month for seasoned	3 months

Canned Corn Chowder

Soups are my go-to dinner during the winter because of their warmth, yes, but also because they're just so easy to make. This is especially true when you've got the soup base stored safe and sound on your pantry shelves and all you have to do is add a little cream, cracked black pepper and chili powder.

Makes 8 pint (500-ml) jars

For the Chowder

3 cups (711 ml) vegetable or chicken broth

2 cups (474 ml) water

3 cups (500 g) corn kernels (approximately 4–5 ears)

1 lb (453 g) chopped onions

¾ cup (112 g) diced sweet peppers

1 cup (140 g) diced carrots

1 lb (453 g) potatoes, cut into ½-inch (12-mm) cubes

½ cup (60 g) diced celery

1 bay leaf

1 tsp dried thyme

4 cloves garlic, minced

2 tbsp (36 g) salt

1 tsp ground black pepper

For Serving

¼ cup (59 ml) heavy cream, half and half or milk per jar of soup

Dried Chili Powder (page 222) or cracked black pepper

Small sprigs of thyme

For the chowder, prepare the pressure canner. Rinse it and its rack, place the bottom rack inside and fill the canner with a few inches of water, according to the manufacturer's instructions. Put the pressure canner on the stove over low heat while you prepare the jars. This is a hot-pack recipe, so the water in the pressure canner needs to be about 180°F (82°C) before you put the jars into the canner.

Wash eight pint (500-ml) jars in hot, soapy water and check for any nicks or cracks in the jars. Rinse the jars in clean water and set them aside. Wash the lids in hot, soapy water, rinse them and set them aside.

In a large stockpot, bring the broth and the water to a low boil over medium-high heat. When the liquid is boiling, add the corn, onions, peppers, carrots, potatoes, celery, bay leaf, thyme, garlic, salt and pepper. Simmer the mixture for 15 minutes, stirring occasionally.

Remove the pot from the heat and ladle the soup into the prepared jars, leaving 1 inch (2.5 cm) of headspace. Remove the air bubbles with a bubble remover tool or chopstick and recheck the headspace. If you run out of the broth and water mixture before each jar is filled properly, top off the jars with boiling water.

Process the jars, according to the manufacturer's instructions, at 10 psi (69 kPa) for 55 minutes for pints (500 ml), adjusting for altitude (page 25), if necessary. Let the pressure canner depressurize naturally (page 25). Arrange a folded towel on the counter or table. Open the canner and remove the jars, using a jar lifter.

Place the jars on the towel, and let them cool for at least 12 hours. Remove the bands, check the seals and store the jars for up to 1 year. If any jars failed to seal, put them in the refrigerator to use first.

For serving, empty a jar of corn chowder into a medium stockpot and heat the chowder over medium heat for 10 minutes, until the chowder is bubbling. Add the cream to the chowder and give it another stir. Sprinkle a little chili powder on top and add a small sprig of thyme.

Canned Sweet and Zesty Corn Salad

Corn salad is one of those versatile recipes that can turn my pantry into a deli. This zesty salad is fantastic straight out of the jar and added to burrito bowls and tacos.

Makes 3 pint (500-ml) or 6 half-pint (250-ml) jars

2 tbsp (36 g) salt

4 tsp (8 g) ground mustard

4 cups (948 ml) apple cider vinegar

1 cup (237 ml) water

⅔ cup (134 g) sugar

5 cups (830 g) corn kernels (approximately 17–19 ears)

1 cup (150 g) diced peppers, a mix of sweet and hot, seeds removed from hot peppers if you prefer milder flavor

6–8 cloves garlic, minced

Prepare the water bath canner by filling it halfway with water and putting it on the stove to simmer. Check three pint (500-ml) or six half-pint (250-ml) jars for any nicks or cracks, wash them in hot soapy water and rinse them in hot water. Keep the jars hot until it's time to use them. Wash the lids in hot soapy water, rinse them and set them aside.

Combine the salt, mustard, vinegar, water and sugar in a large stockpot and bring the mixture to a boil, stirring occasionally. Add the corn, peppers and garlic, and bring the mixture back to a boil. Reduce the heat to low and simmer the mixture for 20 minutes.

Remove the stockpot from the heat, and fill the jars with the corn salad, leaving ½ inch (12 mm) of headspace. Remove the air bubbles with a bubble remover tool or chopstick and recheck the headspace; add more brine if necessary. Wipe the rims with a clean cloth, put the lids on the jars and screw on the bands. Place the jars in the prepared hot water bath canner, making sure that the jars are covered by at least an inch (2.5 cm) of water.

Bring the water to a full rolling boil and put the lid on the canner. Process the jars for 15 minutes, adjusting for altitude (page 17), if necessary. Arrange a folded towel on the counter or table. Remove the jars, using a jar lifter, and place them on the towel. Let the jars cool for at least 12 hours.

Once the jars are cooled, remove the bands and check the seals. If any jars failed to seal, put them in the refrigerator to use first. Wipe the jars with a clean cloth and store them for up to a year.

Serving Suggestions: *Garnish with Dried Chili Powder (page 222) and serve as a cold side dish. Use the salad to top eggs, or mix it with a can of black beans and diced tomatoes for a quick and fun salsa.*

Frozen Creamed Corn

There are as many versions of creamed corn as there are people who make it. This recipe uses the cream in the corn cob to make a simple, delicious and versatile creamed corn for the freezer.

Makes 6 cups (1.44 L)

For the Creamed Corn

8 ears of corn, shucked and silks removed

2 tbsp (28 g) butter

1 tbsp (18 g) salt

1 tsp ground black pepper

For Serving

2 tbsp (30 ml) heavy cream or half and half

½ tsp sugar (optional)

Dash of garlic powder (optional)

Cracked black pepper or chili powder

Using a cutting board and a sharp knife or corn cutter, cut the kernels off the cob. What makes creamed corn "creamed corn" is using the milky liquid called *corn cream* that is still on the cob after you remove the kernels. To get to the sweet, milky liquid, over a large bowl, rub the knife up and down each cob with the flat side of the knife. Don't cut into the cob, just remove the liquid and the bits of corn left on the cob. Add the kernels to the corn cream in the bowl.

Melt the butter in a large stockpot, then add the corn and corn cream. Bring the mixture to a simmer over medium heat; add the salt and pepper. Simmer the mixture for 10 minutes while stirring. You'll notice that the mixture will begin to thicken and the color will deepen.

Remove the pot from the heat, let the creamed corn cool and put it into freezer-safe containers. If you're using glass jars, be sure to leave ½ inch (12 mm) of headspace for expansion. Put the jars into the refrigerator to cool overnight, and then transfer them to the freezer. Creamed corn can be stored in the freezer for up to a year.

For serving, thaw the frozen creamed corn in the refrigerator overnight. Put the creamed corn in a small stockpot and warm it over medium heat until it simmers. Stir in the heavy cream to make it creamier, and the sugar and the garlic powder, if desired. Garnish the creamed corn with the cracked pepper.

Canned Spicy Corn Cob Jelly

There is no need to toss the corn cobs after the kernels are all gone. Instead, use them to make corn cob jelly! The sugar in this recipe balances the heat from the peppers and the result is a flavorful, not overly sweet, jelly.

Makes 5 half-pint (250-ml) jars

10–12 corn cobs, cut into 4-inch (10-cm) lengths; kernels reserved for another use

2 quarts (2 L) water

6 tbsp (54 g) pectin

½ tsp red pepper flakes

3 cups (600 g) sugar

Serving Suggestions: *This jelly is really great on a breakfast biscuit or peanut butter sandwich. It can also be used as a glaze on meats, served on crackers with soft cheese or added to vinegar and oil to make a salad dressing.*

Prepare the water bath canner by filling it halfway with water and putting it on the stove to simmer. Check five half-pint (250-ml) jars for any nicks or cracks, wash them in hot soapy water and rinse them in hot water. Keep the jars hot until it's time to use them. Wash the lids in hot soapy water, rinse them and set them aside.

Put the corn cobs and water in a large stockpot. Bring the water to a boil, then reduce the heat to medium and simmer the mixture for 40 minutes. Turn off the heat and strain the juice through a jelly bag or double layer of cheesecloth into a large measuring cup or bowl. Just let the juice drip through the bag; pressing or squeezing the bag will make the jelly cloudy.

You will need 3 cups (711 ml) of corn cob juice to make the jelly. If you don't have enough juice after straining out the solids, you can add water to make up the difference.

Put the measured juice in a stockpot, stir in the pectin and red pepper flakes and bring the mixture to a boil. Add the sugar and bring the mixture to a rolling boil, while stirring. Boil the mixture for 5 minutes, then remove the pot from the heat.

Pour the hot jelly immediately into the hot jars, leaving ¼ inch (6 mm) of headspace. If there is any scum on the top of the jelly, remove it with a spoon or spatula. Wipe the rims of the jars with a clean cloth, put on the lids and screw on the bands. Place the jars in the prepared hot water bath canner and process them for 10 minutes.

Arrange a folded towel on the counter or table. After 10 minutes of processing, remove the jars from the water bath canner, using a jar lifter, and place them on the folded towel. Let the jars cool for at least 12 hours. Once they are cooled, remove the bands and check the seals. If any jars failed to seal, put them in the refrigerator to use first. Wipe the jars with a clean cloth and store for them for up to a year.

*In the photo, the jelly is shown in the jar on the left.

Fermented Corn Salsa

This tangy salsa is fantastic on tacos or nachos. Its short fermentation time keeps the sweetness of the corn but shortens its storage time. Make this salsa as you need it instead of making large batches for storing.

Makes 1 quart (1 L)

3 cups (500 g) corn kernels (approximately 4–5 ears)

¼ cup (40 g) chopped onion

1 tbsp (3 g) chopped fresh cilantro

2 tbsp (30 ml) lime juice

4 tsp (24 g) sea salt

2 cups (474 ml) filtered water

Put the corn kernels in a wide-mouth quart (1-L) Mason jar. Add the onions, cilantro and lime juice to the jar.

Mix the salt into the water to make the brine. Fill the jar with the brine, making sure to cover the corn and onions but leaving room for the weight and expansion. Put a weight in the jar to keep everything under the brine, and top the jar with a fermentation lid. Put the jar on a plate or small cookie sheet to catch any overflow.

Set the jar in a cool place, out of direct sunlight, for 4 to 6 days. You can taste the salsa any time after 4 days. If it needs to ferment longer, replace the weight and the fermentation lid and ferment for a few more days. When the salsa is to your liking, replace the weight and fermentation lid with a plastic storage lid. Store the salsa in the refrigerator for up to 4 months.

*See the photo on page 143 (this recipe is shown in the jar on the right).

Serving Suggestions: *Enjoy straight from the jar, as a cold side dish or sprinkled on a salad. This salsa can also be mixed with canned beans that have been rinsed to make a tangy corn and bean salsa.*

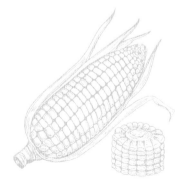

Dried Chili-Lime Corn Snacks

There's something about the combination of chili, lime and corn that is so very good. The first time I made these snacks, one of my sons ate the whole batch when they came out of the dehydrator—before they had time to cool and before anyone else got to try them. Sneaky guy—he knew I'd have to make more.

Makes 1 half-pint (250 ml)

3 ears of corn

1 tbsp (15 ml) lime juice

½ tsp salt

½ tsp chili powder

Fill a stockpot about halfway with water and bring it to a boil over high heat. When the water is at a full boil, put the corn into the pot and blanch the corn for 4 minutes. While the corn is in the boiling water, prepare a large bowl of ice water. Take the corn out of the boiling water, using tongs. Immediately put the corn into the bowl of ice water to stop the cooking.

While the corn is cooling, mix the lime juice, salt and chili powder in a medium bowl.

Remove the corn from the ice water and pat it dry with a clean kitchen towel. Using a sharp knife, cut the kernels off the corn cob and measure out 2 cups (330 g); you may have extra corn for another use. Carefully add the measured corn to the bowl with the seasonings, and mix to coat all the pieces.

Lay the seasoned corn kernels on a dehydrator tray. You can put the pieces close together, as they will shrink considerably. Dehydrate at 125°F (52°C) for 10 to 12 hours, or until the kernels are brittle. When fully dry, the kernels should be crisp and brittle.

When the kernels are fully dry, remove the tray from the dehydrator and let the corn cool. Put the kernels in a glass jar with a tight-fitting lid and label the jar. Use the corn within a month.

Serving Suggestions: *Several of my children like to eat this as a snack right out of the jar, but these can be a little hard, so be forewarned. The seasoned kernels can be crushed or ground in a spice grinder and used to garnish soups, added to sour cream to make a dip or added to cream cheese to make a spread.*

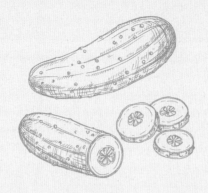

cucumbers
More Than Just Pickles

Cucumbers get a bad rap sometimes, mostly because they cause some people to burp, but also because people think you must either eat them plain or pickle them. While I agree with the burping—much to the delight of my children when they were small—I don't agree with the lack of versatility. Cucumbers are good for more than just pickles.

Cucumbers are members of the *cucurbit* family, along with melons and squashes, and come in a variety of shapes and sizes. There are two basic varieties of cucumber: those grown for pickling and those grown for eating fresh (called *slicing cucumbers*).

Pickling cucumbers are smaller than slicing cucumbers and have thin skins and small seeds. Their flesh is firmer than that of slicing cucumbers; this helps them hold up better when pickled. Instead of being dark green like most cucumbers you'll find in the grocery store, pickling cucumbers are lighter with yellow undertones. The skin might even be dappled. As the pickling cukes get bigger, their skin will turn from green to a creamy yellow.

Slicing cucumbers range from the thick-skinned, dark green cucumbers you'll find in any grocery store to the thin-skinned, 30-inch (76.2-cm)-long Armenian cucumbers that you can grow or find at the farmers' market. Slicing cucumbers tend to dehydrate quickly, so most of them found in stores have been coated with wax to help prevent moisture loss.

Overgrown slicing cucumbers will also turn from green to yellow and their seeds will get very large and tough.

Growing

Cucumbers are easy to grow. The main thing to be aware of is that, when they get stressed, cucumbers get bitter. Cucumbers need rich, loose soil and consistent watering to keep from getting stressed.

I like to grow cucumbers on a trellis to keep the fruit off the ground. It doesn't have to be anything fancy; a chain link fence will do just fine. You'll be able to find the cucumbers that are hiding under leaves more easily if you grow cucumbers upright on a trellis.

You can start cucumbers indoors about 4 weeks before your average last frost date. If you have a long growing season, you can direct-seed cucumbers once all danger of frost has passed. Most cucumber plants will start producing 50 to 70 days after the plant has its first set of true leaves. They'll continue producing until the first frost.

However, if you live in a climate with long, hot summers, cucumbers might stop producing way before the first frost. You can start new seeds and grow a second crop for the fall garden.

Cucumbers are susceptible to the cucumber beetle, powdery mildew, aphids and blight. You can hand-pick cucumber beetles and squish the eggs they lay on the underside of leaves to help control them. You can also use diatomaceous earth to help control them and aphids. Blight is a soil-borne pathogen, so don't plant cucumbers where other members of the cucurbit family, including squash and melon, have been planted in the last three seasons. Also, water the soil, not the leaves, to help reduce powdery mildew.

Cucumber Varieties to Try

I like to choose cucumber varieties that mature early, are prolific and tend to not get bitter when they're large.

For slicing cucumbers, Marketmore 80 and Straight Eight are prolific and produce good-flavored cucumbers. Both mature in about 70 days, although Straight Eight will sometimes mature in as early as 50 days.

If you want to pickle small whole cucumbers, try Parisian Pickle, which is a small gherkin variety and will mature in about 60 days. For larger pickles, Russian Pickling cucumber is a good choice and matures in as little as 50 days.

If you have room for only one cucumber variety, plant Muncher cucumbers. This is a dual-purpose variety that is great for pickling, but also has a nice flavor for eating fresh. The Muncher cucumber matures in 60 days.

For fun, I like to grow round-shaped lemon cucumbers (so named for their yellow color, not lemon flavor), a white variety named Salt and Pepper and Armenian cucumbers. I don't grow them every year, and, when I do grow them, I grow only a couple of plants.

Harvesting

Harvest pickling cucumbers when they are the size of "pickles," which is about 3 inches (7.6 cm). Most slicing cucumbers are best harvested at 5 to 6 inches (12.7 to 15.2 cm) long. The long Armenian cucumbers will be harvested at 20 to 24 inches (50.8 to 61 cm).

When you harvest, try not to pull the cucumber off the vine: I can't tell you how many times I've yanked on a cucumber and pulled the entire vine off the trellis. Instead, use gardening shears and cut the cucumbers off the vine, or hold the vine in one hand and twist and pull the cucumber off with the other hand.

If you find an overgrown, yellow cucumber, don't compost it! Unless it's rotten, you can still use it to make senfgurken, which is a German pickle made with overgrown cucumbers (Fermented German Mustard Pickles, page 154). Senfgurken is similar to watermelon rind pickles.

Buying

If you are buying cucumbers, your best bet is to go to the farmers' market and buy pickling cucumbers or unwaxed slicing cucumbers while they are in season. Look for small, firm cucumbers that do not have shriveled skin—make sure to look at the tips, too.

If you are buying cucumbers at the grocery store, they will be waxed; even organic ones. Organic cucumbers are waxed with a non-synthetic wax and are a better option than conventionally grown cucumbers.

If you can't grow cucumbers or buy them from a farmers' market, you can still preserve cucumbers. Simply remove the wax by pouring boiling water over the cucumbers. This will melt the wax and wash it off down the drain. Then, scrub the cucumber with a loofah or vegetable brush to loosen any leftover wax and pour boiling water over it again. Be careful not to soak the cucumbers in boiling water, as you don't want to cook them.

If you use waxed cucumbers with the wax removed for fermenting or pickling, try a small batch first to see how it goes. Waxed cucumbers are not recommended for pickling, since the brine can't penetrate the wax. But you can certainly preserve waxed cucumbers by freezing and dehydrating them.

What to Do with Bitter Cucumbers

Bitterness in cucumbers is caused by a natural organic compound called *cucurbitacin*. While cucurbitacin is found mainly in the leaves, roots and stem, it can spread to the fruit, especially if the plant has been stressed.

If a cucumber is bitter, it's most likely just bitter on the stem end and in the skin. Cutting the stem end off and peeling the cucumber should take away the bitterness. Try a small slice of every cucumber before preserving it. If it's bitter, peel it before preserving it.

Preserving

Cucumbers don't store long because they dehydrate quickly. If you can't preserve the cucumbers right away, store them in the crisper of your refrigerator. They really need some humidity to stay fresh. If it's going to be more than 2 days before you can get to them, put a damp cloth in the crisper with the cucumbers.

Canning

Cucumbers are a low-acid food, canned in a vinegar brine and processed in a water bath. Cucumbers are the classic vegetable for pickles and relishes. There are no recommendations for pressure canning cucumbers, as they would turn to mush.

Cucumbers can be canned whole, speared, sliced or chopped. They can be canned in a savory brine or a sweet brine. They can be made with or without peppers. You can add any number of spices to them, such as mustard seed, celery seed, peppercorns, garlic or the iconic dill. Truly, the choices are limitless.

Our favorite pickle is my Canned Granny's Bread-and-Butter Pickle (page 151). To spice them up, I'll sometimes substitute jalapeños for some of the cucumber or add red pepper flakes to the jars.

The most important thing to remember when canning cucumbers is that you need to have a safe low-acid food (cucumbers, onions, peppers) to vinegar ratio. You can add or leave out spices as you like. You can add sugar or leave it out. But you cannot use less vinegar than the recipe calls for.

Freezing

People are always shocked when I tell them I freeze cucumbers. My goal is to not buy things we can grow, so if I want cucumber-infused water or Frozen Cucumber Tzatziki (page 158) all year long, I have to freeze cucumbers.

There are several ways to freeze cucumbers. You can freeze them in ice cube trays by putting chopped cucumbers in the ice cube tray and pouring water over them. Once they are frozen, you can pop them out of the tray and store them in a freezer bag.

Another way to freeze cucumbers is to shred them as you would a zucchini. Put the shredded cucumber in a freezer bag and freeze.

My favorite way to freeze cucumbers is to freeze slices. I've found that this is the most versatile and fastest way to get the job done. To freeze slices, line a baking sheet with parchment paper and lay cucumber slices on it. Put the baking sheet in the freezer for several hours, until the cucumbers are fully frozen. Once the slices are frozen, transfer them to a freezer bag and store them in the freezer for up to a year.

When cucumbers thaw, they will release much of their water content. They will no longer be crisp and won't be good for eating plain. They are good for any dish in which you want the cucumber flavor, but don't need the cucumber texture.

Dehydrating

Cucumbers make a nice dehydrated chip that can be used for dipping in sauces, powdered and added to homemade salad dressings or rehydrated, which will give you the fresh cucumber flavor but a limp texture.

To dehydrate cucumbers, slice them into ¼-inch (6-mm) rounds and lay them on the dehydrator trays without letting them touch. Dehydrate the slices for 4 to 6 hours at 135°F (57°C), until they easily snap in half when bent. Let the slices cool, then store them in glass jars with tight-fitting lids.

To rehydrate cucumber slices, soak them in cool water for 30 to 60 minutes. You can also use your favorite pickle brine instead of water to make them pickle-flavored.

Fermenting

Fermented cucumbers are the original "pickle" and have been around for thousands of years, dating back to 2000 BC in India. Over time, they have made their way around the world and now are a staple in many homes. Fermented cucumbers may taste very much like canned cucumber pickles, but there are some marked differences.

The most notable difference is that some nutritional value is lost in the canning process and nutritional value is added in the fermenting process. To can pickles, you must use vinegar. But to ferment pickles, you use a saltwater brine. Also, canned pickles are shelf-stable, while fermented pickles will probably need to be stored in the refrigerator to last the year.

It's important to use pickling cucumbers for fermenting, as slicing cucumbers tend to turn soft in the brine. Also, if you must buy cucumbers, make sure they are not waxed and, if you can find them, buy cucumbers grown with organic practices. For fermented cucumbers, it's best to just rinse the cucumber and not wash them. The bacteria that is naturally on the cucumber will help with the fermentation process.

Cucumbers can be fermented whole, speared, sliced or chopped as a relish. The most popular ways are whole and sliced.

To make fermented cucumbers, put rinsed cucumbers, either whole or sliced, in a clean Mason jar and cover them with a 3 percent brine (page 51). You can add flavor to the cucumbers with onions, garlic, spices such as dill, bay leaves, peppercorns, mustard seed, red pepper flakes or ginger—or a small bit of horseradish before adding the brine. Cover the top of the jar with grape, oak or horseradish leaves or a silicone cover to help keep the pickles crisp. Add a weight and an airlock fermenting lid.

Put the fermenting cucumbers on a plate or small cookie sheet to catch any overflow, and store the jar out of direct sunlight. After about 4 days,

the cucumbers will be half sour, and after about 6 days, they will be full sour. Test the cucumbers each day until they are as sour as you like, being sure to replace the leaves, weight and fermenting lid each time you check them. When the pickles are ready, remove the leaves, weight and fermenting lid and add new leaves, if you have them, and a plastic storage lid. Store the pickles in the refrigerator for up to a year.

Preserving Cucumbers Cheat Sheet

	Water Bath Canning	Pressure Canning (Not recommended)	Freezing	Dehydrating	Fermenting 3% brine
How to prepare	Whole or slices	N/A	No blanching required; slices	No blanching required; slices	Whole or slices
Flavors	Pickled, savory or sweet	N/A	Plain	Plain or seasoned	Seasoned with herbs
Length of processing	10 minutes	N/A	—	4–6 hours	4–6 days
Storage life	12 months	N/A	8–12 months	12 months for plain; 1 month for seasoned	12 months

Canned Granny's Bread-and-Butter Pickles

Bread-and-butter pickles are a throwback to the Depression Era. The stories vary about why these pickles are named bread-and-butter, but one thing all the stories have in common is a mention of how delicious they are! The pickles are sweet, but not too sweet. They're great on sandwiches or a relish tray, even on plain buttered bread.

Makes 8 pint (500-ml) jars

6 lbs (2.75 kg) medium pickling cucumbers, cut into ⅛–¼-inch (4–6-mm) slices

2 lbs (907 g) onions, cut into ⅛–¼-inch (4–6-mm) slices

¼ lb (113 g) sweet or hot peppers, seeds removed from hot peppers if you prefer milder flavor, cut into ⅛–¼-inch (4–6-mm) slices

½ cup (145 g) sea salt

5 cups (1 kg) sugar

3 cups (711 ml) apple cider vinegar

½ tsp turmeric

2 tbsp (24 g) mustard seed

2 tbsp (18 g) celery seed

½ tbsp (3 g) ground cloves

Serving Suggestions: *These pickles are good straight out of the jar or added to burgers. You can chop them up and use them in dishes that call for relish.*

Put the cucumbers, onions and peppers in a large bowl or dish pan; stir to combine them. Sprinkle the cucumber mixture with the salt, cover the mixture with ice and mix it well. Let the mixture stand for 3 hours.

Prepare the water bath canner by filling it halfway with water and putting it on the stove to simmer. Check eight pint (500-ml) jars for any nicks or cracks, wash them in hot soapy water and rinse them in hot water. Keep the jars hot until it's time to use them. Wash the lids in hot soapy water, rinse them and set them aside.

After the vegetables have been salted, drain them in a colander to let the juices run off. Rinse them with cold water and drain again.

In a large stainless-steel pot, combine the sugar, vinegar, turmeric, mustard seed, celery seed and cloves. Bring the mixture to a boil. Add the vegetables, bring to a boil again and remove from the heat.

Fill the hot jars with the cucumber mixture. Push the vegetables down tightly and pour the brine over them, leaving ½ inch (12 mm) of headspace. Remove the air bubbles with a bubble remover tool or chopstick and recheck the headspace; add more brine if necessary. Wipe the rims with a clean cloth, put the lids on the jars and screw on the bands. Place the jars in the prepared hot water bath canner, making sure that the jars are covered by at least an inch (2.5 cm) of water.

Bring the water to a full rolling boil and put the lid on the canner. Process the jars for 10 minutes, adjusting for altitude (page 17), if necessary. Arrange a folded towel on the counter or table. Remove the jars, using a jar lifter, and place them on the towel. Let the jars cool for at least 12 hours.

Once the jars are cooled, remove the bands and check the seals. If any jars failed to seal, put them in the refrigerator to use first. Wipe the jars with a clean cloth and store them for up to a year.

*See photo on page 152 (this recipe is shown in front of the bowl).

Fermented Cucumber Relish

Whenever possible, I prefer to make fermented relish rather than canned relish to increase our probiotic intake. This fermented relish can easily pass for "regular" relish in salads that call for it and on burgers and hot dogs. This is one of those recipes: "I won't tell, if you won't tell."

Makes 1 quart (1 L)

2 cups (270 g) chopped cucumbers

¼ cup (37 g) sweet or hot peppers, seeds removed from hot peppers if you prefer milder flavor

⅓ cup (35 g) sliced onion

1 tsp dill seed

1 tsp mustard seed

1 tbsp (18 g) sea salt

2 cups (474 ml) filtered water

Pack the cucumbers, peppers, onion, dill and mustard seed into a wide-mouth jar, leaving 2 inches (5 cm) of headspace.

Mix the salt into the water to make the brine, then pour it into the jar, making sure to cover the vegetables but leaving room for a weight and expansion. Put a weight in the jar to keep everything under the brine and top the jar with a fermentation lid. Put the jar on a plate or small cookie sheet to catch any overflow.

Set the jar in a cool place, out of direct sunlight, for 5 to 7 days. You can taste the relish any time after 5 days. If it needs to ferment longer, replace the weight and fermentation lid and ferment for a few more days.

When the relish is to your liking, replace the weight and fermentation lid with a plastic storage lid, label the jar and store it in the refrigerator for up to 12 months.

*In the photo, the relish is in the bowl.

Serving Suggestions: *This savory relish can be added to deviled eggs or pasta, potato or tuna salad.*

Fermented German Mustard Pickles

While looking for ideas for using overgrown cucumbers, I came across a recipe for canned German mustard pickles, senfgurken. I decided to alter the recipe for fermenting and it worked out great! I make a quart (1 L) of these tasty pickles whenever I harvest an overgrown cucumber.

Makes 1 quart (1 L)

Approximately 1 lb (453 g) overgrown cucumber, peeled, seeded and cut into 1-inch (2.5-cm) slices

½ cup (57 g) onion slices

1 tsp black peppercorns

1½ tsp (6 g) mustard seed

2–3 sprigs fresh dill weed

1 bay leaf

1 clove garlic

1 tsp coriander seed

1 tbsp (15 ml) honey

1 tbsp (18 g) sea salt

2 cups (474 ml) filtered water

Put the cucumber into a wide-mouth quart (1-L) jar. Add the onion, peppercorns, mustard seed, dill, bay leaf, garlic, coriander and honey to the jar.

Mix the salt into the water to make the brine. Then fill the jar with the brine, making sure to cover the cucumbers and onions but leaving room for a weight and expansion.

Put a weight into the jar to keep everything under the brine, and screw on a fermentation lid. Put the jar on a plate or small cookie sheet to catch any overflow. Set the jar in a cool place, out of direct sunlight, for 10 to 21 days. You can taste the pickles any time after 10 days. If they need to ferment longer, replace the weight and fermentation lid and ferment them for a few more days.

When the pickles are to your liking, replace the weight and fermentation lid with a plastic storage lid. Store the pickles in the refrigerator for up to 12 months.

*See photo on page 152 (this recipe is shown to the right of the bowl, behind the Bread-and-Butter Pickles [page 151].

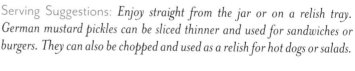

Serving Suggestions: *Enjoy straight from the jar or on a relish tray. German mustard pickles can be sliced thinner and used for sandwiches or burgers. They can also be chopped and used as a relish for hot dogs or salads.*

Dried Cucumber-Dill Chips

Surprise the dill pickle lover in your life with these cucumber chips they can eat anywhere. These chips pack a classic dill pickle flavor and will satisfy your desire for a crunchy snack. Did I mention that they're also healthy? A win all-around!

Makes 1 pint (500 ml)

1 tbsp (15 ml) apple cider vinegar

1 tsp onion powder

1 tsp garlic powder

1 tbsp (1 g) dill weed

2 lbs (907 g) cucumber, cut into ⅛-inch (4-mm) slices

Put the vinegar, onion powder and garlic powder in a large bowl. Add the dill weed, rubbing it between your fingers to break up the leaves a bit. Stir the mixture until it is well-combined. Carefully add the cucumbers to the bowl and mix to coat all the pieces.

Lay the cucumber slices on a dehydrator tray. You can put the pieces close together, as they will shrink considerably. Dehydrate the slices at 125°F (52°C) for 10 to 12 hours or until they are brittle. When the cucumber slices are done, they should break when bent.

When the cucumber slices are fully dry, remove the tray from the dehydrator and let the slices cool. Put the dried cucumber slices in a glass jar with a tight-fitting lid and label the jar. Use the dried slices within a month.

Serving Suggestions: *Eat as a crispy snack. These can also be served on a chip and dip platter with Frozen Cucumber Tzatziki (page 158).*

Canned Cucumber-Jalapeño Jam

Cucumber jam is a unique and tasty way to preserve cucumbers—whenever I take this to get-togethers, people rave about how delicious it is. This is a sweet and tangy jam, with just a bit of a kick from the jalapeños, and it pairs well with goat cheese or cream cheese. You can adjust the heat by using hotter or milder peppers.

Makes 6 half-pint (250-ml) jars

3½ cups (465 g) chopped cucumbers

½ cup (45 g) sliced jalapeños, seeds removed if you prefer milder flavor

½ cup (118 ml) lemon juice

½ cup (118 ml) apple cider vinegar

6 tbsp (54 g) pectin

4 cups (800 g) sugar

Prepare the water bath canner by filling it halfway with water and putting it on the stove to simmer. Check six half-pint (250-ml) jars for any nicks or cracks, wash them in hot soapy water and rinse them in hot water. Keep the jars hot until it's time to use them. Wash the lids in hot soapy water, rinse them and set them aside.

Combine the cucumbers, jalapeños, lemon juice, vinegar and pectin in a stockpot and bring the mixture to a boil over medium-high heat, stirring often. After it begins to boil, add the sugar, bring the mixture back to a rolling boil and boil it for 1 minute, while continually stirring.

Remove the pan from the heat and ladle the jam into the hot jars, leaving ¼ inch (6 mm) of headspace.

Wipe the rims with a clean cloth, put on the lids and screw on the bands. Place the jars in the prepared hot water bath canner and process them for 10 minutes. Arrange a folded towel on the counter or table. Remove the jars, using a jar lifter, and place them on the towel. Let the jars cool for at least 12 hours.

Once the jars are cooled, remove the bands and check the seals. If any jars failed to seal, put them in the refrigerator to use first. Wipe the jars with a clean cloth, label them and store the jam for up to a year.

Serving Suggestions: *Serve over a block of cream cheese with crackers, or use as a topping for crackers and goat cheese. This jam can also be blended and combined with vinegar and oil for a nice salad dressing or dipping sauce.*

Frozen Cucumber Tzatziki

Tzatziki is a Mediterranean dip that is used for dipping pita, vegetables and chips. It's usually made with fresh cucumbers, but we make it with frozen cucumber slices when we don't have any cucumbers available in the garden.

Tzatziki also makes a fantastic salad dressing or dipping sauce. It's super versatile. My teenage son calls it a better version of ranch dressing. Yes, it's that good.

Makes ¾ cup (177 ml)

4–5 oz (115–142 g) frozen cucumber slices (¼ medium cucumber)

½ cup (118 ml) plain full-fat Greek yogurt or full-fat sour cream

2 cloves garlic

2 tsp (10 ml) lemon juice

2 tsp (1 g) fresh dill weed or ¾ tsp dried dill weed

¼ tsp salt

⅛ tsp ground black pepper

1 tsp olive oil

Sprig of fresh dill weed (optional)

Thaw the cucumbers in a bowl. The cucumbers will release quite a bit of liquid as they thaw. Use only the thawed cucumbers, reserving the liquid only if you would like to thin the dip into a salad dressing.

In a small blender, combine the cucumbers, yogurt, garlic, lemon juice, dill, salt and pepper. Blend until the dip is creamy. There will be some small cucumber bits and that's OK. Transfer the tzatziki to a dipping bowl and drizzle the olive oil on top. Garnish the dip with the dill weed, if desired.

*See photo on page 299 (this recipe is shown behind the zucchini fries).

Serving Suggestions: *Serve tzatziki as a dip for vegetables, pita, crackers or chips. It is also fantastic on flatbread wraps or thinned and used as a salad dressing.*

green beans
And Other Snap, Shell and Dry Beans

Beans are right up there with tomatoes and corn as one of the most popular crops among home vegetable gardeners. It's no wonder; they're easy to grow, super prolific and quite tasty. There are three types of beans: snap beans, shell beans and dry beans.

Snap beans, including green beans, are picked when the pod is immature, before the seeds start filling out, and the entire pod is eaten. Shell beans are the mature fresh seeds whose pod has not dried out, and dried beans are the mature seed that has dried in the pod. In theory, you can plant just one variety of bean and, by harvesting it at different stages of maturity, get snap beans, shell beans and dry beans. In reality, some bean varieties are best eaten as snap beans; other varieties make good shell beans or dried beans.

Snap beans go by several names, including green beans, string beans and wax beans. *Snap beans* is because of the snap sound they make when you snap the tip off. *Green beans* is because green is the most common color, although they can come in yellow, which are called *wax beans*, purple and red. And *string beans* is because older varieties have a string that runs down each side of the pod; it needs to be removed before cooking. Many modern varieties have had this trait bred out of them, although most pods will have a string if you let them reach maturity.

If you don't harvest beans before the seed matures, you get shell beans. Shell beans can be used exactly the same as dry beans; however, they will not swell and they don't require soaking and a long cooking time.

If the bean is allowed to fully mature and the pod dries out on the plant, you have dry beans. These are a wonderful source of protein and are great for your food-storage supply. Nature did the preserving for you, so the beans just need to be taken out of the pod and stored in a glass jar with a tight-fitting lid.

Growing

A bean plant will either be a vine, called a *pole bean,* or a small bush, called a *bush bean.* Both truly need some support, as bean plants tend to fall over. Pole beans will need to be grown on a trellis. Bush beans don't need a trellis; they can be planted a little closer together than the seed packet recommends so they can lean against each other for support. I prefer to grow pole beans, even though they need a trellis, because I can see them better when I'm harvesting and I'm less likely to end up with shell beans.

Bush beans tend to produce a lot of beans in a short amount of time, then one or two smaller harvests. Pole beans continue to produce pods all through the season, although production will slow down once the temperatures exceed 90°F (32°C).

Beans can be planted as soon as there's no danger of frost and can be directly seeded in the garden. They can also be started indoors and then transplanted to the garden.

Plant beans in well-draining soil in full sun. Beans don't need super fertile soil, since they take nitrogen from the air. They are nitrogen fixers and will add nitrogen to the soil, just like peas do.

When you water beans, try to water the soil and not the plant, as beans are prone to mildew. The biggest problem I tend to have with beans is cutworms getting to them when they're young. Because of this, I sow more seeds than I need and then thin the plants to the proper spacing.

Harvesting

Harvesting beans is a two-handed job: one hand for tugging on the bean pod and the other for holding the plant. It's easy to yank a stem off instead of just a bean pod if you harvest with just one hand.

All beans, regardless of whether they are snap, shell or dry, should be harvested the same way; break off the green bean just above where it attaches to the stem.

For snap beans, harvest when the pod is slender and the beans have not started to plump up. If you come across bean pods that are starting to get plump, you can either harvest them and use them as shell beans, let them dry on the vine and use them as dry beans or save them for planting next season.

If you are intentionally growing shell beans, harvest them when the bean is plump and the pod is still fresh looking. If the pod starts to dry out, the bean will also be somewhat dried out. If you're growing dry beans, don't pick them until the pod is completely dried out.

Bean Varieties to Try

If you want to try growing just one bean variety and use it for all three types of beans, try Black Coco bush bean or Painted Pony. Otherwise, choose bean varieties based on what you're going to do with them.

You also want to consider your climate when you choose what beans to grow. Some beans, like fava, can handle colder and damper soil temperatures better than other beans. Some varieties, like the yard-long beans, will continue producing in the heat of the summer when other varieties are taking a break.

I like to plant Emerite and Purple Podded beans for snap beans. Both of these varieties are pole beans and are quite prolific. The Emerite beans tend to produce sooner than the Purple Podded beans, but the purple beans are easier for me to see, so I don't overlook as many when I'm harvesting.

I also plant Scarlet Runner beans, which are beautiful and attract hummingbirds. Runner beans are a perennial in many areas with warm winters. The above-ground parts will die back, but the roots won't, and new plants will emerge in the spring.

If you want to grow bush beans, Provider is a good one to try. It's prolific, germinates well in cool soil and is resistant to powdery mildew.

For shelling beans, Cannellini is a good choice, as it does double duty as a dry bean. It's very prolific and the bush grows upright and off the ground. Lima beans are also a good double-duty choice. When they're harvested as shelling beans, the beans are green. When they're harvested as dry beans, the beans are a creamy white and usually called *butter beans*.

If you want to grow dry beans, consider Cranberry or Black Turtle beans; both are bush beans.

Buying

When buying snap beans, look for beans that look fresh and still have a snap when bent. Of course, don't go around just breaking beans in half. But, if you're in doubt, bend one and see what it does.

The beans should be barely formed; avoid beans that have thick pods and large seeds. Ideally, you'll be able to sort through the beans as you shop. If the farmer doesn't have a verified scale, he might already have the beans portioned out and you won't be able to sort through them. That's fine, but ask if you can open the bag and take a peek.

It's hard to find shell beans at the market or grocery store. If you do find them, choose shell beans that are well filled out and have fresh looking pods without brown streaks, a sign of age.

Most dry beans will be bought at the grocery store. Check the dates on the packages and choose the freshest beans available.

Preserving

At the height of their season, beans are heavy producers. They don't store well without being preserved. If you are not going to use the snap beans the day you pick or buy them, store them unwashed in a container with a lid or in a plastic bag and place them in the crisper part of the refrigerator. They need the moisture so they don't dry out, but check them to make sure they don't rot from too much moisture. If you didn't wash them, they should keep for a week in the refrigerator.

Ideally, you will shell and use or preserve shell beans the day you pick or buy them. If not, store them unwashed in a paper bag in the refrigerator. Use or freeze them within 3 days.

If the bean pods have strings, remove them before preserving the beans. Break the top of the bean just under the stem and cap and pull the string down. Then turn the bean over, snap the little tail off and pull down.

For the purposes of this book we're going to focus on preserving snap beans. I'll also share how to freeze shell beans.

Canning

Snap beans can be canned in a pressure canner using the hot-pack or raw-pack method (page 24). They can also be canned in a water bath canner if you pickle them.

It takes an average of 9 pounds (4 kg) of snap beans to fill nine pint (500-ml) jars and 14 pounds (6.4 kg) to fill seven quart (1-L) jars. To safely use a pressure canner, you need to have at least two quarts (1 L) or four pints (500 ml) to process.

Before canning snap beans, you'll need to wash them and remove the stems and strings, if they have strings. Unless you have a lot of beans that are the same size and they will fit in a jar standing up, you'll probably want to cut the beans into 1- to 2-inch (2.5- to 5-cm) pieces.

To pressure can snap beans, first decide if you want to use the hot-pack or raw-pack method (page 24). After the jars are filled, use the bubble remover tool to remove the air bubbles and make sure the jars have 1 inch (2.5 cm) of headspace. Wipe the rims of each jar and put a lid and band on the jar. Process the jars, according to the manufacturer's instructions, at 10 psi (69 kPa) for 20 minutes for pints (500 ml) and 25 minutes for quarts (1 L). Adjust for altitude (page 25).

Pickled snap beans are often called *dilly beans*. If you like cucumber pickles, consider substituting snap beans for cucumbers in your favorite recipe. When I make dilly beans, I like to use whole snap beans so they stand up in the jar. They look pretty this way and make a fun gift for a fellow pickle lover.

Freezing

People often have strong opinions about frozen snap beans: they either like them or they don't. My family prefers canned snap beans, because frozen snap beans have what they affectionately call a squeak to them when you chew.

However, some people prefer frozen snap beans because they are more firm than canned beans when cooked. Freezing snap beans also requires less hands-on time than canning does, which is a huge benefit during the height of the harvest season.

It's recommended that snap beans be blanched for 3 minutes (page 34) before freezing; however, many people skip this step, including me. I've tried it both ways and haven't found there to be a difference in texture or flavor. However, my frozen snap beans get used within a few months. I don't know how they would compare if they were stored for a year or so.

If you're interested in skipping the blanching step, I recommend that you test both ways to see if there's any noticeable difference to you before you freeze a large amount of snap beans that haven't been blanched.

Snap beans need to be washed and have the stems and strings, if any, removed before freezing. You can cut them into pieces or leave them whole. If you're going to blanch them, they need to be blanched for 3 minutes. After blanching, put them into an ice bath to stop the cooking process.

Lay the snap beans on a clean kitchen towel and dry them before freezing them. This will help keep ice crystals from forming on them. If you want to make sure the beans don't freeze in a big clump, then lay them out on a baking sheet to freeze them individually before you transfer them to a labeled freezer-safe container.

To freeze shelled beans, remove them from the pod and put them in a freezer-safe container. It's that simple.

Dehydrating

Snap beans can be dehydrated and reconstituted to be used just like fresh beans. If you don't like canned snap beans and want shelf-stable beans, dehydrating is the way to go. Another bonus is that dried snap beans take up half the space that canned beans require.

The snap beans will need to be washed and have their stems and strings removed. It's best if all the beans are roughly the same size, so they dehydrate evenly. Therefore, cut the beans into 2-inch (5-cm) pieces.

The snap beans will need to be blanched for 3 minutes (page 24). I've tried skipping the blanching step when I dehydrate snap beans, and the result is not nearly as good as when I blanch them. So, I always blanch snap beans before dehydrating them.

After blanching the beans, put them into a bowl of ice water to stop the cooking process. When they're cooled, lay them out on a kitchen towel and pat them dry. Transfer the beans to a dehydrator tray lined with the mesh insert. Dehydrate at 135°F (57°C) for 8 to 12 hours.

To reconstitute the beans, put them in a bowl and cover them with warm water. Cover the bowl and let the beans soak for 30 to 60 minutes.

Dehydrated beans can be added directly to soup while it's cooking—just be aware that the beans will soak up the liquid and make the soup thicker.

Fermenting

Snap beans are some of the earliest summer vegetables that I harvest from my garden and they need only a few days to ferment. This makes fermented snap beans a good fill-in-the-gap food for us.

I like to leave snap beans whole to ferment them; just remove the stems and strings. Ideally, the beans will all be about the same length and thickness so that they'll ferment evenly. They need to be short enough that they can stand up in the jar and leave at least 1 inch (2.5 cm) of headspace. If they're too tall, I trim them to the right length and add the trimmings to the bag of Frozen Summer Garden Mix (page 170) in the freezer.

To make fermented beans, put rinsed beans, either whole or slices, in a clean Mason jar and cover them with a 2 percent brine (page 51). You can add onions, garlic and spices, such as dill, bay leaves, peppercorns, mustard seed, red pepper flakes and ginger, to the jar before adding the brine. I like to make Fermented Thai Green Beans (page 166) that are spicy and have just a bit of fish sauce in them. Add a weight and an airlock fermenting lid.

Put the fermenting beans on a plate or small cookie sheet to catch any overflow and store the jar, out of direct sunlight, for 6 to 10 days. After 6 days, test the beans each day until they are as sour as you like, being sure to replace the weight and fermenting lid each time you test. When the beans are ready, remove the weight and fermenting lid, add a plastic storage lid to the jar and store the jar in the refrigerator for up to a year.

Preserving Beans Cheat Sheet

	Water Bath Canning	Pressure Canning	Freezing	Dehydrating	Fermenting 2% brine
How to prepare	Whole or pieces	Whole or pieces	3-minute blanching recommended; in pieces	3-minute blanching required; in pieces	Whole or pieces
Flavors	Savory, pickled with herbs	Plain or seasoned	Plain or in tomato sauce	Plain or seasoned	Savory with herbs
Length of processing	15 minutes	Pints (500 ml): 20 minutes Quarts (1 L): 25 minutes	—	10–12 hours	6–10 days
Storage life	12 months	12 months	8–12 months	12 months for plain; 1 month for seasoned	3–9 months

Canned Three Bean Salad

While pickled snap bean recipes are easy to find, tested recipes that use dry beans or shell beans and are processed in a water bath canner are rare to find. When I found one, I had to try it. It was good but not quite right for our family, so I made a few tweaks within the approved guidelines and created a new family favorite. This recipe is a two-day process, as the beans need to marinate overnight, but it's worth the effort.

Makes 11–12 half-pint (250-ml) or 5–6 pint (500-ml) jars

3 cups (330 g) snap beans, chopped, blanched for 3 minutes (page 34) and cooled

3 cups (770 g) canned and drained or cooked kidney beans

2 cups (480 g) canned and drained or cooked garbanzo beans

1 cup (150 g) chopped onion

⅔ cup (98 g) chopped sweet pepper

1 cup (237 ml) red wine vinegar (5% acidity)

1 cup (237 ml) bottled lemon juice

1½ cups (300 g) sugar

½ cup (118 ml) olive oil

1 tsp sea salt

2½ cups (593 ml) water

Combine the snap beans, kidney beans, garbanzo beans, onion and pepper in a bowl and set it aside.

In a nonreactive stockpot (like stainless streel), combine the vinegar, lemon juice, sugar, olive oil, sea salt and water. Bring the mixture to a boil over medium-high heat. Then, add the bean mixture and let it simmer over medium heat for 15 minutes. Remove the pot from the heat, let the beans cool to lukewarm, then refrigerate the beans for 12 to 14 hours to marinate them.

The next day, prepare the water bath canner by filling it halfway with water and putting it on the stove to simmer. Check the jars for any nicks or cracks, wash them in hot soapy water and rinse them in hot water. Keep the jars hot until it's time to use them. Wash the lids in hot soapy water and rinse them.

Bring the bean mixture to boil and then ladle the mixture into the prepared jars, leaving ½ inch (12 mm) of headspace. Remove the air bubbles with a bubble remover tool or chopstick and recheck the headspace; add more brine if necessary. Wipe the rims with a clean cloth, put the lids on the jars and screw on the bands. Place the jars in the prepared hot water bath canner, making sure that the jars are covered by at least 1 inch (2.5 cm) of water.

Bring the water to a full rolling boil and put the lid on the canner. Process the jars for 10 minutes, adjusting for altitude (page 17), if necessary. Arrange a folded towel on the counter or table. Remove the jars, using a jar lifter, and place them on the towel. Let the jars cool for at least 12 hours.

Once the jars are cooled, remove the bands and check the seals. If any jars failed to seal, put them in the refrigerator to use first. Wipe the jars with a clean cloth, and store them for up to a year.

Serving Suggestions: *This bean salad is great as a cold side dish for a sandwich or salad supper. Garnish it with chopped fresh parsley.*

Fermented Thai Green Beans

Many Thai-inspired ferments rely on adding just a Thai pepper and calling it good. This recipe uses naturally fermented fish sauce to create an authentic Asian-flavored ferment. Fish sauce has a unique odor, but don't let that fool you! It tastes wonderful when used sparingly, as in this recipe.

Makes 1 quart (1 L)

¾ lb (340 g) green beans

¼ cup (22 g) sliced onion

1 dried Thai chili pepper or another hot pepper

2 tsp (10 ml) fish sauce

4 tsp (24 g) sea salt

2 cups (474 ml) filtered water

Rinse the snap beans and remove the stem end. Cut them so that they can stand up in a quart (1-L) wide-mouth Mason jar and still leave 2 inches (5 cm) of headspace.

Fill the jar with the green beans, onion, pepper and fish sauce. Mix the salt with the water to create a brine and pour it into the jar, covering all the vegetables. Put a weight in the jar to keep everything under the brine and top the jar with a fermentation lid. Put the jar on a plate or small cookie sheet to catch any overflow.

Set the jar in a cool place, out of direct sunlight, for 6 to 10 days. Taste the beans after 6 days. If they need to ferment longer, replace the weight and fermentation lid and ferment for a few more days. When the beans are to your liking, replace the weight and fermentation lid with a plastic storage lid and store the jar in the refrigerator. These are best eaten within 3 months.

Serving Suggestions: *Enjoy these as you would any other pickle, either straight out of the jar or on a relish tray. These are also nice as a cold side dish for sandwiches.*

Canned Lemon–Garlic Green Beans

While most would agree freshly cooked green beans are the best, there's something truly wonderful about opening a jar of lemon–garlic green beans and eating them straight out of the jar. These savory beans are perfect for the person who wants cold green beans for salads, but doesn't care for pickled food.

Makes 6 pint (500-ml) jars

For the Beans

4 cups (948 ml) water

2 cups (474 ml) vegetable or chicken broth

1½ tsp (1 g) grated lemon zest

4 tbsp (59 ml) lemon juice

1½ tsp (5 g) garlic powder

3 tsp (18 g) sea salt

Cracked black pepper or ground black pepper

2 lbs (907 g) green beans, cut into 1-inch (2.5-cm) pieces

For Serving

Cracked black pepper

Lemon slices

Serving Suggestions: *Enjoy straight out of the jar as a cold side for salads and sandwiches. Or heat the beans on the stovetop and serve them as a hot side dish.*

To prepare the pressure canner, rinse it and its rack, place the bottom rack inside and fill the canner with a few inches of water, according to the manufacturer's instructions. Put the pressure canner on the stove over low heat while you prepare the jars. This is a raw-pack recipe, so the water in the pressure canner needs to be no higher than 140°F (60°C) before you put the jars into the canner.

Wash six pint (500-ml) jars in hot, soapy water and check for any nicks or cracks in the jars. Rinse the jars in clean water and set them aside. Wash the lids in hot, soapy water, rinse them and set them aside.

Mix the water, broth, lemon zest, lemon juice, garlic powder, salt and pepper in a large pot and bring the mixture to a boil over high heat. Add the green beans to the broth mixture and bring it back to a boil. Turn the heat off and divide the green beans and broth among the jars, leaving a generous 1 inch (2.5 cm) of headspace. Remove the air bubbles with the bubble remover tool or a chopstick, and recheck the headspace. If you run out of the broth and water mixture before each jar is filled properly, top off the jars with boiling water.

Process the jars, according to the manufacturer's instructions, at 10 psi (69 kPa) for 30 minutes for pints (500 ml), adjusting for altitude (page 25), if necessary. Let the pressure canner depressurize naturally (page 25). Arrange a folded towel on the counter or table. Open the canner and remove the jars, using a jar lifter.

Place the jars on the folded towel, and let them cool for at least 12 hours. Remove the bands, check the seals and store the jars for up to a year. If any jars failed to seal, put them in the refrigerator to use first.

For serving, garnish the beans with the cracked pepper and lemon slices.

*In the photo, the canned green beans are in the jar on the left.

Frozen Summer Garden Mix

At the beginning and end of the gardening season, we often find ourselves with not quite enough of any one vegetable to preserve or prepare as a side dish for dinner. When this happens, or when I find myself with leftover odds and ends from other preservation recipes, I make and use bags of Frozen Summer Garden Mix. This is more of a process than an exact recipe, so feel free to experiment with it.

Makes Varied Amounts

For the Vegetable Mix

Snap beans, cut into 1-inch (2.5-cm) pieces

Carrots, cut into ¼-inch (6-mm) slices

Onions, chopped

Summer squash, cut into ¼-inch (6-mm) slices

For Serving

2 tbsp (30 ml) olive oil, butter or bacon grease

Salt

Ground black pepper

Garlic powder or dried thyme

I like to use a gallon (4-L) freezer bag for this recipe because it will hold about 1 pound (453 g) of vegetables. Also note that, while blanching is usually recommended for most of these vegetables, this recipe does not call for blanching. I promise they will taste great when you cook them and the texture will be good, even though they weren't blanched.

Put some of each vegetable into the freezer bag, remove the air and seal the bag. Label the bag and put it in the freezer. Use the vegetable mix within 6 months.

For serving, heat the olive oil over medium-high heat in a large skillet. Empty the bag of summer garden mix into the skillet and sauté. Some of the vegetables will be frozen together, but they will get unstuck as they cook. Stir the vegetables occasionally so that they cook evenly. Season with the salt, pepper and garlic powder. You'll notice quite a bit of water being released from the vegetables. Continue to cook the vegetables until all the water evaporates and the vegetables are caramelizing, which should take about 15 minutes.

*See photo on page 168 (this recipe is shown in the jar on the right).

Serving Suggestions: *This makes a great side dish or stir-fry, served over rice or noodles. The summer garden mix can also be added directly to soups. The vegetables will thaw out and cook as the soup simmers.*

Frozen Snap Beans and Tomatoes

Green beans and tomatoes are a classic combination and they are often canned together. I prefer to bypass the pressure canner and freeze this combo.

Makes 4 cups (948 ml)

2 cups (474 ml) tomato sauce

3 cups (330 g) snap beans, cut into 1-inch (2.5-cm) pieces

½ cup (75 g) chopped onions

1½ cups (270 g) chopped tomatoes

Heat the tomato sauce in a medium saucepan over medium-high heat until it's at a low boil. Add the snap beans, onions and tomatoes and cook the mixture for 3 minutes.

Remove the pan from the heat and let the mixture cool. Put the bean mixture into freezer-safe containers. I like to freeze this recipe in 2-cup (474-ml) portions in zippered freezer bags, because that is a good serving size for our family. Consider your family's needs when you decide on a container. Remember to label the container with the contents, the quantity and the date.

Serving Suggestions: *Thaw the green beans and tomatoes in the refrigerator overnight. Put the mixture in a saucepan and heat it over medium heat for 10 to 15 minutes, or until the beans are cooked to your preferred texture. Serve over prepared rice or pasta.*

Dried Parmesan Bean Crisps

Sometimes healthy, crunchy snacks are hard to come by. Fortunately, it's easy to season and dehydrate a nutritious food like snap beans and turn them into a snack that is healthy, crunchy and tastes great.

Makes 1 pint (500 ml)

1 lb (453 g) snap beans, cut into 1-inch (2.5-cm) pieces

1 tbsp (15 ml) Frozen Carrot Top Pesto (page 115) or other prepared pesto

1 tbsp (15 ml) lemon juice

¼ cup (32 g) finely grated Parmesan cheese

Fill a medium stockpot about halfway with water and bring it to a boil over high heat. Put the beans into the pot and blanch them for 3 minutes. While the beans are in the boiling water, prepare a bowl of ice water. After 3 minutes, use a slotted spoon to transfer the beans from the pot immediately into the bowl of ice water to stop the cooking.

While the beans are cooling, mix the pesto and lemon juice in a large bowl.

Drain the water from the beans, put the beans onto a clean kitchen towel and pat them dry. Carefully add the beans to the bowl with the seasoning mixture, and mix to coat all the pieces.

Lay the pieces on a dehydrator tray and sprinkle them with the Parmesan cheese. Dehydrate at 125°F (52°C) for 10 to 12 hours, or until the beans are brittle. The beans should easily snap in half when bent.

When the beans are fully dry, remove the tray from the dehydrator and let them cool. Put the dried beans in a glass jar with a tight-fitting lid and label the jar. Use the bean crisps within 1 month.

The bean crisps are best eaten within a few days. If they lose their crispiness, they can be put into the dehydrator on high for 15 to 30 minutes to crisp them.

Serving Suggestions: *These are great as a snack right out of the jar. They can also be crushed and added to salads or soups to add texture.*

kale, spinach and other greens

Adding Superfoods to Your Daily Life

In my opinion, greens are the unsung hero of the home garden. They are some of the most nutritious vegetables and are easy to grow. There's a green that will grow in every climate and, in some climates, you can grow various greens year-round. Some are extremely cold tolerant and will even survive under a blanket of snow, while others are heat tolerant to over 100°F (38°C).

What exactly are greens? To me, greens are any vegetable grown primarily for its leaves, including tender greens like lettuce and hardy greens like kale and mustard greens. Swiss chard, spinach, collard greens and the greens from root vegetables, such as turnips, beets and radishes, are also in the greens family.

Many of these plants are not related. For instance, kale and mustard greens are *Brassicas,* Swiss chard is related to beets and spinach is in the *Amaranth* family. Nevertheless, they have similar growing needs, and most can be used interchangeably. For this reason, I'm including them all in one chapter.

Growing

All greens prefer cooler weather, though some will tolerate hot weather. Greens grown in the fall and picked after the first frost will have a mild, sweeter flavor than those picked before the first frost or grown over the summer months.

Greens like loose, well-draining, rich soil. The soil needs to stay moist while the seeds germinate; consider covering the soil with burlap to retain the moisture until the seeds sprout. I've found that getting the seeds to sprout is the hardest part of growing greens. One thing I do is keep an eye on the weather. When the weather forecast calls for rain for 3 to 4 days in a row, I'll sow seeds on day one, or even the day before, and just water them, even if it's a little early.

Because greens like cold weather, they are ideal for fall planting. Even if you have really harsh winters, you might be able to keep greens growing under protection for most of the winter. At some point, when it gets too cold or the days get too short, they will stop maturing until it warms up or the days get longer.

Greens can also be started indoors and transplanted to the garden in the early spring, before the average last frost date arrives.

Greens are mostly water and will dehydrate quickly, so be sure to water them regularly. Greens are one of the few plants that like having their leaves wet, so you don't need to be as careful about watering only the soil, as you do with other plants.

For the most part, the greens I've grown are relatively free of pests. When summer is in full force, we do have issues with aphids on the kale and Swiss chard, but since I've been growing those plants since the previous fall, we just pull them up and give them to the chickens. If aphids attack younger greens that you are growing for the fall, spray them off with a water hose.

Harvesting

Try to harvest greens after the first frost for the best flavor. However, in a climate like mine that might not get a first frost until December, we often harvest greens before the frost and they're just fine, mainly because they are from young plants. So, this isn't a hard-and-fast rule.

Start harvesting the outer leaves first, allowing the inner leaves to remain on the plant. This will give you a continual harvest for the entire growing season. To harvest the leafy green leaves, either break or cut the leaf off an inch (2.5 cm) or so above the soil. The leaves can be harvested as soon as the plant has four to five real leaves; just don't harvest so much that the plant can't continue to grow. Limit yourself to harvesting one or two leaves per plant from young plants.

Greens dehydrate quickly after harvesting, so it's best to cook or preserve them right away. If it's going to be a while, stick the leaves in a container of water, like you would cut flowers, to keep them hydrated.

Greens Varieties to Try

Kale is probably the most popular green right now, which is good since there are so many varieties to choose from. Dinosaur kale has large, flat leaves that are good for making wraps. Blue Curled Scotch kale is beautiful, with frilly leaves, and it looks lovely in a flower bed. Scarlet and Red Russian kales are other curly varieties that can be planted in a flower bed. Most kale varieties take 75 to 80 days to mature.

Of all the greens, spinach has the most varieties from which to choose. Fortunately, spinach doesn't take up much space, so it's easy to experiment with different varieties. Bloomsdale Long Standing spinach is mature in less than 50 days and slow to bolt, making this a good all-purpose variety; it's especially good for gardens in areas with a very short spring. A good spinach variety for growing for salads is Renegade. Malabar spinach is an Asian vine variety that grows through the heat of the summer without going bitter. This is a good variety for those who live in hot climates and want to grow spinach in the summer.

Chard is so very beautiful that is makes a great addition to any flower bed, so if you have limited garden space, consider planting chard in flower beds instead of in the vegetable garden. Most varieties have large leaves with colored ribs: white, yellow, orange, pink and deep red are all available. When cooked, chard has a spinach-like texture. Bright Lights is probably my favorite chard variety simply because I like its colorful stalks. If you have limited space, you might try Lucullus or Barese, which have white ribs and smaller leaves. Fordhook Giant Swiss chard is another white-ribbed variety, but it grows large leaves. Most chard varieties will mature in 55 to 60 days.

There are only a few collard varieties, with Georgia Southern being the most popular. Collards often have a bitter taste, which is good for your digestion. But if you aren't used to bitter food, it can be hard to overcome. If you want to plant a less bitter variety, try the Yellow Cabbage collard variety. Collard matures more slowly than other greens, taking 85 to 90 days to reach maturity.

Mustard greens have a spicy, pungent flavor that other greens don't have. A favorite variety is Southern Giant Curled mustard, which has large leaves with a curly texture and hot flavor that mellows when it's cooked. Ruby Streaks mustard is a red variety with a sweet but somewhat pungent flavor. Mustard is one of the fastest growing greens, reaching maturity in only 30 to 40 days.

Buying

You can buy greens year-round at most grocery stores and, for eating raw, that's a huge blessing. However, for preserving greens, you'll want to purchase them when they're in season, which is the winter months.

Look for leaves that are crisp with no signs of yellow on them. Yellowing means the greens are old and they will have a bitter taste. Avoid wilted leaves and leaves that have begun to deteriorate.

When you get home with the greens, either use them quickly or store them in a plastic freezer bag or closed container in the refrigerator for a couple of days. You can store greens with long stems in a container of water, like you would cut flowers, for a day, if needed.

Preserving

Preserving greens is a great way to make sure you have these nutrient-dense foods all year long. Greens can be canned, dehydrated, frozen and fermented. They can be preserved plain or as part of a stand-alone dish.

Before preserving, the greens should be washed several times and spun in a salad spinner. This will remove any grit or pests hiding in them; curly-leaf varieties might need to be washed and spun a few times.

If the green has a hard rib, remove it, as it might cause bitterness. Some greens—chard and beet greens—have edible ribs that are not bitter and make a good preserve (Fermented Leafy Greens and Stems, page 184), but the rest need to be removed.

Canning

Canned greens are convenient and make a great addition to soups and casseroles. When canning greens, use the freshest greens possible, as older greens will have a strong, bitter flavor after canning.

Greens must be canned using a pressure canner; they cannot be water bath canned in a vinegar brine, like most other vegetables. The only green I can is kale (Canned Kale with Lemon, page 182) because it holds its texture better than chard or spinach. But all greens can be pressure canned using the same procedure.

It takes approximately 18 pounds (8 kg) of fresh greens to fill nine pints (500 ml) and 28 pounds (13 kg) of fresh greens to fill seven quarts (1 L). You can safely pressure can as few as four pints (500 ml) or two quarts (1 L) at a time, using 2 pounds (907 g) of fresh greens per pint (500 ml) and 4 pounds (1.8 kg) of fresh greens per quart (1 L) as a guide.

Before canning greens, they first need to be steamed or wilted for 3 to 5 minutes; you will need to work in small batches, as fresh greens are bulky. Once the greens are wilted, loosely pack them into the prepared jars and pour fresh boiling water over them, leaving 1 inch (2.5 cm) of headspace. You can add ¼ teaspoon of salt per pint (500 ml) and ½ teaspoon of salt per quart (1 L) to each jar. Wipe the rims of each jar and put a lid and band on the jar. Process the jars, according to the manufacturer's instructions, at 10 psi (69 kPa) for 70 minutes for pints (500 ml) and 90 minutes for quarts (1 L). Adjust for altitude (page 25), if necessary.

Freezing

Frozen greens are so very versatile and, in my opinion, are closer in texture to the fresh vegetable than canned greens. Kale especially retains its texture when frozen.

Tender greens, like spinach and chard, need to be blanched or steamed for 2 minutes before they are frozen; hardier greens, like kale and collards, need 3 minutes (page 35).

I prefer to steam-blanch greens instead of boiling them; I think it helps them retain more nutrients and be less mushy.

Once the greens have been blanched, put them in an ice bath to stop the cooking process. When they are cool, put them in a salad spinner or colander to drain and dry.

Portion out the greens into servings for your family; to help you out, 1½ cups (340 g) of cooked greens is equivalent to approximately 1 pound (453 g) of fresh greens. Put the cooked and dried greens in freezer bags, remove all the air and seal. Don't forget to label the bag with its contents and quantity. These should last for a year in the freezer.

If you're freezing greens because you want to add small amounts to soup or smoothies, then consider freeing them in ice cube trays or silicone muffin tins instead of freezer bags. Once they are frozen, you can pop them out of the tray or tin and put the chunks of frozen greens in a freezer bag.

A practical way that I like to freeze greens, especially spinach, is to make a pot of Frozen Creamy Spinach Rice (page 181) and then freeze it in meal-sized portions.

Dehydrating

Dehydrating greens is my favorite way to preserve them. It's quick, and the end result is very versatile. In fact, I use dehydrated greens in some way almost every day. One way I don't use them, though, is to rehydrate them and serve them like I would canned or frozen greens.

Yes, it can be done, but it's not very practical to me; dehydrated greens are just too fragile. They're fine if you're going to use them right away, but every time you move the jar or reach into the jar to get a few leaves, leaves are going to break. Eventually, you'll have a jar of green flakes or powder instead of green leaves.

That's why I make Dried Superfood Green Powder (page 179) with any and every green that needs to get preserved quickly. This could be because I picked too much kale or chard for dinner and realized it when all the greens wouldn't fit in the pan. Or because I've harvested radishes or carrots and don't need any more pesto. Or because I bought spinach for salad in the heat of the summer, and we're not eating it fast enough. There are many reasons that greens find their way into the jar.

Before dehydrating, blanch greens for 3 minutes, then cool them in an ice-water bath. Spin the cooled greens in a salad spinner or put them in a colander to drain. Lay the greens on dehydrator trays and dehydrate at 125°F (52°C) for 4 to 6 hours, or until they are brittle. Put the dried leaves in a glass jar with a tight-fitting lid and store it for up to a year.

To rehydrate greens, put the dried greens in a small bowl and pour boiling water over them. Let them soak until they are soft, which will take 30 to 45 minutes.

Fermenting

Fermenting greens can be hit or miss. You can end up with jar of amazing leaves and stems (Fermented Leafy Greens and Stems, page 184) or end up with a slimy, odiferous mess. I've mentioned before that, of all the preserving methods, fermenting has the most variables that can impact the end product. Sometimes there needs to be a little trial and error; just be sure to ferment the trials in small batches and not get discouraged by any errors, as they are learning opportunities.

That being said, fermenting greens is pretty straightforward. Chop clean greens, put them in a clean jar with spices, herbs or other vegetables, pour a 2 percent brine (page 51) solution into the jar, add weight and a fermentation lid and wait for 4 days. When you open the jar, you'll know if you have a winner or not.

When choosing spices and herbs, you want bold ones that can hold their own against the strong flavor of the greens; try garlic, curry, chiles and strong onions. Chop the greens fairly small, especially those with tougher leaves, such as kale. Instead of making a jar with only greens, use a small portion of them in sauerkraut, kimchi or another ferment.

Try blanching tough leaves for 1 minute, then cooling them in an ice bath before fermenting them. If you do this, you'll need to add some brine or whey from another ferment to the jar, since the blanching kills the beneficial microbes needed for fermenting.

Preserving Greens Cheat Sheet

	Water Bath Canning (Not recommended)	Pressure Canning	Freezing	Dehydrating	Fermenting 2% brine
How to prepare	N/A	Whole or pieces	Blanching recommended; whole or chopped	Blanching recommended; in pieces	Chopped
Flavors	N/A	Plain, in soups or seasoned	Plain	Plain or seasoned	Seasoned with herbs
Length of processing	N/A	Pints (500 ml): 70 minutes Quarts (1 L): 90 minutes	—	4–6 hours	4–7 days
Storage life	N/A	12 months	8–12 months	12 months for plain; 1 month for seasoned	6–12 months

Dried Superfood Green Powder

This is the easiest and most versatile recipe I have—in fact, it's not really a recipe. Green powder is extremely expensive in the store, but you can easily make your own. I use green powder every single day in my home.

The greens can be kale, Swiss chard, spinach, mustard greens, turnip greens, beet greens, cabbage, carrot top greens, radish greens . . . you get the idea; any leftover leafy green can be used.

It's recommended that the greens be blanched before dehydrating; however, I've found that since I turn these dehydrated greens into powder, the quality is not comprised by not blanching them. If you want to take the time to blanch them, you certainly can.

If you want to be able to just crush the dried leaves into a coarse powder, then remove the stems from the leaves before dehydrating them. The stems can still be dehydrated, but they will need to be powdered or they will look like little sticks in your food.

Wash the greens and spin them in a salad spinner to remove any grit or pests that may be hiding in them. Tear any large leaves into smaller pieces and lay the greens on the dehydrator tray. Dehydrate the leaves at 125°F (52°C) for 2 to 3 hours, or until they are brittle. The leaves should easily crumble when they are completely dry.

When the leaves are dry, remove the tray from the dehydrator and let the dried greens cool. Put the leaves in a clean jar with a tight-fitting lid, crushing them down as you add more. Two pounds (907 g) of dehydrated greens should easily fit in a quart-sized (1-L) Mason jar. Remember to label and date the jar.

You can make a finer powder by putting the greens in a blender or food processor and giving them a whirl. Put the powder in a glass jar with a tight-fitting lid and label the jar.

The powder can be stored for up to 12 months. That being said, I keep a perpetual green powder jar in my kitchen. Whenever I dehydrate greens, I just add them to the jar and give the jar a few shakes to mix everything up.

Serving Suggestions: *Use the superfood green powder in dishes such as soups, rice, eggs, meatloaf, spaghetti sauce and casseroles. It can also be added to smoothies, muffins, pancakes and fruit leathers, or used as a green garnish instead of dried parsley.*

Frozen Creamy Spinach Rice

Side dishes can make or break a meal, can't they? When unexpected guests arrive at dinnertime or you have to grab a rotisserie chicken on the way home because your day was crazy, having ready–made sides keeps dinner from getting chaotic. This spinach and rice side dish has saved my day more times than I want to remember.

Makes 2 pint (500-ml) jars

2 cups (474 ml) water or broth

1 cup (200 g) short grain white or brown rice

½ tsp salt

½ cup (75 g) chopped onion

1 lb (453 g) spinach leaves

Bring the water to a boil in a medium stockpot, add the rice, salt and onion and give it a stir.

If you are using white rice, place the spinach leaves in the pot, put the lid on the pot and cook the mixture for 15 minutes without lifting the cover.

If you are using brown rice, let the rice mixture cook with a lid on the pot for 30 minutes. Then lift the lid, quickly put the spinach in the pot and replace the lid. Cook the mixture for another 15 minutes.

When the rice is cooked, remove the pot from the heat. Stir the spinach into the rice, and let the mixture cool without the lid on the pot for 15 to 20 minutes.

When the rice is cooled, put it into freezer-safe containers in serving-size portions. If you're using glass jars, be sure to leave ½ inch (12 mm) of headspace for expansion. Put the containers into the refrigerator to cool overnight, and then transfer them to the freezer. Spinach and rice can be stored in the freezer for up to 6 months.

To serve the spinach and rice, thaw the spinach and rice in the refrigerator overnight. To heat the spinach and rice in the microwave, transfer the mixture to a microwave-safe bowl and heat it for 2 minutes, stirring at the halfway mark. To heat the spinach and rice on the stove, cover the bottom of a small stockpot with ¼ inch (6 mm) of water, and bring it to a simmer over medium heat. Add the spinach and rice and heat over medium heat for 15 minutes for white rice or 45 minutes for brown rice, until the rice is fluffy. Stir the mixture often to prevent it from sticking to the pan.

Serving Suggestions: *Serve the spinach and rice as a side dish with ¼ cup (59 ml) of cream or milk stirred in. Garnish the dish with sliced almonds.*

Canned Kale with Lemon

This recipe can be used with any greens, but my favorite is kale because it holds up to the canning process the best. The lemon, onions and garlic make this one of our favorite easy side dishes.

Makes 4 pint (500-ml) jars

8 lbs (3.6 kg) kale leaves, stemmed and roughly chopped

1 tsp garlic powder, divided

1 tsp salt, divided

4 tsp (20 ml) lemon juice, divided

1 cup (150 g) chopped onion, divided

3 cups (711 ml) boiling water

Serving Suggestions: *Canned kale can be heated and served as a side dish; garnish it with slivers of red onion and almonds. It can also be mixed with drained Canned Potatoes with Herbs (page 231) and cooked sausage links for a quick dinner.*

To prepare the pressure canner, rinse it and its rack, place the bottom rack inside and fill the canner with a few inches of water, according to the manufacturer's instructions. Put the pressure canner on the stove over low heat while you prepare the jars. This is a hot-pack recipe, so the water in the canner needs to be about 180°F (82°C) before you put the jars in.

Wash four pint (500-ml) jars in hot, soapy water and check for any nicks or cracks in the jars. Rinse the jars in clean water and set them aside. Wash the lids in hot, soapy water, rinse them and set them aside.

Put about an inch (2.5 cm) of water in a large stockpot and add some of the kale. Wilt the leaves, turning them several times so as not to overcook them. When the leaves are wilted, remove the pan from the heat. Cut through the greens with two sharp knives a few times before packing them into the jars.

Pack the kale into the hot jars, dividing the kale among the jars. Add ¼ teaspoon of the garlic powder, ¼ teaspoon of salt, 1 teaspoon of lemon juice and ¼ cup (37.5 g) of the onion to each jar.

Add the boiling water to the jars, leaving 1 inch (2.5 cm) of headspace. Remove the air bubbles with the bubble remover tool or a chopstick and check the headspace.

Process the jars, according to the manufacturer's instructions, at 10 psi (69 kPa) for 70 minutes for pints (500 ml) and 90 minutes for quarts (1 L), adjusting for altitude (page 25), if necessary. Let the pressure canner depressurize naturally (page 25). Arrange a folded towel on the counter or table. Open the canner and remove the jars, using a jar lifter.

Place the jars on the towel and let them cool for at least 12 hours. Remove the bands, check the seals and store the jars for up to 1 year. If any jars failed to seal, put them in the refrigerator to use first.

*In the photo, the canned kale is in the jar on the right.

Fermented Leafy Greens and Stems

There are times when I get overzealous picking greens for dinner and I end up with more greens than we can eat in one sitting. Fermenting them is a great way to use them up. Because the stems will ferment slower than the leaves, this recipe has a lot of texture. Using beet greens along with the stems will produce a pretty purple color.

Makes 1 quart (1 L)

3 cups (150 g) chopped greens and stems

¼ cup (40 g) chopped onion

1 tbsp (18 g) salt

2 cups (474 ml) filtered water

Pack the greens and onion into a quart (1-L) jar. Mix the salt into the water to make the brine. Fill the jar with the saltwater brine, making sure to cover the greens but leaving room for the weight and expansion.

Put a fermentation weight in the jar to keep everything under the brine and top the jar with a fermentation lid. Put the jar on a plate or small cookie sheet to catch any overflow.

Set the jar in a cool place out of direct sunlight for 4 to 10 days. You can taste them any time after 4 days. If they need to ferment longer, replace the weight and fermentation lid and ferment for a few more days.

When the greens are to your liking, replace the weight and fermentation lid with a plastic storage lid. Store the fermented greens in the refrigerator for up to 12 months.

*See photo on page 183 (this recipe is shown in the jar on the left).

Serving Suggestions: *Serve as a cold side or use the greens to top sandwiches or tacos. The fermented greens can also be chopped into small pieces and stirred into sour cream with garlic powder to make a dip.*

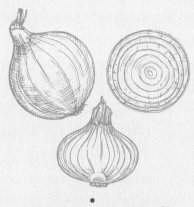

onions

The Sweet and the Savory

"Every meal begins with an onion." This is what a friend once told me, and it changed the way I cooked. Now onions play an indispensable role in our daily meals and in the food we preserve. I've been amazed at how this one change has made our food more flavorful.

Like all members of the *Allium* family, onions aren't just tasty, they also promote good cardiovascular health and offer anti-inflammatory and antibacterial benefits. They deserve a place in the garden and in the pantry.

There are various types of onions, such as chives; scallions or bunching onions; spring onions; bulb onions such as storage and sweet onions; and shallots.

Bulb onions are probably what you think of when you think of onions. They can be white, yellow or red and can have a strong, biting flavor or a mild, sweet flavor. These are the onions we're going to focus on in this book.

Scallions are also called *bunching onions* or *green onions*. These onions are thin, with long tender green leaves, and will never produce a bulb. They can be grown year-round in many climates. We have grown these for years, allowing the plants to flower

and then drop their seeds and grow new plants. It's my perpetual onion patch.

Spring onions are the same as storage onions, but they are harvested before they've formed a bulb. These look like green onions and are often called *green onions*, but if you leave them in the ground, they will form a bulb when they mature. We don't specifically grow spring onions, but if I notice that some of the onions weren't thinned quite enough, I'll harvest spring onions.

Growing

Onions are easy to grow—as long as you plant the right kind for your climate. If you're buying local plants to transplant into your garden, then you'll be fine, as they'll stock the right varieties. If you are ordering them, you need to know if you need long-day or short-day onions, since bulb formation is triggered by day length.

Long-day onions need 14 to 15 hours of daylight to bulb and are grown by those gardening in the North. Short-day onions will bulb when the day length is 10 hours; they are grown by gardeners in the South. There are also day-neutral onions, also called *intermediate-day* onions, that will bulb with 12 to 14 daylight hours.

You can plant seeds, transplants or sets to grow onions. They each have benefits and drawbacks. If you plant seeds, you need to start them indoors 4 to 6 weeks before you want to plant them outside. Transplants are seeds that have already been started for you; they're sold in bundles of about 50 onions. I believe this is the surest option for growing onions. Sets are bulbs that were started the previous year and allowed to dry out. They grow really well, but are more likely to flower than transplants and the sets are more expensive.

Onions take 100 to 175 days to mature. Depending on your climate, you might need to plant onions in the fall and let them overwinter in the garden under straw. If you don't plant in the fall, definitely plant onions before the average last frost date.

When you plant onions, be sure to mix some compost into the soil. Onions grow very close to the surface and they need the nutrients at the surface, since their roots aren't very deep. Plant in loose, well-draining soil that has been weeded. Onions don't compete well with weeds, and it's hard to weed around the plants when they're young, so it helps to start with a bed free of weeds.

Onions need about an inch (2.5 cm) of water a week during their growing season. When the tops of the onions begin to fall over, it's time to stop watering them. They are done growing and need to begin to dry out. If you continue watering them, they'll rot.

Fortunately, not many pests bother onions. Cutworms like to chew off the soft green leaves of young plants. You can sprinkle diatomaceous earth or crushed eggshells around the young plants to deter the cutworms. Ask other local gardeners if your area has a problem with onion maggots. If so, then cover your onions with a floating row cover after you plant them.

Harvesting

When onions start to bulb, the bulb will push out of the top of the soil and the skin will start to brown. Don't cover them up with more soil; they need sun exposure to continue growing the bulb. When the green tops fall over, they can be harvested. You can keep them in the ground until the tops are almost all brown, but you run the risk of them rotting, especially if there is an unexpected rainstorm.

To harvest onions, just pull them up by the greens. They should easily lift out of the ground since the bulb is halfway out already. If you aren't storing the onions, you can peel and use them right away.

If you're going to store the onions, they need to be cured by laying them out in the sun for a few days to dry out. I lay ours on a tarp under a tree so they get a little protection from our harsh sun. If you have mild summer heat, then they can be laid out in full sun.

After a few days, gather the onions and dust off the dirt. The onions are dry enough if the dirt is easily removed and not sticking to the dry outer leaves. Trim the roots and cut the tops about an inch (2.5 cm) from the bulb. Store the dried onions in wire baskets in a cool dark place.

Onion Varieties to Try

There are so many onion varieties that it can be hard to decide which ones to plant, especially if you're growing them from seed. I suggest starting by talking to other local gardeners, your county extension agent or local nursery about what varieties do well in your area. One of the great things about onions is that you don't need to worry about cross-pollination, since they don't bloom until their second year. So, try experimenting with several varieties.

Because onions don't store well in our hot climate, bunching onions fill the fresh-onion gap for my cooking. I use the onion greens for many dishes that call for bulb onions and it works just fine. Tokyo Long bunching onions are heat tolerant and are good for those who have long, hot summers and mild winters. Evergreen Bunching onions can be planted in the spring or fall and over winter better than Tokyo Long onions do.

Sweet bulb onions have a milder flavor than storage onions and are great for cooking fresh or preserving. Sweet onions can be red, yellow or white. Since I'm a little willy-nilly in my planting, I like to grow red sweet onions and yellow or white storage onions, so I can easily tell them apart. Red Burgundy is a good short-day variety that has a very mild and sweet flavor, perfect for Canned Caramelized Maple Onions (page 192). Walla Walla is a good long-day sweet variety that will keep in storage for about a month.

Storage onions not only store longer, but also are better when canning foods such as Canned Mexican Salsa (page 278) because they hold their flavor better than sweet onions do. Some popular long-day varieties are Yellow Globe, Southport White Globe and Brunswick, which is a red variety. It's harder to find short-day storage varieties, as most onions in the south need to be planted in the fall and are harvested in early summer. However, Red Creole is a red variety that can be stored for up to 6 to 7 months and Cipollina Borettana is a creamy yellow onion that can be stored for about 5 months.

Buying

If you're buying bulb onions, look for ones that feel firm and hard and don't have any signs of sprouting. A soft bulb onion is a sign that it's probably spoiled. Smell the onion and put back any that have a scent; properly cured onions that have not been cut into should not give off a smell. Where the stem meets the bulb is susceptible to rot, so check the stem for any soft spot.

If you're buying from a local farmer, talk to him about how he grows and cures the onions. You might find that he just harvested the onion the day before, and you will need to cure them if you plan on storing them.

Preserving

I realize that some people will question my love of preserving onions. After all, they're usually grown for storing. However, onions don't store well in every climate; especially in tropical and subtropical climates. Where we live, most of us don't have root cellars or basements, and the garage is too hot for storing food. Add that to the fact that there aren't many short-day storage onions that will store for more than a few months, and you now have a need to preserve onions.

If onions store well in your area, you will still need to preserve onions that don't store well, such as sweet onions and underdeveloped storage onions.

To prepare onions for preserving, they will need to be peeled and rinsed. Large onions will need to be chopped or sliced.

Canning

Using a pressure canner, small onion bulbs can be canned, and onions can be added to other vegetables that are being pressure canned. Onions can be canned using a water bath canner if they are pickled, jammed or part of a relish or salsa recipe that is sufficiently acidified.

For canning plain onion bulbs, the bulbs need to be 1 inch (2.5 cm) in diameter or less; there's no recommendation for pressure canning onion slices or bulbs larger than 1 inch (2.5 cm) in diameter. To can the small onion bulbs, they need to be peeled and rinsed, then boiled in water for 5 minutes before they are packed into hot jars. Pour fresh boiling water over the bulbs in the jars, leaving 1 inch (2.5 cm) of headspace, wipe the rims and add the lids. Process pints (500 ml) or quarts (1 L) for 40 minutes at 10 psi (69 kPa), adjusting for altitude (page 25), if necessary. Remember, you need at least four pints (500 ml) or two quarts (1 L) to properly run your pressure canner. That's a lot of small onion bulbs.

I'm going to be honest. I think pressure canning small onion bulbs is too much work for such a small reward. I would much rather ferment small onion bulbs (page 189) to preserve them for eating them raw in salads. But if you have a lot of small onions and want to pressure can them, you certainly can.

If you are canning sauces or salsas and want a more distinct onion flavor, then use storage onions instead of sweet onions. The sharp, almost biting flavor of onion mellows when cooked; if you start with a mild onion, you won't have much onion flavor when the canning is done.

Freezing

Freezing is how we preserve most of our onions. We freeze them plain, but we also freeze them as Frozen Spicy Fajita Veggie Mix (page 194) with peppers and seasoning. I use the frozen onions almost daily when fresh onions aren't available.

To freeze onions, they need to be peeled, rinsed and then cut. Chopped and thinly sliced onions do not need to be blanched before freezing, which makes this a superfast way to preserve a lot of onions. Unless I'm freezing them with other vegetables, I freeze them chopped and not in slivers or slices. If you have a lot of onions to process, especially stronger storage onions, consider wearing googles and using a food processor. You'll look funny, but you won't be crying.

After cutting the onions, I put them in labeled freezer bags or vacuum bags in 1-cup (150-g) portions, which is approximately half of a regular-sized onion. The bags go straight into the freezer. I don't worry about the onions clumping together, because this is an amount that I can use for many recipes. However,

if you do worry about them clumping, you can first freeze the chopped onions on a baking sheet lined with parchment paper, then transfer the frozen onions to freezer bags.

While it's not the best way to freeze onions, they can be frozen whole after being blanched. Blanch small onions for 3 minutes, medium onions for 5 minutes and large onions for 7 minutes (page 35). Whole onions need to be heated all the way to the center; therefore, you'll need to cut an onion in half to check for doneness. If it's not heated to the center, put the onions back into boiling water and heat for another minute.

Dehydrating

Onions don't need to be blanched before dehydrating, making this another way to preserve onions with very little hands-on time.

To dehydrate plain onions, cut them into ⅛-inch (4-mm) or ¼-inch (6-mm) slices or slivers, lay the pieces on the dehydrator tray and dehydrate them at 125°F (52°C) for 3 to 9 hours. The finished onions should be brittle and snap in half when dry.

You can chop the onions and dehydrate them in smaller pieces. I find dehydrated chopped onions to be the most versatile, and I can get more onions on the trays than I can with slices or slivers.

To rehydrate the dried onion pieces, put them in a bowl and pour hot water over them. Let them soak for 30 to 45 minutes, or until they are fully rehydrated. They can also be added directly to soups or casseroles and will rehydrate as they cook.

Use a small electric coffee grinder to grind the dried onions to a powder, and then transfer the powder to a small jar. Unlike commercial onion powder, homemade onion powder doesn't have anti-caking agents, and it will start to cake together over time. It's fine, just use a spoon to scrape it apart or regrind it.

Fermenting

One year, I planted onions late—really late—and many of them did not make bulbs and, if they did, they were super small. I left them in the ground as long as I could. Still, the bulbs were tiny. On a whim, I decided to put them in a wide-mouth Mason jar with a few spices to see what would happen. When I opened the jar, I knew fermenting was going to be my go-to way of preserving small bulbs in the future.

To ferment onions, they need to be peeled and rinsed. If you're fermenting small bulbs 1 inch (2.5 cm) or smaller in diameter, then you can leave them whole. If not, slice or chop the onions. Put the onions in a wide-mouth Mason jar and pour a 2 percent brine (page 51) over them. Insert a fermentation weight to keep everything under the brine and screw on a fermentation lid. Put the fermenting onions on a plate or small cookie sheet to catch any overflow. Let the onions ferment, out of direct sunlight, for 3 to 7 days. You can test them any time after 3 days. If they aren't fermented enough for you, put the weight and lid back on and let them ferment longer. When the onions are ready, remove the weight and fermenting lid, add a plastic storage lid to the jar and store the jar in the refrigerator for up to 9 months.

Preserving Onions Cheat Sheet

	Water Bath Canning	Pressure Canning	Freezing	Dehydrating	Fermenting 2% brine
How to prepare	Whole small bulbs or sliced	Whole: small bulbs only	No blanching required; sliced or diced	No blanching required; sliced or diced	Whole: small bulbs only; sliced or diced
Flavors	Pickled, savory or sweet jam	Plain: small bulbs only; as an ingredient in other preserves	Plain or with other vegetables	Plain or seasoned	Seasoned with herbs
Length of processing	15 minutes	Pints (500 ml): 40 minutes Quarts (1 L): 40 minutes	—	3–9 hours	3–14 days
Storage life	12 months	12 months	8–12 months	12 months for plain; 1 month for seasoned	6–9 months

Fermented Onion Bulbs

Small onions don't store well, so whenever we harvest small onions, I make fermented onion bulbs. You can use this process to ferment pearl onions, Egyptian onions and even sliced storage onions. This is one of my very favorite ferments to use for making salad dressing.

Makes 1 quart (1 L)

1 lb (453 g) small onion bulbs or onion slices

2 tsp (8 g) black peppercorns

½ tsp red pepper flakes

½ tsp ground mustard

1 bay leaf

1 tbsp (15 ml) honey

1 tbsp (18 g) salt

2 cups (474 ml) filtered water

Put the onions in a clean quart (1-L) jar. Add the peppercorns, red pepper flakes, mustard, bay leaf and honey to the jar.

Mix the salt into the water to make the brine. Fill the jar with the saltwater brine, making sure to cover the onions but leaving room for the weight and expansion.

Put a weight in the jar to keep everything under the brine and top the jar with a fermentation lid. Put the jar on a plate or small cookie sheet to catch any overflow. Set the jar in a cool place, out of direct sunlight, for 3 to 7 days. After 3 days, taste a bulb to see if it is to your liking. If the onions need to ferment longer, replace the weight and fermentation lid and ferment for a few more days.

When the onions are to your liking, replace the weight and fermentation lid with a plastic storage lid and store the jar in the refrigerator for up to 12 months.

* In the photo, the onion bulbs are in the jar on the right.

Serving Suggestions: *These onions are great sliced and used in a tossed salad or on a sandwich. They can also be chopped and added to potato, pasta or tuna salads. Mix the brine with a little olive oil for a tasty salad dressing.*

Canned Caramelized Maple Onions

These caramelized maple onions are a staple in my kitchen. Of course, we serve them with hamburgers and flatbread wraps, but I also use them to glaze chicken and pork. And, every so often, you'll find us having an afternoon snack of crackers and cream cheese topped with these sweet onions.

Makes 4 half-pint (250-ml) jars

1 tbsp (15 g) butter

3 lbs (1.4 kg) onions, cut into ½-inch (12-mm) slices

¾ cup (177 ml) apple cider vinegar

1½ cups (356 ml) maple syrup

¾ cup (150 g) sugar

2 tsp (12 g) salt

½ tsp ground black pepper

Melt the butter in a large stockpot over medium-high heat and add the onions. Sauté the onions until they start to brown, about 7 to 10 minutes. Add the vinegar, maple syrup, sugar, salt and pepper to the onions. Reduce the heat and simmer the mixture for 45 to 60 minutes, stirring occasionally; the liquid will reduce and thicken during this time.

While the onions are simmering, prepare the water bath canner by filling it halfway with water and putting it on the stove to simmer. Check four half-pint (250-ml) jars for any nicks or cracks, wash them in hot soapy water and rinse them in hot water. Keep the jars hot until it's time to use them. Wash the lids in hot soapy water, rinse them and set them aside.

Ladle the onions into the prepared jars, leaving ½ inch (12 mm) of headspace. Wipe the rims with a clean cloth, put on the lids and screw on the bands. Place the jars in the prepared hot water bath canner and process them for 15 minutes, adjusting for altitude (page 17), if necessary. Arrange a folded towel on the counter or table. Remove the jars, using a jar lifter, and place them on the towel. Let the jars cool for at least 12 hours.

Once the jars are cooled, remove the bands and check the seals. If any jars failed to seal, put them in the refrigerator to use first. Wipe the jars with a clean cloth, label them and store them for up to a year.

*See photo on page 190 (this recipe is shown in the jar on the left).

Serving Suggestions: *Spread soft cheese on slices of baguette, and top the cheese with these sweet onions. These onions also dress up burgers, sandwiches or tacos.*

Dried Seasoned Onion Crisps

Seasoned onion crisps are extremely versatile and have become a pantry staple in my home. They can be eaten as a snack right out of the jar or crushed and used to garnish soups or salads. But my favorite thing to do with them is to blend them into a powder and use the powder to season cream cheese or sour cream for a quick spread or dip.

Makes 1 pint (500 ml)

1 tbsp (15 ml) olive oil

3 tbsp (45 ml) tamari

2 tsp (10 ml) lemon juice

½ tsp garlic powder

1 lb (453 g) onions, cut into ⅛–¼-inch (4–6-mm) slices

Mix the olive oil, tamari, lemon juice and garlic powder in a large bowl. Carefully add the onions to the bowl, and mix to coat all the onions with the seasoning mix.

Lay the seasoned onion slices on a dehydrator tray. You can put the pieces close together, as they will shrink considerably. Dehydrate at 125°F (52°C) for 6 to 8 hours, or until the onions are brittle. They should easily snap in half when bent.

When the onion slices are fully dry, remove the tray from the dehydrator and let the onions cool. Put the dried onion slices in a glass jar with a tight-fitting lid and label the jar. Use the onion crisps within 1 month.

The onion crisps are best eaten within a few days. If they lose their crispiness, they can be put into the dehydrator on high for 15 to 30 minutes to crisp them.

Serving Suggestions: *Onion crisps make a tasty snack or can be used to add crispiness to sandwiches, wraps, salads and soups. They can also be powdered and used as a seasoning.*

Frozen Spicy Fajita Veggie Mix

Nothing dresses up fajitas more than grilled onions and peppers. While most fajita vegetables are a combination of onions and bell peppers, the beauty of making your own mix is that you can use the peppers your family loves and leave out those they don't love.

Makes 1 quart (1 L)

For the Veggie Mix

1 medium onion, cut into ¼-inch (6-mm) slices (see Note)

1 sweet pepper, cut lengthwise into ¼-inch (6-mm) slices

1 hot pepper, seeds removed if you prefer milder flavor, cut lengthwise into ¼-inch (6-mm) slices

3 cloves garlic, minced

1 tsp ground cumin

1 tsp chili powder

¾ tsp salt

½ tsp paprika

½ tsp dried Mexican oregano

For Serving

1 tbsp (15 ml) olive oil

For the veggie mix, put the onion and peppers in a quart (1-L) freezer bag and add the garlic, cumin, chili powder, salt, paprika and oregano. Close the bag and give it a few shakes to mix the spices with the vegetables. Open the bag just a bit, gently squeeze out excess air and reseal the bag. Label the bag and put it in the freezer for up to 12 months.

For serving, heat the olive oil over medium-high heat in a medium skillet. When the oil is warm, add the frozen fajita mix to the skillet and sauté until the edges of the onions and peppers are brown. This will take some time, about 15 to 20 minutes, since the onions and peppers will release liquid from being frozen before they start to brown. Don't worry, the liquid will evaporate and the onions and peppers will caramelize just fine.

Note: *It's recommended that onions be blanched for 10 to 15 seconds before freezing them (page 35). However, I've found that they cook up just fine in this recipe without blanching. You can blanch the onions slices if you wish, but I choose not to.*

Serving Suggestions: *Serve with fajitas, tacos or burritos. This mix can also be cooked and added to omelets, rice and beans.*

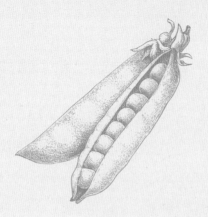

peas
In and Out of the Pod

I hated peas growing up. While the rest of my family happily munched on bowls of pea salad at dinner, I tried to look inconspicuous as I passed the bowl without taking a spoonful. I still don't care for peas by the spoonful.

But, fresh peas in the garden are a totally different story. Most of our peas don't make their way inside; instead, we enjoy eating them as we pick them from the vine.

There are several varieties of peas: garden peas, sugar snap peas and snow peas. Black-eyed peas, a popular variety of cowpea, are referred to as a pea, but it is a bean and is grown and shelled just like other dry beans (page 159).

Garden peas are what most people think of when they think of peas: small, round, plump green balls. Garden peas go by several different names, including English peas, sweet peas and shelling peas. The pods of garden peas are not really edible; while they are smooth, they are also tough and fibrous. But they can be used to make Frozen Pea Pod Soup Concentrate (page 205). Garden peas are great for shelling because they have more peas in each pod than sugar snap peas.

Garden pea varieties will either have wrinkled or smooth peas. The wrinkled pea varieties are sweeter and are eaten fresh. The smooth pea varieties are starchier and are great for drying and using for split pea soup.

Sugar snap peas have an edible pod and plump, round peas. These are great in salads, on vegetable trays and sautéed with other vegetables. To me, sugar snap peas are the best of both worlds. We can eat them when they are immature like snow peas or let them mature and eat the plump peas like English peas. If you let snap peas mature, they will have a string that will need to be removed before you preserve them.

Snow peas have thin-skinned pods with flat peas inside. The immature pods are often used in Asian stir-fries but are a nice addition to any sautéed dish. Mature snow peas can be shelled and eaten like garden peas.

Growing

Peas love cool, wet weather and are some of the first seeds that can be sown when the ground thaws. They are frost tolerant, so there's no need to worry about a late-season frost damaging the plants. If you live in a climate that has moderate winters, you can plant peas in the fall and grow them all winter.

Like beans, peas have pole varieties and bush varieties. Pole varieties will need a trellis to grow on. Bush peas don't need a trellis, but do need some support. If you plant them a little closer than the recommended spacing, they will prop each other up.

Even though peas like wet weather, they don't like waterlogged soil. Sow peas in loose, well-draining soil so they don't rot. Many people use a powdered legume inoculant to help the plants convert nitrogen from the air into food for the plant. I rarely use this, because we've built healthy soil over the years; however, if you are planting in an area that doesn't have great soil, using an inoculant is a good idea.

The biggest issue I've had with growing peas is that cutworms really like them, too! For this reason, I plant them closer than recommended so that plenty will survive. Peas can also fall victim to various fungi, blights, mosaics and rots. Most of these diseases live in the soil, so it's imperative that peas are on a 5-year rotation plan if you have any of these diseases in your area. Peas can also be affected by pests such as Mexican bean beetles, aphids, thrips and leaf miners.

Pea Varieties to Try

When I'm choosing pea varieties, I look for ones that are pole peas because I can grow them on our arched trellises instead of using a whole garden bed for them. If you don't already have trellises, you might prefer bush varieties. I also look for pea varieties that are resistant to at least a few common pea diseases.

My favorite peas to plant are sugar snap peas, because I think they are the most versatile when harvested. If you're looking for a fun garden pea variety that can double as a snow pea, then plant Blue Shelling peas, a pole variety. They are a pretty blue-purple color with an edible pod when immature and 7 to 9 plump peas when mature. They will turn green when cooked. If garden peas were my family's favorite vegetable, I would plant those for freezing, as they have more peas per pod than snap peas do.

Improved Maestro Garden pea is an heirloom bush variety that has some resistance to common pea diseases. A popular pole garden pea variety is Laxton's Progress No. 9 Garden pea. Both are heavy producers and will fill your freezer faster than letting snap peas mature.

If you want to plant snow peas, Oregon Sugar Pod II is a pole variety that is delicious and a heavy producer. If you're looking for a novelty snow pea, the Golden Sweet pea is a creamy yellow and retains its color when cooked.

Harvesting

Harvesting peas is a two-handed job. Peas have shallow roots, and, if you try to pull peas off the plant without holding the vine, you run the risk of pulling the whole plant up. I know it sounds silly, but trust me on this one.

Peas can be harvested at any time depending on how you're going to use them. If you want to eat the whole pod, harvest before the peas start filling out. Even some garden pea varieties will have an edible pod when immature. The best thing to do is to just snap a few peas of various sizes off the vine and taste them to decide which size pod you like best.

If you want to shell the peas and just eat the plump seeds, then wait for them to fill out. The pods should not be dry or yellowing; those will be too mature and starchy. Leave those to dry on the vine and save the seeds for planting next year. When you open the pod, the peas should be bright green and glossy. If they're dull looking, they will be starchy.

Peas are sweetest when they are first picked and will lose their sweetness the longer they're off the vine. It's best to pick peas as close to serving time as possible.

If you happen to miss a few days of picking peas when they are coming in full-force, you'll end up with some that are overripe. I like to use these to make Frozen Pea Pod Soup Concentrate (page 205), as they add flavor and creaminess to the soup.

Buying

While peas are certainly sweetest right off the vine, there are times when we need to purchase peas. Just don't expect them to taste as good.

Look for peas that are bright green in color and have crisp flesh with pods that snap, not bend. Old peas look scalded, spotted or limp. Don't buy peas that have already been shelled—they'll taste old. It's tempting, but it's worth shelling them yourself to get a fresher flavor.

The best place to buy peas is a you-pick farm, where you'll know exactly when they were picked and how they were handled after picking. The next best place would be a farm stand that picks daily.

Because peas are somewhat labor-intensive to pick, many market farmers will need to pick peas a day or two before market days. This is perfectly fine for most vegetables, but since peas lose their sweetness over time, it's good to ask when they were picked.

Of course, market peas picked a day or so ago are better than what you can find in the regular grocery store, which is my least favorite place to buy peas—even locally grown peas.

Preserving

Pea plants are usually heavy producers and, at the height of pea season, I'll sauté them with carrots for dinner and serve them with Frozen Cucumber Tzatziki (page 158) for lunch. And we still can't eat them all. The excess peas need to be preserved to make the most of the pea's sweetness.

If you let snap pea or snow peas mature, they will probably have a string on each side that will need to be removed before you preserve them. To remove the strings, pinch off the tip of the pea pod and pull the string downward. Turn the pod over and do the same on the other side.

Canning

Peas can be pressure canned and pickled for processing in a water bath canner. Unless you've grown or purchased garden peas specifically for canning, it might to be hard to get enough peas in one day's harvest to fill the four pints (500 ml) you need in order to properly pressure can peas. It takes 20 pounds (9.1 kg) of peas still in their pods to fill nine pint (500-ml) jars and 32 pounds (14.5 kg) to fill seven quart (1-L) jars.

To can garden peas, they first need to be shelled. Garden peas can be hot packed or raw packed (page 24) into the jars. You can add ½ teaspoon of salt to each pint (500 ml) and 1 teaspoon of salt to each quart (1 L).

When the jars are filled, use the bubble remover tool or a chopstick to remove the air bubbles, and make sure the jars have 1 inch (2.5 cm) of headspace. Wipe the rim of each jar and put a lid and band on the jar. Process the jars, according to the manufacturer's instructions, at 10 psi (69 kPa) for 40 minutes for pints (500 ml) and 40 minutes for quarts (1 L). Adjust for altitude (page 25), if necessary.

It is not recommended that snow or snap peas be pressure canned, as they tend to get mushy. However, there is no safety reason for not canning them. I've found that pressure Canned Snap Peas and Carrots (page 204) turn out just fine for us.

Snow peas and snap peas can be pickled and processed in a water bath canner. However, unless I have a lot of peas to preserve, I think it's easier to ferment them.

Freezing

Freezing peas is a great way to retain the sweet pea flavor and bright green color. Peas can be frozen in their pod or shelled.

Peas need to be blanched (page 35) before they're frozen. Snow peas or immature, thin-skinned pea pods need to be blanched for 1 minute. Snap peas and garden peas that have been shelled need to be blanched for 1½ to 2 minutes.

After blanching, use a clean kitchen towel to dry the peas before you put them in freezer-safe containers. This will help keep ice crystals from forming in the containers. I freeze peas in small serving-sized portions instead of large portions, so I don't worry if the peas freeze together in a clump.

If you want to make sure the peas don't freeze in a clump, lay them on a baking sheet lined with parchment paper and freeze them. Once they're frozen, transfer them to a freezer-safe container for storage.

I also like to make Frozen Pea Pod Soup Concentrate (page 205). This is a great use of peas that are a little overripe and of the pods from shelled peas.

Dehydrating

Shelled garden peas can be dehydrated and then reconstituted for use in soups. They need to be blanched for 3 minutes before being dehydrated (page 35). Dehydrated peas get pretty small, so be sure to put a mesh sheet under them to keep them from falling through the dehydrator trays.

Dehydrated garden peas can also be powdered and used to add nutrition and color to homemade pastas and smoothies. Dehydrated peas can even be used to make a quick pea soup.

Snap peas and snow peas can also be dehydrated; they will need to be blanched for 2 minutes before being dehydrated (page 35). These can be reconstituted and used in stir-fries or soups.

Fermenting

All peas can be preserved by fermentation—garden peas will be shelled; snap and snow peas will be fermented whole.

You can add spices, such as garlic, peppers, dill, rosemary, lemon zest and thyme, to the fermentation jar to add flavor. Carrots and onions also make great fermenting companions with peas.

Peas are fermented in a 2 percent brine (page 51). If you want to add spices, add them to the jar of peas before adding the brine.

Put the jar of fermenting peas on a plate or small cookie sheet to catch any overflow and store the jar out of direct sunlight. Let the peas ferment for 5 to 8 days, then do a taste test. If the peas need to ferment more, replace the weight and fermenting lid and let the jar sit for another day or two. When the peas have fermented to your liking, remove the weight and fermenting lid, add a regular storage lid and store them in the refrigerator for up to a year.

Preserving Peas Cheat Sheet

	Water Bath Canning (Snap and snow peas only)	Pressure Canning	Freezing	Dehydrating	Fermenting 2% brine
How to prepare	Shelled or whole	Shelled or whole	Blanching recommended; shelled or whole	Blanching required; shelled or whole	Shelled or whole
Flavors	Pickled	Plain or with other vegetables	Plain or soup concentrate	Plain or seasoned	Seasoned with herbs
Length of processing	15 minutes	Pints (500 ml): 40 minutes Quarts (1 L): 40 minutes	—	8–10 hours	5–8 days
Storage life	12 months	12 months	8–12 months	12 months for plain; 1 month for seasoned	3–4 months

Dried Asian Snap Pea Chips

The first time I asked my husband to try these, he didn't look very excited. Then he tasted them. Then he put the jar in his lunch the next day. That's when I knew this recipe was a keeper.

Makes 1 pint (500 ml)

1 lb (453 g) snap peas, stems removed

2 tsp (10 ml) toasted sesame seed oil or olive oil

2 tsp (10 ml) tamari

1 tsp grated Parmesan cheese

Fill a medium stockpot about halfway with water and bring it to a boil over high heat. Put the snap peas into the boiling water and let it come back up to a boil. Cover the pot and blanch the snap peas for 3 minutes. While the peas are in the boiling water, prepare a bowl of ice water. Using a slotted spoon, immediately transfer the snap peas from the boiling water into the ice bath to stop the cooking.

While the snap peas are cooling, mix the sesame seed oil, tamari and Parmesan in a large bowl.

Drain the peas, put them on a clean kitchen towel and pat them dry. Carefully add the peas to the bowl with the seasoning mixture. Mix well to coat all the pieces.

Lay the seasoned peas on a dehydrator tray. You can put the pieces close together, as they will shrink considerably. Dehydrate at 125°F (52°C) for 8 to 10 hours, or until crispy. The chips should easily snap in half when bent.

When the peas are fully dry, remove the tray from the dehydrator and let the peas cool. Put the dried peas in a glass jar with a tight-fitting lid and label the jar. Use the seasoned snap peas within a month.

These are best eaten within a few days. If they lose their crispiness, they can be put into the dehydrator on high for 15 to 30 minutes to crisp them.

Serving Suggestions: *These are really great as a chip substitute and go well with hummus or Frozen Creamy Broccoli Dip (page 89). The chips can be crushed and sprinkled on soups or salads. They can also be used in sandwiches or flatbread wraps to add texture.*

Canned Snap Pea Pickles

Similar to dilly beans, these snap pea pickles are sure to win over those who say they don't like peas. These pickles are crisp and not overly "pea" flavored.

Makes 2 pint (500-ml) jars

2 cups (474 ml) white vinegar

1 cup (237 ml) water

½ tsp dried dill weed

½ tsp black peppercorns

1 clove garlic, sliced

¾ lb (340 g) snap peas

½ cup (45 g) sliced jalapeños

Prepare the water bath canner by filling it halfway with water and putting it on the stove to simmer. Check two pint (500-ml) jars for any nicks or cracks, wash them in hot soapy water and rinse them in hot water. Keep the jars hot until it's time to use them. Wash the lids in hot soapy water and rinse them.

Combine the vinegar, water, dill weed, peppercorns and garlic in a stockpot and bring the mixture to a boil, stirring occasionally.

Divide the peas and jalapeños between the jars and use a ladle to pour the brine into the jars. Leave ½ inch (12 mm) of headspace. Remove the air bubbles with a bubble remover tool or chopstick and recheck the headspace; add more brine if necessary. Wipe the rims with a clean cloth, put the lids on the jars and screw on the bands. Place the jars in the prepared hot water bath canner, making sure that the jars are covered by at least an inch (2.5 cm) of water.

Bring the water to a full rolling boil and put the lid on the canner. Process the jars for 15 minutes, adjusting for altitude (page 17), if necessary. Arrange a folded towel on the counter or table. Remove the jars, using a jar lifter, and place them on the towel. Let the jars cool for at least 12 hours.

Once the jars are cooled, remove the bands and check the seals. If any jars failed to seal, put them in the refrigerator to use first. Wipe the jars with a clean cloth and store them for up to a year.

* In the photo, the snap pea pickles are in the jar on the right.

Serving Suggestions: *Snap pea pickles are a great ingredient in burrito bowls. We serve them as a cold side dish with a squeeze of lime or lemon juice. They can also be used in tacos or flatbread wraps.*

Canned Peas and Carrots

Peas and carrots go together, well, like peas and carrots. Instead of using garden peas in this classic combination, I like to use snap peas. They're much less work and retain their texture just fine, even in the pressure canner.

Makes 6 pint (500-ml) jars

6–8 cups (1.4–1.9 L) water

2 lbs (907 g) snap peas, stems removed

2 lbs (907 g) sliced carrots

1 onion (150 g), sliced

1½ tsp (9 g) salt, divided

To prepare the pressure canner, rinse it and its rack, place the bottom rack inside and fill the canner with a few inches of water, according to the manufacturer's instructions. Put the pressure canner on the stove over low heat while you prepare the jars. This is a raw-pack recipe, so the water in the pressure canner needs to be no higher than 140°F (60°C) before you put the jars into the canner.

Wash six pint (500-ml) jars in hot, soapy water and check them for any nicks or cracks. Rinse the jars in clean water and set them aside. Wash the lids in hot, soapy water, rinse them and set them aside.

Put the water in a pot and bring it to a boil. Divide the snap peas, carrots and onion among the jars. You don't want them super tight, so don't push them down. Peas soak up quite a bit of the liquid, and you want plenty of room for them to swell.

Once the jars are filled with the vegetables, add ¼ teaspoon of salt to each pint (500 ml). Pour the hot water into the jars, leaving 1 inch (2.5 cm) of headspace. Remove the air bubbles with a bubble remover tool or a chopstick and check the headspace.

Serving Suggestions: Heat the peas and carrots with the liquid from the jars in a pot on the stove. You can add cracked black pepper and other seasonings, such as thyme, garlic or lemon juice. These peas and carrots can also be added to soups or drained and sautéed for a quick stir-fry.

Process the jars, according to the manufacturer's instructions, at 10 psi (69 kPa) for 40 minutes for pints (500 ml) and quarts (1 L), adjusting for altitude (page 25), if necessary. Let the pressure canner depressurize naturally (page 25). Arrange a folded towel on the counter or table. Open the canner and remove the jars, using a jar lifter.

Place the jars on the folded towel, and let them cool for at least 12 hours. Remove the bands, check the seals and store the jars for up to 1 year. If any jars failed to seal, put them in the refrigerator to use first.

*See photo on page 202 (this recipe is shown in the jar on the left).

Frozen Pea Pod Soup Concentrate

Pea pod soup is a great way to use overgrown peas or leftover pods. This makes a quick freezer preserve on pea-shelling day. Tossing in some overgrown peas makes it even creamier.

Makes 2 cups (474 ml)

For the Soup Concentrate

1 tbsp (15 ml) olive oil

⅔ cup (100 g) diced onion

2 cloves garlic, diced

1 cup (237 ml) chicken or vegetable broth

1 tbsp (15 ml) lemon juice

½ lb (226 g) pea pods and overgrown peas, stems and strings removed

For Serving

3 cups (711 ml) chicken or vegetable broth

Canned Hot Pepper Sauce (page 218)

Sprig of fresh thyme

Sourdough bread, toasted

For the concentrate, in a medium stockpot, heat the oil over medium heat. Lightly sauté the onion and garlic just until the onion is translucent, about 5 minutes. Add the chicken broth, lemon juice and pea pods and simmer the mixture for 25 to 30 minutes, until the pea pods are quite soft.

When the pods are soft, remove the pan from the heat and puree the soup. You can use an immersion blender or ladle the soup into a blender. After the soup is pureed, you can strain the solids by using a mesh strainer and gently pushing the soup through the mesh, or use a food mill with a berry cone.

Allow the strained soup to cool, then put it into freezer-safe containers, such as half-pint (250-ml) Mason jars or plastic freezer bags. Label the containers. If you're using glass jars—wide-mouth jars with no shoulder would be best for this recipe—be sure to leave 1 inch (2.5 cm) of headspace for expansion. Put the pea soup concentrate into the refrigerator to cool overnight and then transfer it to the freezer. It can be stored in the freezer for up to a year.

For serving, thaw the soup concentrate overnight in the refrigerator. Put the soup in a medium stockpot, stir in the chicken broth and heat the mixture over medium heat until the soup bubbles, about 10 minutes. Garnish the soup with a drop or two of the hot pepper sauce and a sprig of thyme. Serve with the bread. This soup is also lovely served cold.

Fermented Snow Peas

Snow peas are often used in Asian stir-fry, and I think it's fitting that fermented snow peas get seasoned with tamari and fish sauce, two naturally fermented Asian sauces. These fermented snow peas have a crisp pickle flavor and make a fun addition to any charcuterie board.

Makes 1 quart (1 L)

½ lb (226 g) snow peas, stems removed

¼ cup (40 g) sliced onion

1–2 cloves garlic

1 tbsp (15 ml) tamari

½ tsp fish sauce

1 tbsp (18 g) salt

2 cups (474 ml) filtered water

Put the peas and onion in a wide-mouth quart (1-L) jar and add the garlic, tamari and fish sauce to the jar.

Mix the salt with the water to make the brine. Fill the jar with the saltwater brine, making sure to cover the peas and onion but leaving room for the weight and expansion.

Put a weight in the jar to keep everything under the brine and top the jar with a fermentation lid.

Put the jar on a plate or small cookie sheet to catch any overflow, then set it in a cool place, out of direct sunlight, for 5 to 7 days. You can taste the peas any time after 5 days. If they need to ferment longer, replace the weight and fermentation lid and ferment the peas for a few more days.

When the peas are to your liking, replace the weight and fermentation lid with a plastic storage lid and store the peas in the refrigerator for up to 4 months.

Serving Suggestions: *Enjoy straight from the jar or on a relish tray. These make a nice cold side dish for stir-fry and rice. We also enjoy the fermented peas in flatbread wraps.*

Dried Spiced Pea Crisps

This recipe is for shelled garden peas, but snap peas or snow peas can easily be substituted. Even though I'm not a fan of garden peas, I love these garlicky pea crisps. They have a great pea flavor, but not the pea texture.

Makes 1 half-pint (250 ml)

¾ lb (340 g) shelled garden peas

1 tbsp (15 ml) melted coconut oil

½ tsp salt

1 tsp garlic powder

Fill a medium stockpot about halfway with water and bring it to a boil over high heat. Add the shelled peas to the pot, and blanch them for 2 minutes. While the peas are in the boiling water, prepare a bowl of ice water. After 2 minutes, use a slotted spoon to immediately transfer the peas from the boiling water to the bowl of ice water to stop the cooking.

While the peas are cooling, mix the coconut oil, salt and garlic powder in a medium bowl.

Drain the water from the bowl, pour the peas out onto a clean kitchen towel and pat them dry. Carefully add the peas to the bowl with the seasoning mixture. Mix well to coat all the pieces.

Lay the seasoned peas on a dehydrator tray. You can put the pieces close together, as they will shrink considerably. Dehydrate the peas at 125°F (52°C) for 8 to 10 hours, or until they are crispy. Fully dried peas should easily shatter when hit with a small hammer.

When the peas are fully dry, remove the tray from the dehydrator and let the peas cool. Put the dried peas in a glass jar with a tight-fitting lid and label the jar. Use the peas within a month.

These are best eaten within a few days. If they lose their crispiness, they can be put into the dehydrator on high for 15 to 30 minutes to crisp them.

Serving Suggestions: *These can be eaten right out of the jar as a snack, but they're also really great powdered and sprinkled on pea soup (page 205). The powder can also be added to sour cream to make a dip for potato chips, Dried Asian Snap Pea Chips (page 201) or other dehydrated snacks.*

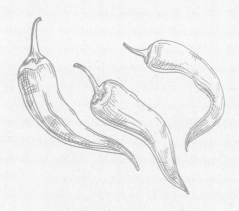

peppers

Adding Spice to Your Life

Peppers can be confusing. When I think of peppers, I always think of hot or spicy peppers, probably because I grew up in South Texas. But I have friends who always think of sweet bell peppers and call any hot pepper a chile, not a pepper. There are literally hundreds of varieties of peppers, some are sweet and some are hot, but they all are members of the *Capsicum* family.

Sweet peppers are definitely in the minority in the family, as most peppers have at least a bit of heat to them. But peppers such as bell, gypsy and some bananas have pepper flavor without the heat.

Hot peppers range from mildly hot to you-need-to-go-to-the-hospital hot, and there's an index, called the Scoville scale that measures peppers by Scoville Heat Units. We've included a copy of the scale (page 211) to help you decide which peppers to plant and preserve. This copy does not include every pepper, just the most common ones, to give you a reference point.

For the most part, peppers can be used interchangeably. If a recipe calls for jalapeño, you can substitute gypsy pepper for a no-heat flavor,

poblano for a mild flavor, a serrano for a hotter flavor or a habanero for a my-mouth-is-on-fire flavor. Of course, there are some variances in the actual flavor of the peppers, but, for the most part, peppers are chosen by how hot you want the dish.

Growing

The great thing about growing peppers is that you can grow a much greater variety than you can find in your local store. You can also let them get fully ripe before they are harvested. Ripe peppers are actually red, yellow or orange, not green. When they ripen and change color, the flavor intensifies: sweet peppers get sweeter and hot peppers have more flavor, but not more heat.

Peppers are heat-loving plants that are usually grown as annuals. Peppers need 70 to 80 days to mature. If you have a short summer season, you will need to start seeds indoors about 4 to 6 weeks before your average last frost. Do not put the pepper in the ground before the average last frost date, and be ready to protect them in the event of a late frost. Pepper plants are very frost tender.

In warmer climates, you can direct-seed peppers after the danger of frost is over, or you can start them inside 4 to 6 weeks before your average last frost date.

Peppers like rich, well-draining soil, so add compost to the soil before you plant them. Even though peppers like the heat of summer, they also like regular watering and a thick layer of mulch. Be sure to water the soil and not the leaves or fruit.

Ironically, this plant that's known for loving hot weather will probably stop producing when temperatures rise above 90°F (32°C). At this temperature, the pollen can become sterile and the flowers will drop. Keep watering the plant so it stays alive until the heat breaks. It will produce again.

Pepper plants can get leggy and topple over, so use tomato cages or stake them so they grow upright.

The only problem we really have with peppers is that occasionally some will get blossom-end rot, a brown or yellow water-soaked spot that appears at the end of the pepper. This is usually caused by inconsistent watering, but it can also be caused by a calcium deficit. If you think it's from a calcium deficit, you can sprinkle dolomite limestone on the soil surrounding the pepper plants. Some people have had success sprinkling powdered eggshells or pouring milk on the soil.

Harvesting

Use garden clippers to harvest peppers to reduce the chance of damaging the plant and cut about an inch (2.5 cm) up the stem instead of right beside the fruit. You can begin harvesting peppers whenever they reach full size or even a little smaller, but still a good size for eating. Most commercially sold peppers are picked green; you can let them fully ripen.

When peppers set their first fruits, we pick them green to encourage the plant to set more. After that, we let them ripen because we prefer the more developed flavor of the ripe peppers. If you let the first fruits fully ripen before picking them, they won't set more fruit as quickly and your harvest will be much smaller.

Be careful when you harvest hot peppers. The capsicum from the peppers can get on your hands, and it needs to be washed off, preferably with dish soap, before you touch sensitive body parts, like your eyes. Using clippers reduces this risk but doesn't eliminate it.

Once harvested, peppers can be stored in the refrigerator for a couple of weeks or on the counter for a few days. They will begin to dry out and shrivel up if left on the counter too long.

Pepper Varieties to Try

There are thousands of varieties of peppers, each with its own flavor and level of heat. I suggest that you talk with other gardeners in your area and ask which peppers they grow and why. Then experiment until you know what peppers work well for your family.

Chili Pequin grows as a perennial in our area. The peppers are tiny, about the size of a BB pellet, but can be hotter than a cayenne. The little bush produces hundreds of peppers each year. We also grow jalapeño, Thai, poblano, serrano and other hot peppers, depending on the year and what I need them for. No one in my family really cares for bell peppers, so we grow mild banana peppers and gypsy peppers as our sweet peppers.

If you live in the north, you'll want to try early-maturing peppers, such as Lady Bell, Ace or King of the North for sweet peppers. For hot peppers, choose Anaheim, Hungarian Hot Wax and Early Jalapeño.

Also be aware that some peppers have different names when they're dried. For example, an Ancho pepper is a dried Poblano pepper. Sometimes it also depends on when the pepper is picked and then dried.

If you have space for only a few pepper plants, I suggest growing ones that are hard to find locally and that you can use on a regular basis. For instance, if you want to make Dried Chili Powder (page 222), then grow Hatch, Mirasol and Poblano peppers. You can use them fresh as you would jalapeño in any recipe and leave the seeds in to increase the spice. Then you can dry what you need to make chili powder or Frozen Harissa Paste (page 215).

Fresh Name	Dried Name
Jalapeño	Chipotle picked very ripe and smoked
Poblano	Ancho that is picked when very ripe
Chilaca	Pasilla
Anaheim	Colorado
Mirasol	Guajillo
Serrano	Chili Seco
Bola	Cascabel
Hatch	New Mexico

Scoville Heat Units	Pepper Name
15,000,000–16,000,000	Pure Capsicum
2,500,000–3,000,000	Standard US Grade Pepper Spray
2,200,000	Carolina Reaper
2,009,231	Trinidad Moruga Scorpion
1,463,700	Trinidad Scorpion Butch T
800,000–1,001,300	Bhut Jolokia or Ghost Pepper

Scoville Heat Units	Pepper Name
350,000–575,000	Red Habanero
250,000–400,000	White Bullet Habanero
150,000–325,000	Orange Habanero
100,000–300,000	Datil
50,000–100,000	Thai
30,000–60,000	Chili Pequin
30,000–50,000	Cayenne
15,000–50,000	Pencil Hot
12,000–30,000	Manzano
8,000–22,000	Serrano
5,000–15,000	Hungarian Wax Pepper
5,000–15,000	Caribe
2,500–10,000	Red Fresno
2,500–8,000	Jalapeño
2,500–5,000	Cherry Bomb
2,500–5,000	Mirasol
1,000–5,000	Hatch Chile
500–2,500	Anaheim
500–2,000	Padron
1,000–2,000	Poblano
500–1,000	Santa Fe
100–1,000	Italian Long Hot
100–1,000	Shishito
100–500	Pimento
100–500	Pepperoncini
0–1,000	Cubanelle
0–500	Banana
0 no heat	Gypsy Pepper
0 no heat	Bell Pepper

Buying

When you buy peppers, look for ones that have firm, smooth skin, and avoid any that have started to dry out. If you're buying them from a grocery store, you will probably have only underripe green or yellow peppers to choose from.

If you're buying from a farmer, you'll likely have more choices of ripeness and variety. If you want fully ripe peppers, you might need to ask the farmer to let some ripen for you.

If you find some that have already started to turn red, they will continue ripening over the next few days. However, they will dry out; what you gain in ripeness, you lose in moisture.

When you bring peppers home, they can be stored at room temperature for a few days or in the refrigerator for a week or two.

Preserving

The pepper season is fleeting, but most pepper plants produce a lot of peppers, making preserving them for the future easy. How you want to use them will determine how you preserve them.

To prepare peppers for preserving, you'll need to remove the stems and rinse the peppers. If you are preparing a lot of hot peppers or have sensitive skin, you'll want to wear gloves when you cut them. The capsicum from the peppers can burn your skin.

If you want to reduce the spice in hot peppers, then remove the seed bundle inside the peppers. The capsicum is located in this bundle, so removing it and the membrane that holds it to the pepper will reduce the heat of the dish. Even though the seeds are edible, they can also be bitter, which is another reason to remove them.

Some recipes will call for removing the skin of the pepper, and some people just prefer to remove the skin. To easily skin a pepper, char whole peppers either outside on the grill or in a hot oven; if you have a gas stove, you can use tongs and char peppers one at a time over the burner. Once the skin bubbles, remove the peppers from the heat, put them in a pan and cover them with a damp cloth until they're cool enough to handle. The cloth will keep them moist. Then peel off the skin with your hands.

Some recipes will call for roasting fresh peppers. Put them in a baking dish and roast them in a preheated 400°F (204°C) oven until their skins blister and the peppers are soft; this should take about 10 minutes. When the peppers are done, transfer them to a bowl and cover the bowl while the peppers cool.

Canning

Peppers can be water bath canned as jelly or jam, and they can be pickled in a vinegar brine. They can also be canned plain in a pressure canner.

While it may not seem like it when they're fresh, the skin of some peppers is tough. The National Center for Home Food Preservation recommends removing the skin before canning most peppers, especially larger ones. However, I believe it is a quality recommendation, not a safety recommendation. You can peel the peppers before canning or not, depending on your preference.[5]

Peppers can be used in jams and jellies such as Canned Cucumber-Jalapeño Jam (page 156) or Canned Banana Pepper and Mint Jam (page 217). Dried pepper flakes can be used just like other dried spices and safely added to canned goods. This can create an interesting twist on an old favorite like Canned Spicy Corn Cob Jelly (page 142).

---

[5]   https://nchfp.uga.edu/how/can_04/peppers.html

Pickling peppers is a good shelf-stable way to preserve them. Small peppers can be pickled whole with slits in them; the slits allow air in the pepper to escape. Larger peppers need to be sliced. You can also make Canned Hot Pepper Sauce (page 218) that is similar to Tabasco with your peppers and process it in the water bath canner.

To pressure can peppers, you need about 9 pounds (4 kg) of peppers to fill nine pint (500-ml) jars; the USDA does not recommend quart (1-L) jars for canning peppers. You can mix and match pepper varieties or put one variety of pepper per jar. Peel peppers that have tough skins (page 212) and remove the seeds if you wish. Small peppers can be left whole, but put two to four slits in each one and flatten them. Large peppers need to be quartered or sliced.

You can add ½ teaspoon of salt to each pint (500 ml) jar. Loosely fill the jars with prepared peppers and add freshly boiled water, leaving 1 inch (2.5 cm) of headspace. When the jars are filled, use the bubble remover tool or a chopstick to remove the air bubbles. Wipe the rims of each jar and put a lid and band on the jar. Process the jars, according to the manufacturer's instructions, at 10 psi (69 kPa) for 35 minutes for pints (500 ml) or half-pints (250 ml). Adjust for altitude (page 25), if necessary.

Freezing

All peppers can be frozen without blanching, although some people prefer to remove the skin on peppers (page 212) before freezing them.

Freezing peppers is as easy as slicing them, removing the seeds if you wish and putting them in a labeled freezer bag. If you're worried about them sticking together, you can freeze them on a baking sheet lined with parchment paper, then transfer the frozen peppers to labeled freezer bags.

Pepper sauce, such as Frozen Harissa Paste (page 215), is also good to keep in the freezer.

Dehydrating

Dehydrated peppers are so good to have on hand for adding to other preserved food and making spice mixes, such as Dried Chili Powder (page 222). Peppers don't need to be blanched or have their skin removed before dehydrating, which makes preserving them super fast.

One way of dehydrating peppers is to tightly tie strings around their stems and hang them out of direct sunlight in an area where there is airflow. You need them tied tightly because, as they dehydrate, the stem will shrink and the pepper can fall out. It will probably take at least a week for them to dry out, and, if you live in a humid area, there's a risk that they'll mold.

You can also use a dehydrator; peppers can be dehydrated whole or in slices. I think whole peppers dehydrate better when they've been slit on one side. For sliced peppers, cut them into ¼-inch (6-mm) slices. Dehydrate peppers at 125°F (52°C) for 8 to 12 hours, or until they are brittle.

Peppers can be charred or smoked before dehydrating if you want them to have a smoky flavor. You can also remove the seeds if you want.

To rehydrate peppers, put them in a bowl and pour boiling water over them. Let them soak until fully hydrated, which will take about an hour. Dried peppers can also be added to soups or casseroles and will rehydrate as they cook.

Fermenting

Fermented peppers are the first fermented food I was able to convince my husband to try. He hates pickles and all things vinegar. But he's a lover of hot peppers, so he would suffer through canned peppers and some hot sauces—if they weren't too vinegary—when fresh peppers weren't available. Now that we have fermented peppers, he no longer has to suffer.

You can ferment peppers whole or in slices. If you use whole peppers, you'll want to put some slits in them, so they ferment evenly, and remove the stems. You can put a variety of peppers in each jar or just one variety per jar. Put sliced or whole peppers in a wide-mouth jar and pour 2 percent brine (page 51) over them. Add a fermentation weight and lid, put the jar of fermenting peppers on a plate or small cookie sheet to catch any overflow and store the jar out of direct sunlight. Let the peppers ferment for 7 days, then do a taste test. If the peppers need to ferment more, replace the weight and fermenting lid and let the jar sit for up to 7 more days. When the peppers have fermented to your liking, remove the weight and fermenting lid, add a regular storage lid and store them in the refrigerator for up to 1 year.

Preserving Peppers Cheat Sheet

	Water Bath Canning	Pressure Canning	Freezing	Dehydrating	Fermenting 2% brine
How to prepare	Whole or sliced; peeling recommended for some	Whole or sliced; peeling recommended for some	No blanching required; whole or slices	No blanching required; whole or slices	Whole or slices
Flavors	Pickled or as a jam	Plain	Plain or with other vegetables	Plain	Seasoned with herbs
Length of processing	15 minutes	Pints (500 ml): 35 minutes	—	8–12 hours	7–14 days
Storage life	12 months	12 months	8–12 months	12 months or longer	12 months

Frozen Harissa Paste

Harissa is a spicy North African paste that can add heat to any meal. But it's not just heat: harissa is packed full of flavor. You can use any combination of fresh and dried peppers and any combination of sweet and hot peppers. Here's a basic recipe to get you started.

Makes approximately 2 half-pint (250-ml) jars

½ tsp cumin seed

½ tsp coriander seed

½ tsp caraway seed

4 oz (113 g) mixed roasted (page 212) fresh and reconstituted dried hot peppers

1 lb (453 g) roasted (page 212) red bell or other sweet pepper

2–3 cloves garlic

3 tbsp (45 ml) lemon juice

1 tbsp (16 g) tomato paste

¼ cup (59 ml) olive oil

Toast the cumin, coriander and caraway seeds in a small skillet over medium-low heat for 5 minutes, until the seeds begin to release their fragrance. This is an optional step, but it improves the flavor of the paste so much you will be glad you did it.

Combine the toasted seeds, hot and sweet peppers, garlic, lemon juice and tomato paste in a food processor. Blend until you have a textured but somewhat smooth paste. Add the olive oil and blend again. This will not be a super smooth paste like hummus; it will have some texture, like pesto. You can add more olive oil if it's needed to achieve that texture.

Put the harissa into freezer-safe containers, such as 4-ounce (125-ml) Mason jars or plastic freezer bags, and label the containers. If you're using glass jars, be sure to leave ½ inch (12 mm) of headspace for expansion. Put the harissa in the refrigerator overnight to cool it, then transfer it to the freezer. Harissa can be stored in the freezer for up to 6 months.

Serving Suggestions: *Harissa can be used as a dipping sauce or a condiment. It can be thinned, if needed, and served with pita or breadsticks as a dipping sauce. Use harissa as a spread on sandwiches or flatbread wraps and to spice up soups and other dishes.*

Canned Banana Pepper and Mint Jam

Pepper jam is a party favorite that's often served with cream cheese and crackers. It's delicious, but usually spicy. This jam uses banana peppers instead of hot peppers, so you get all the pepper flavor without the heat. Don't let the mint scare you; the minty flavor is muted and refreshing, not overpowering at all.

Makes 6 half-pint (250-ml) jars

1 cup (30 g) roughly chopped fresh mint leaves

¾ cup (177 ml) water

3 cups (370 g) sliced banana or gypsy peppers

1¼ cups (296 ml) apple cider vinegar

½ cup (118 ml) lemon juice

6 tbsp (54 g) pectin

4 cups (800 g) sugar

Prepare the water bath canner by filling it halfway with water and putting it on the stove to simmer. Check six half-pint (250-ml) jars for any nicks or cracks, wash them in hot soapy water and rinse them in hot water. Keep the jars hot until it's time to use them. Wash the lids in hot soapy water and rinse them.

Put the mint leaves and water in a medium stockpot, bring the water to a gentle simmer, then simmer the mint leaves for 10 minutes. You can leave the mint leaves in the jam or remove them. I usually remove them by pouring the water through a mesh strainer over a bowl to catch the liquid. Press the leaves to remove all of the flavored water.

Put ½ cup (118 ml) of the strained water back into the pot and add the peppers, vinegar, lemon juice and pectin. Bring the mixture to a boil over medium-high heat, stirring often. After the mixture begins to boil, add the sugar, bring the mixture to a rolling boil and boil it for 1 minute, while continually stirring.

Remove the pan from the heat, and ladle the jam into the hot jars, leaving ¼ inch (6 mm) of headspace. Wipe the rims with a clean cloth, put on the lids and screw on the bands. Place the jars in the prepared hot water bath canner and process them for 10 minutes, adjusting for altitude (page 17), if necessary.

Arrange a folded towel on the counter or table. Remove the jars, using a jar lifter, and place them on the towel. Let them cool for at least 12 hours. Once the jars are cooled, remove the bands and check the seals. If any jars failed to seal, put them in the refrigerator to use first. Wipe the jars with a clean cloth, and store for up to a year.

Serving Suggestions: *Serve with soft cheese and crackers or on a turkey and hard cheese sandwich or flatbread wrap.*

Canned Hot Pepper Sauce

Hot pepper sauce graces our table at every meal, as some of my people put a little dab on everything but desserts. This hot sauce is similar to Tabasco sauce, but without the overwhelming vinegar flavor. To be sure, there's still a vinegar flavor since the vinegar is what makes this safe for canning. But using apple cider vinegar instead of white vinegar reduces the harshness of the vinegar flavor.

Makes 2 half-pint (250-ml) jars

½ lb (226 g) sliced peppers, a mixture of sweet and hot, seeds removed from hot peppers if you prefer milder flavor

½ cup (118 ml) apple cider vinegar

½ cup (118 ml) white vinegar

½ cup (75 g) chopped onion

½ tsp garlic powder

½ tsp ground cumin

½ tsp ground mustard

½ tsp ground turmeric

½ tsp salt

¼ tsp ground cloves

¼ tsp ground allspice

2 tsp (10 g) sugar

Serving Suggestions: Use hot pepper sauce as a condiment for soups, pasta, sandwiches, tacos, eggs . . . pretty much anything. It can also be used to spice up the Canned Mexican Salsa (page 278), for those who like a spicier salsa.

In a medium stockpot, combine the peppers, cider vinegar, white vinegar, onion, garlic powder, cumin, mustard, turmeric, salt, cloves, allspice and sugar. Put the lid on, bring the mixture to a simmer over medium heat, then simmer the sauce for 20 minutes.

While the hot sauce is simmering, prepare the water bath canner. Fill it halfway with water and put it on the stove to simmer. Check two half-pint (250-ml) jars for any nicks or cracks, wash them in hot soapy water and rinse them in hot water. Keep the jars hot until it's time to use them. Wash the lids in hot soapy water and rinse them.

After 20 minutes, remove the pan from the heat and puree the pepper mixture. You can use an immersion blender or ladle the mixture into a blender to puree it.

Pour or ladle the hot sauce into the prepared jars, leaving ¼ inch (6 mm) of headspace. Remove the air bubbles with a bubble remover tool or chopstick and recheck the headspace. Wipe the rims with a clean cloth, put the lids on the jars and screw on the bands. Place the jars in the prepared hot water bath canner, making sure that the jars are covered by at least an inch (2.5 cm) of water.

Bring the water to a full rolling boil and put the lid on the canner. Process the jars for 10 minutes, adjusting for altitude (page 17), if necessary. Arrange a folded towel on the counter or table. Remove the jars, using a jar lifter, and place them on the towel. Let the jars cool for at least 12 hours.

Once the jars are cooled, remove the bands and check the seals. If any jars failed to seal, put them in the refrigerator to use first. Wipe the jars with a clean cloth and store them for up to a year.

* In the photo, the hot pepper sauce is shown in the bottle on the left.

Canned Whole Pickled Peppers

This is the easiest and prettiest way to can a lot of peppers. You can leave small ones whole and slice larger ones. Use a variety of peppers to make interesting jars of pickled peppers to give as gifts. The sugar in this recipe is purely optional; it softens the harshness of the vinegar a bit but doesn't make the peppers or brine taste sweet. Taste the brine before pouring it over the peppers; if it's too harsh for your liking, add the sugar.

Makes 4 pint (500-ml) jars

5 cups (1.2 L) white vinegar

1 cup (237 ml) water

4 tsp (24 g) salt

2 tbsp (30 g) sugar (optional)

3 lbs (1.4 kg) small or medium peppers, a mixture of sweet and hot

Serving Suggestions: *Use the pickled peppers whole on a relish tray or slice them to add to salads, sandwiches, tacos and flatbread wraps.*

Prepare the water bath canner by filling it halfway with water and putting it on the stove to simmer. Check four pint (500-ml) jars for any nicks or cracks, wash them in hot soapy water and rinse them in hot water. Keep the jars hot until it's time to use them. Wash the lids in hot soapy water and rinse them.

Combine the vinegar, water, salt and sugar, if desired, in a stockpot, and bring the mixture to a boil over medium heat, stirring occasionally.

Cut 2 to 4 long slits in each pepper. If you're working with a lot of hot peppers, you might want to wear gloves.

Pack the peppers into the jars and pour the brine into the jars, using a ladle. Leave ½ inch (12 mm) of headspace. Remove the air bubbles with a bubble remover tool or chopstick and recheck the headspace; add more brine if necessary. Be patient with this step; it will take a bit for the brine to fully settle into the peppers, so spend a little more time removing air bubbles than you normally do.

Wipe the rims with a clean cloth, put the lids on the jars and screw on the bands. Place the jars in the prepared hot water bath canner, making sure that the jars are covered by at least an inch (2.5 cm) of water. Bring the water to a full rolling boil, and put the lid on the canner. Process the jars for 10 minutes, adjusting for altitude (page 17), if necessary. Arrange a folded towel on the counter or table. Remove the jars, using a jar lifter, and place them on the towel. Let the jars cool for at least 12 hours.

Once the jars are cooled, remove the bands and check the seals. If any jars failed to seal, put them in the refrigerator to use first. Wipe the jars with a clean cloth and store them for up to a year.

*See photo on page 219 (this recipe is shown in the jar on the right).

Fermented Green Hot Sauce

Fermented hot sauce is a great way to get probiotics into the diets of those who love spicy food but are leery of eating fermented food. You can make this sauce as thick or thin as you want by adjusting the brine you add when you blend it. You can use any combination of hot and sweet peppers to adjust the spice, the flavor and the color.

Makes 1 pint (500 ml)

¼ lb (113 g) sliced green peppers

½ cup (75 g) chopped onion

3 cloves garlic

1 tbsp (15 ml) honey

1½ tsp (9 g) salt

1 cup (237 ml) filtered water

Put the peppers, onion, garlic and honey in a clean wide-mouth pint (500-ml) jar.

Mix the salt into the water to make the brine. Fill the jar with the saltwater brine, making sure to cover the peppers. Press the peppers down if necessary, but leave room for the weight and expansion.

Put a weight in the jar to keep everything under the brine and top the jar with a fermentation lid. Put the jar on a plate or cookie sheet to catch any overflow. Set the jar in a cool place, out of direct sunlight, for 8 to 14 days. You can taste the peppers any time after 8 days. If they need to ferment longer, replace the weight and fermentation lid and ferment for a few more days.

When the peppers are to your liking, pour the ferment into a blender and blend it until the sauce is smooth. Divide the hot sauce into smaller glass bottles that are easier to pour from. You can use cleaned bottles from store-bought salad dressing or hot sauce. Store the sauce in the refrigerator for up to 9 months.

Serving Suggestions: *Use as a condiment for soups, pasta, sandwiches, tacos, or eggs. Just put this sauce on the table for every meal. If you like spicier salsa, add some of this green hot sauce to the Canned Mexican Salsa (page 278).*

Dried Chili Powder

Chili powder is useful for so many things besides making chili. It's often sprinkled, along with lime juice, on corn on the cob or fruit. I like to garnish creamy soups with it or add just a bit to Canned Spicy Corn Cob Jelly (page 142) to balance the sweetness of the jelly. The great thing is, if you can grow peppers, you can grow most of the ingredients for chili powder.

Makes 1 half-pint (250 ml)

3 dried (35 g) Ancho peppers, seeded

3 dried (19 g) Guajillo peppers, seeded

3 dried (56 g) New Mexico peppers, seeded

3 tbsp (6 g) cumin seed

2 tbsp (18 g) garlic powder

1 tbsp (1 g) Mexican oregano

1 tsp smoked paprika

3 whole cloves

2 whole allspice berries or ⅛ tsp ground allspice

Roughly tear or chop any large peppers so they fit in the food processor better.

Put the Ancho peppers, Guajillo peppers, New Mexico peppers, cumin, garlic powder, oregano, paprika, cloves and allspice in a food processor, and process until the mixture is powdered. This will take a bit of time, up to 3 minutes, and there will probably still be some small chunks. Sift the chunks out by putting the powder in a mesh strainer over a bowl. Gently shake the strainer until all the powder has sifted through and you're left with just flakes.

The flakes can be powdered again in the food processor or a spice mill, then sifted again. Continue powdering any flakes until they are gone. It's OK to have some flakes in the chili powder; you just don't want a lot of them.

Put the chili powder in a glass jar with a tight-fitting lid. Label the jar and use the chili powder within 1 year. Since you're not adding an anti-caking agent, which commercial chili powder has, the powder will tend to stick together over time. It's fine, just take a spoon and mix it up whenever you use it.

Serving Suggestions: *Chili powder can be used for more than just seasoning chili con carne. Use it to garnish soups, such as Canned Corn Chowder (page 137); to season vegetables, such as Dried Chili–Lime Corn Snacks before dehydrating it (page 145); or to season cream cheese to make a flavorful spread for crackers or flatbread. Chili powder can be sprinkled on any food to which you want to give a smoky chili flavor.*

potatoes
Our Favorite Meal–Extender Veggie

Unlike cereal crops such as rice, wheat and other grains, potatoes are easily grown in the backyard garden. The United Nations declared 2008 the International Year of the Potato, citing its importance in feeding people: "The potato produces more nutritious food more quickly, on less land and in harsher climates than any other major crop—up to 85 percent of the plant is edible human food, compared to around 50 percent in cereals."[6]

Most grocery stores carry only russet potatoes, which are a low-moisture, high-starch potato that is good for baking, and low-starch varieties, such as red or gold potatoes, that are good for boiling. But there are many more varieties to choose from.

When you grow your own potatoes or purchase them from a farmers' market, you can choose from low-starch, medium-starch or high-starch potatoes. You can choose white-flesh, creamy-flesh, red- or even purple-flesh potatoes, all with a variety of skin colors.

---

[6]   http://www.fao.org/potato-2008/en/aboutiyp/index.html

Growing

Unlike most other vegetables, potatoes are grown from previously harvested potatoes and not from seeds. Potato growers hold back some of their harvest and let the potatoes sprout. These are called *seed potatoes*. When grown from seed potatoes, the new plant will be a clone of the plant from which the seed potato came.

There are times when store-bought potatoes sprout and, if the timing is right, you might be tempted to use them as seed potatoes. Gardening and agricultural experts do not recommend this, because you run the risk of introducing potato blight or other diseases to your property. That said, people do it.

Potatoes are a cool-weather crop and can be planted once the soil temperature reaches 45°F (7°C). In some southern climates, you can plant a spring crop and a fall crop of potatoes.

Potatoes are organized into three groups, based on how long it takes the potato crop to mature. Early-season varieties take 10 to 12 weeks, midseason varieties take 14 to 16 weeks and late-season varieties take 16 to more than 20 weeks.

Plant potatoes in sandy, well-draining soil and go easy on the compost. If the soil is too rich, the plant will put all its energy into growing the above-ground parts, which aren't edible. If you have clay soil, you need to mix in sand or grow your potatoes in containers to reduce the risk of the potatoes rotting.

When you get seed potatoes, it's recommended that you pre-sprout them, also called *chitting*, to help them grow faster. This isn't necessary in every climate, but it might be in a climate with a really short spring. To chit potatoes, look at the potatoes and find the end with the most eyes, called the *rose end*. Set the potatoes rose-end up in a single layer on a tray or in open egg cartons. Put them in a warm, dark area to break their dormancy. The ideal temperature is 70°F (21°C). They should start sprouting within a week. After that, move them to a cooler location, about 50°F (10°C), that has light. This should cause the sprout to turn green.

When you're ready to plant the seed potatoes, cut them into cubes with two to three eyes on each one; the starch in the potato will feed the growing plant. You can let the potatoes dry out for a few days to reduce the likelihood of them rotting; however, I've found that dipping the cut ends in wood ash protects them just as well.

Potatoes like to be planted in hills. You can accomplish this by mounding up more soil around the plant as it grows. It's important to keep the growing potato tubers under the ground as they can get sun-scorched, which will increase their *solanine* levels (we'll talk more about this later). Potatoes also like consistent watering and need about an inch (2.5 cm) a week, so don't let them completely dry out between watering or you'll end up with split potatoes. They'll taste fine but won't be as pretty.

Colorado potato beetles are probably the biggest problem for potatoes. Fortunately, they're slow and easy to spot since they have black and orange strips. They come early in the season to lay eggs.

If you're diligent about picking them off the leaves and killing them and destroying the eggs they lay on the underside of the leaves, you can probably keep them in check without using any pesticides.

Most other problems can be avoided by encouraging beneficial insects, such as ladybugs, praying mantis and spiders, building healthy soil and practicing crop rotation. Avoiding the use of broad-scope insecticides encourages beneficial insects. Do not plant potatoes where any other nightshade plant grew the previous year. Nightshade plants include tomatoes, peppers and eggplants.

Harvesting

You can harvest potatoes at any time by gently digging around a plant and lifting out the tuber. Put the soil back and the plant will continue to grow. But you'll know for sure that it's time to harvest potatoes when the plants begin to die back.

Once harvested, potatoes can be used immediately or left outside in full shade to cure before they are stored. Like onions, potatoes don't store well here, so I leave the biggest ones outside in the shade and bring smaller ones inside to cook or preserve. After the potatoes dry out, we rub the dirt off them and put them in wire baskets lined with fabric or burlap bags, depending on how many we have. We use the "stored" ones first and save the preserved ones for when we run out of fresh potatoes.

Potato Varieties to Try

Choose potato varieties based on how long your growing season is and what you want to do with them. If you're new to growing potatoes and want to get the highest yield, buy from your local nursery or feed store instead of randomly selecting potatoes from a catalog. The local store will stock only what they know will grow well in your area.

A good all-purpose early variety to try is Superior, which has golden-brown skin, white flesh and is resistant to disease. Norland, another early variety, has red skin and white flesh. Early Gem is a high-producing variety that is resistant to scab, a tuber disease that causes brown patches on the potatoes.

There are many midseason potato varieties, such as Yukon Gold, which is a popular variety sold in grocery stores. Chippewa is a heavy producer that does especially well in northern climates. Red Pontiac is a red potato with white flesh that is great for boiling and stores well. The Katahdin potato is adaptable to various climates and is considered the standard for storage potatoes. And then there's the Adirondack Blue potato, which has purple skin and purple flesh, making it fun to experiment with.

The Russet Burbank potato is a late variety that is the most widely grown potato in the US and is resistant to many diseases, including scab, blight, fusarium and blackleg. The Russian Banana potato is a yellow potato with a buttery flavor and is resistant to scab. French Fingerling potatoes are finger-like, yellow-fleshed potatoes with reddish-orange skin that are also resistant to scab.

Buying

When buying potatoes, look for potatoes that are heavy for their size, with smooth skins and no signs of discoloration or sprouting. Gently squeeze the potatoes; they should be firm without any give. If they're soft, they've lost moisture.

If you're buying bagged potatoes, take a minute to look at every potato; there's nothing worse than getting home and seeing rotten potatoes in the bag.

Sometimes, you'll get a potato that looks perfectly good on the outside, but, when you cut it, it has a ring of rot. That's black-rot disease and it can't be detected from external appearances. Do not compost diseased potatoes, either burn them or put them in the garbage.

There is a lot of controversy about eating potatoes that have green under the skin. The green is just chlorophyll, but it indicates the presence of a toxin called *solanine*. Healthy adults can process small amounts of this toxin just fine, but people who have chronic illnesses or are pregnant and children may have a harder time processing the toxin. Peeling the green parts off will remove some but not all of the toxin from the potato. The symptoms of solanine poisoning range from a mild stomachache to paralysis and, occasionally, death. The bottom line is to avoid eating potatoes that have large amounts of green on the skin or have started to sprout. If there is only a small area of green, it's probably safe to just cut out that piece and use the rest of the potato.

For preserving potatoes, buy them only when they're in season in your area. This way, you know you're buying fresh potatoes and not ones that have been sitting in storage.

Preserving

Keeping preserved potatoes on hand makes my life easier. I can have dinner on the table in 15 minutes or less when I serve Canned Potato Soup (page 229). This is a huge time- and money-saver during the rush of the school year. Or, in the time it takes everyone to put away their gear and come to the table, I can make Canned Potatoes with Herbs (page 231) to go with the meat I stewed in the slow cooker.

Before potatoes are preserved, they need to be scrubbed with a vegetable brush and rinsed well. Potatoes tend to darken after they've been cut, so keep a bowl of water with ascorbic acid or lemon juice in it next to the chopping board and put the potatoes in it as you cut them.

Canning

All potatoes can be canned using a pressure canner, but that doesn't mean that they are all good for canning. High-starch potatoes, such as russet, baking potatoes and any potato that tends to fall apart when boiled too long are not ideal for canning.

That said, I've canned many different varieties of potatoes and they were all good. Yes, some are starchier and you can see that in the jar, but they tasted good. If all you have is russets and you want to can them, then go right ahead; they'll be just fine.

Because potatoes are root vegetables and there's a possibility of them having C. botulinum on the skin, it is recommended that all potatoes be scrubbed, peeled and then rinsed again before they are canned. This is a safety recommendation, not a quality recommendation, so be sure to peel the potatoes before canning them.

The peels can be frozen and saved for making broth. It takes about 13 pounds (5.9 kg) of unpeeled potatoes to fill nine pint (500-ml) jars and 20 pounds (9.1 kg) of unpeeled potatoes to fill seven quart (1-L) jars.

To can potatoes, wash and peel them and put them in a bowl of water with ascorbic acid or lemon juice to prevent darkening. Cut the potatoes into ½-inch (12-mm) cubes; potatoes smaller than 2 inches (5 cm) in diameter can be left whole. Fill a stockpot halfway with water and bring it to a boil. Add the potatoes and cook them for 2 minutes. If the potatoes are whole, cook them for 10 minutes. After boiling the potatoes for the recommended time, pour off the water and loosely pack the potatoes into prepared jars. Add ½ teaspoon of salt to each pint (500-ml) jar and 1 teaspoon of salt per quart (1-L) jar. Pour fresh boiling water into each jar, leaving 1 inch (2.5 cm) of headspace. When the jars are filled, use the bubble remover tool or a chopstick to remove the air bubbles and recheck the headspace. Wipe the rims of each jar and put a lid and band on the jar. Process the jars, according to the manufacturer's instructions, at 10 psi (69 kPa) for 35 minutes for pints (500 ml) and 40 minutes for quarts (1 L). Adjust for altitude (page 25), if necessary.

Freezing

Potatoes need to be blanched or cooked in some other way before they are frozen. Potatoes can be frozen whole, in slices or mashed. Low-starch varieties will freeze better than high-starch varieties because they have a lower moisture content.

Whole potatoes will need to be blanched for 3 to 5 minutes, depending on how large they are (page 35). After they've cooled, they can be frozen whole or cut into pieces. Put the potatoes in a labeled freezer bag and store them in the freezer for up to 12 months.

For freezing mashed potatoes, prepare the potatoes as you would normally make mashed potatoes, but instead of using butter, use cream cheese. Put the potatoes in freezer-safe containers and put them in the freezer. When you thaw the mashed potatoes, they will be watery, but that will resolve itself when the potatoes get heated.

Dehydrating

Dehydrating potatoes takes a little more time than freezing them, but it's worth it to have shelf-stable potatoes in the pantry. Potatoes can't be dehydrated whole, but they can be dehydrated in slices or matchsticks, or even shredded.

Before dehydrating potatoes, scrub them with a vegetable brush and prepare a bowl of water with ascorbic acid or lemon juice in it. Cut the potatoes and put them in the bowl of water; sliced potatoes should be about ⅛ inch (4 mm) thick. If you're grating them, use the large holes on your box grater. The potatoes need to be blanched for 3 to 5 minutes (page 35) or they will turn gray while dehydrating. Once the potatoes are cool, lay them on the dehydrator trays and dehydrate them at 135°F (57°C) for 8 to 10 hours. Slices can be laid close to each other but not touching; grated potatoes can overlap some.

While any potato can be dehydrated, low-starch varieties dehydrate better than starchy varieties because they hold their shape better during the blanching process. Starchy potatoes, like russets, dehydrate better in grated, not sliced, form.

Fermenting

Potatoes can be fermented, but they do not keep long, so it's not something you would do for preserving potatoes. Fermenting potatoes is done for dietary reasons to make the potato easier to digest and to reduce the formation of acrylamide

when potatoes are fried or baked. Those reasons are really outside the scope of this book. However, I want to share how to ferment potatoes, in case that's something you want to do.

To ferment potatoes, prepare a 2 percent brine (page 51) and scrub the potatoes. Fill a wide-mouth quart (1-L) jar about halfway with the brine and, as you slice, grate or French-cut the potatoes, add them to the jar. Make sure that the brine completely covers the potatoes. Add a fermentation lid and let the potatoes ferment for up to 48 hours. Either use the potatoes right away or store them in the refrigerator for up to 5 days.

If you're just fermenting enough potatoes for tomorrow night's dinner, you can use any bowl or container that the potatoes and brine will fit in and not use a fermentation lid. As long as the potatoes stay under the brine, they'll be fine.

Preserving Potatoes Cheat Sheet

	Water Bath Canning (Not recommended)	Pressure Canning	Freezing	Dehydrating	Fermenting 2% brine
How to prepare	N/A	Chunks	Blanching required; sliced, French-cut, mashed or grated	Blanching required; sliced, French-cut or grated	Sliced, French-cut or grated
Flavors	N/A	Plain or with herbs	Plain or seasoned	Plain or seasoned	Plain
Length of processing	N/A	Pints (500 ml): 35 minutes Quarts (1 L): 40 minutes	—	8–10 hours	1–2 days
Storage life	N/A	12 months	8–12 months	12 months for plain; 1 month for seasoned	5 days

Canned Potato Soup

There are two soups that I make that everyone in my family loves; potato soup is one of them. It's easy to make fresh, but much faster to make using a canned concentrate. I prefer to use high-starch varieties, such as russet potatoes, for this recipe, as it makes for a creamier soup.

Makes 8 pint (500-ml) or 4 quart (1-L) jars

For the Soup

3 lbs (1.4 kg) peeled potatoes (about 5 lbs [2.3 kg] unpeeled), cut into 1-inch (2.5-cm) cubes

8 cups (1.9 L) vegetable or chicken broth, divided

2 cups (300 g) chopped onions, divided

2 tsp (6 g) garlic powder, divided

4 tsp (24 g) salt, divided

For Serving

1 cup (237 ml) milk per pint (500 ml) of soup

Grated cheddar cheese

Bacon bits

Chives

For the soup, to prepare the pressure canner, rinse it and its rack, place the bottom rack inside and fill the canner with a few inches of water, according to the manufacturer's instructions. Put the pressure canner on the stove over low heat while you prepare the jars. This is a hot-pack recipe, so the water in the pressure canner needs to be about 180°F (82°C) before you put the jars into the canner.

Wash the jars in hot, soapy water and check for any nicks or cracks in the jars. Rinse the jars in clean water and set them aside. Wash the lids in hot, soapy water, rinse them and set them aside.

Fill a large stockpot about halfway with water and bring it to a boil over medium-high heat. Add the potatoes, bring the water back to a boil and boil the potatoes for 10 minutes.

While the potatoes are boiling, put the broth in a small pot and bring it to a boil, then reduce the heat to keep it at a low boil. Fill a small stockpot or teakettle with water, bring it to a boil, then reduce the heat to keep it at a low boil.

Divide the onions among the jars: each pint (500 ml) needs approximately ¼ cup (40 g) and each quart (1 L) needs ½ cup (75 g). Divide the garlic powder and salt among the jars: each pint (500 ml) gets ¼ teaspoon of garlic powder and ½ teaspoon of salt and each quart (1 L) gets ½ teaspoon of garlic powder and 1 teaspoon of salt.

(continued)

Canned Potato Soup (continued)

After the potatoes have cooked for 10 minutes, drain the water and divide the potatoes among the jars. Be careful to not overfill the jars by packing down the potatoes. They should be loose in the jar.

Pour 1 cup (237 ml) of the hot broth into each pint (500-ml) jar or 2 cups (474 ml) into each quart (1-L) jar. Top off the broth, if needed, with the fresh boiling water, being sure to leave 1 inch (2.5 cm) of headspace. Remove the air bubbles, using a bubble remover tool or a chopstick, and check the headspace. Process the jars, according to the manufacturer's instructions, at 10 psi (69 kPa) for 35 minutes for pints (500 ml) and 40 minutes for quarts (1 L), adjusting for altitude (page 25) if necessary. Let the pressure canner depressurize naturally (page 25). Arrange a folded towel on the counter or table. Open the canner and remove the jars, using a jar lifter.

Place the jars on the towel, and let them cool for at least 12 hours. Remove the bands, check the seals and store the jars for up to 1 year. If any jars failed to seal, put them in the refrigerator to use first.

For serving, put the potato soup concentrate and the milk in a medium pot, stir to blend and heat the soup over medium heat for 10 minutes, until it starts to boil. Gently mash some of the potatoes. If you want a creamy potato soup, add more milk or broth and use an immersion blender to blend it. You can add more milk or broth, if needed to get the consistency your family likes. Garnish the soup with the cheese, bacon and chives.

Canned Potatoes with Herbs

In my opinion, potatoes need butter and salt; these two simple things enhance the potato flavor. But when you add rosemary to the mix, you've stepped into a whole new level of potato cooking. It's best to use lower-starch varieties, such as Yukon Gold, for canning these potatoes, especially if you want to fry the potatoes later. If you're going to use them only for mashed potatoes, higher starch russets will work just fine.

Makes 4 quart (1-L) jars

4 lbs (1.8 kg) peeled potatoes (about 6 lbs [2.75 kg] unpeeled), cut into 1-inch (2.5-cm) cubes

2 tsp (6 g) garlic powder, divided

1 tsp onion powder, divided

4 tsp (4 g) dried rosemary, divided

4 tsp (24 g) salt, divided

Serving Suggestions: *These potatoes can be added to soups, mashed with butter or cream cheese to make mashed potatoes or, for an easy side dish, drained and pan fried in butter, oil or bacon grease.*

To prepare the pressure canner, rinse it and its rack, place the bottom rack inside and fill the canner with a few inches of water, according to the manufacturer's instructions. Put the pressure canner on the stove over low heat while you prepare the jars. This is a hot-pack recipe, so the water in the pressure canner needs to be about 180°F (82°C) before you put the jars into the canner.

Fill a large stockpot about halfway with water and bring it to a boil over medium-high heat. Add the potatoes, bring the water back to a boil, then boil the potatoes for 10 minutes.

Boil more water in a medium stockpot or teakettle; this will be used for filling the jars.

While the potatoes are boiling, divide the spices among the jars; each jar should have approximately ½ teaspoon of garlic powder, ¼ teaspoon of onion powder, 1 teaspoon of rosemary and 1 teaspoon of salt.

After the potatoes have cooked for the 10 minutes, drain the water and divide the potatoes among the jars. Be careful to not overfill the jars by packing down the potatoes. They should be loose in the jar.

Pour the fresh boiling water into each jar, leaving 1 inch (2.5 cm) of headspace. Remove the air bubbles using a bubble remover tool or a chopstick, and check the headspace.

Process the jars, according to the manufacturer's instructions, at 10 psi (69 kPa) for 35 minutes for pints (500 ml) and 40 minutes for quarts (1 L), adjusting for altitude (page 25), if necessary. Let the pressure canner depressurize naturally (page 25). Arrange a folded towel on the counter or table. Open the canner and remove the jars, using a jar lifter.

Place the jars on the towel, and let them cool for at least 12 hours. Remove the bands, check the seals and store the jars for up to 1 year. If any jars failed to seal, put them in the refrigerator to use first.

Dried Scalloped Potatoes

I'm not sure there's any food more comforting than creamy, rich scalloped potatoes. Plus, they're a perfect way to use dehydrated potatoes. When you store the seasoning with the jar, you have a side dish that you don't have to fuss over. I like to use lower-starch potato varieties for this recipe, as the potatoes hold their shape better than higher-starch varieties.

Makes 1 quart (1 L)

For the Potatoes

¼ cup (30 g) dried milk

2 tbsp (15 g) cornstarch

2 tbsp (17 g) flour

1 tsp onion powder

1 tsp garlic powder

1 tbsp (0.5 g) dried chives

½ tsp dried thyme

½ tsp ground mustard

½ tsp salt

⅛ tsp ground black pepper

3 cups (130 g) dehydrated potato slices (page 226)

For Serving

1 cup (237 ml) vegetable or chicken broth

1¾ cups (414 ml) water

¼ –½ cup (30–60 g) grated cheddar cheese (optional)

For the potatoes, mix together the milk, cornstarch, flour, onion powder, garlic powder, chives, thyme, mustard, salt and pepper in a small bowl. When it's well-mixed, pour it into a small plastic storage bag.

Put the dehydrated potato slices into a wide-mouth quart (1-L) jar, and add the bag of seasonings to it. Put a tight-fitting lid on the jar, label it, including cooking directions, and store the jar for up to 12 months, although it's best if you cook the potatoes within 6 months.

For serving, preheat the oven to 350°F (177°C). Put the dehydrated potato slices in a casserole dish. In a medium bowl, whisk together the bag of seasonings with the broth and water until there are no lumps. Pour the mixture over the dried potato slices. Sprinkle the cheese on top, if desired. Bake the potatoes for 45 to 50 minutes, or until a knife can easily be inserted into the center. Let the potatoes rest for 5 minutes before serving them.

Frozen Hash Brown Patties

Making homemade hash browns for the freezer is incredibly easy, and I'm giving you more of a process than an exact recipe. Russet potatoes are usually used for hash browns, because they create a crispy outside and creamy inside. But they don't always hold their shape well. If holding shape is important to you, use a lower-starch variety, such as Yukon Gold.

Makes 6 patties per pound (453 g) of potatoes

For the Patties

Potatoes, scrubbed clean

Salt

Ground black pepper

For Serving

1–2 tbsp (14–28 g) butter, oil or bacon grease (per 4 patties)

Serving Suggestions: *Serve with ketchup, barbecue sauce or Canned Mexican Salsa (page 278).*

Preheat the oven to 350°F (177°C). Using a fork, poke holes in each side of the potato, about 8 times or so total. Put the potatoes on a baking sheet and bake them for 1 hour, or until you can easily pierce a potato with a knife. Let them cool at room temperature for 25 to 30 minutes. Transfer the potatoes to a bowl and refrigerate them overnight.

The next day, grate the potatoes using a box or cheese grater. There's no need to peel the potatoes; as you grate them, the skin will come off and you can either cut it up and add it to the mix or remove it.

Line a baking sheet with parchment paper and set it aside. Weigh the grated potatoes, then put them into a large bowl. Add ½ teaspoon of salt and ¼ teaspoon of pepper for each pound (453 g) of grated potato. Mix the potatoes and seasonings well.

To make the patties, I like to use a regular-mouth Mason jar lid and band. Oil the inside of the band and the lid so the potatoes don't stick. Put some of the potato mixture in the lid and gently push it down—but don't pack it tightly.

Turn the lid with the potato mixture onto the prepared baking sheet, then remove the band and then the lid. Repeat until of all the hash brown mixture has been used.

Put the baking sheet into the freezer and freeze the patties overnight. The next day, transfer the frozen hash browns to freezer containers and label them. Using a vacuum sealer and plastic bags or zipper freezer bags work well for these. The hash browns can be frozen for up to 12 months.

For serving, thaw the patties overnight in the refrigerator. Once thawed they will be crumbly; just pat them back together with your hands. Melt the butter in a skillet over medium-high heat. Put the hash brown patties in the pan and fry them for 3 to 5 minutes, until the bottom is browned; When the underside is lightly brown, flip the patty over and brown the other side. Keep flipping the patty until the inside is warmed through, being careful not to burn the outside.

pumpkins and other winter squash

From Acorn to Spaghetti

As a new gardener, I thought winter squash was grown during the winter and summer squash was grown during the summer. I excitedly planted pumpkins and spaghetti squash in late September in my fall and winter garden, only to have them die when the first freeze came in early December. I was so disappointed.

Then I found out that winter squash is named *winter squash* because it's stored over the winter, not because it's grown during the winter. All squash is grown during the heat of the summer, but unlike summer squash, winter squash matures on the plant before it's picked and stored away.

While these crops are usually grown for keeping in cold storage and eating fresh through the winter, they can also be preserved and used through the year to cover any gaps in your garden harvest.

Growing

All squash and edible gourds are members of the *Cucurbit* family, which also includes melons and cucumbers. This means that growing winter squash is going to be very similar to growing melons, cucumbers and summer squash. The main difference is that you're not going to harvest winter squash until it's fully mature.

Depending on the variety, winter squash can take up to 110 days to mature. If you have a short growing season, you'll need to start seeds indoors 6 to 8 weeks before the average last frost date and transplant them into the garden once all danger of frost is gone. If you have a longer growing season, you can sow seeds directly in the garden in the spring, after the last frost date.

Ideally, winter squash is harvested in fall before the first frost. However, if you live in a warm climate, as I do, timing winter squash to be ready in the fall can be tricky. For instance, if I want pumpkins to be ready to pick in September, I need to plant them in May. But by the time May is here, our daytime temperatures are already above 90°F (32°C) and will only get hotter. By the time August gets here, most of the garden is burned up, and that includes the winter squash. I've decided it's best to just accept the limitations of the plants and my climate and plant winter squash in the spring and harvest it mid-summer.

Winter squash plants are heavy feeders and like rich, well-draining soil. They need consistent watering of about an inch (2.5 cm) per week; make sure you water the soil and not the leaves. While they tend to have similar problems with pests and diseases as summer squash (page 291), some winter squash is more resistant to vine borers because their stems tend to be thicker and tougher.

One problem winter squash has that summer squash doesn't seem to have is pill bugs and earwigs boring inside the fruit. Because winter squash sits on the ground ripening for so long, they can become a buffet for bugs. Whenever I notice a winter squash forming on the vine, I put a piece of thick cardboard under it. This helps keep it off the soil and deters many of the bugs.

Most winter squash will grow on a vining plant rather than a bush plant. If you have limited space, use a trellis and grow them vertically. You'll probably need to help it out at the beginning by weaving the vines through the trellis.

Harvesting

Winter squash is ready to harvest when the skin is thick enough that it can't be pricked with a fingernail. If your fingernail can puncture the skin, it needs to stay on the vine longer. Don't worry, the puncture will heal as the squash continues to mature.

Because of our climate, I usually don't harvest winter squash until the plant begins to die. If you live in a cooler climate and are harvesting in the fall, you can leave the winter squash in the garden until the first frost. A light frost will kill the plant but shouldn't harm the fruit.

When you harvest the squash, use garden clippers and clip the stem an inch (2.5 cm) or so away from the squash. If you break the stem off the squash, you run the risk of wounding the squash and encouraging rot.

Once the squash is harvested, I wipe them down with rubbing alcohol. I've found that they'll store better for me if I do this. However, I do not wipe down squash I'm going to ferment. I add a small piece of squash skin to the ferment to add bacteria to the jar; I can't do this if I've killed the bacteria by wiping the squash with rubbing alcohol.

Winter Squash Varieties to Try

There are so many varieties of winter squash, it's hard to believe that they are all related. Some are familiar, some are beautiful and some are neither familiar nor beautiful. I'm going to share the varieties that I think are the most practical for preserving.

The most familiar winter squash is, of course, pumpkin and there are dozens of pumpkin varieties. Not all of them are edible, and some are edible but not tasty. Pie pumpkins are small, sweet pumpkins that are not stringy. They are your best choice for cooking and for making Frozen Winter Squash Butter (page 243). Pie pumpkins need about 100 days to mature. If you want to grow just one pumpkin variety and want pumpkins for both carving and eating, the Connecticut Field pumpkin is a good choice. These pumpkins are large enough to carve, but their meat does not get stringy, as does that of other large pumpkin varieties. It matures in about 110 days.

Spaghetti squash is our family's favorite winter squash. Because it is so stringy, it's not as versatile as other winter squashes are, but it freezes well and, when tossed with pesto (page 245), it makes a quick side dish. Spaghetti squash matures a little faster—in about 85 days— than pumpkins.

Waltham Butternut squash has a sweet, creamy flavor that is perfect for soup (page 240), although it can also be used to make Frozen Winter Squash Butter (page 243). This variety matures in about 100 days and is resistant to vine borers.

Pink Banana squash is both versatile and beautiful. This variety can be used in any recipe calling for pumpkin, butternut, acorn or other winter squashes, with the exception of spaghetti squash. Banana squash matures in about 100 days.

Acorn squash are smaller than other winter squashes, but each plant will produce five to eight squash. The plants are smaller than most other winter squash plants and mature earlier, 80 days, making it a good choice for those with limited space or a short growing season.

Buying

When buying winter squash, look for squash that has hard skin and is heavy for its size. It's good to be familiar with what the coloring of the squash is when it's harvested. For instance, acorn squash is a deep green color when harvested, but will turn orange the longer it's stored; you would want to avoid acorn squash that has any orange on it.

Try to buy squash that still has its stem attached and gently press where the stem attaches to make sure there's no sign of rot.

For preserving, buy fresh winter squash whenever it's in season in your area from the farmers' market; even if it's in the middle of the summer. Depending on the variety, it can be kept at room temperature for a month or two. If you buy winter squash offseason at the grocery store, you have no idea how long it has been stored.

Preserving

Because winter squash stores so well, there aren't many recipes for preserving them. Personally, I think it's best to focus on preserving winter squash in ways to make the most of your garden harvest, instead of trying to put up a year's supply like you would tomatoes.

As a general rule, you want to use varieties that have a string-less, mature pulp for preserving. Of course, this would not apply to spaghetti squash.

Before winter squash can be preserved, it will need to be rinsed and cut open. Remove the seeds and the stringy pulp surrounding them and peel the squash. If you are making a preserve, such as Frozen Winter Squash Butter (page 243) or fruit leather (page 44), you'll need to make squash puree first.

To make puree, I like to bake the squash after cutting it in half and removing the seeds. Put the cut sides down on a baking sheet and bake them at 350°F (177°C) until a knife will easily pierce through; this usually takes 45 to 60 minutes. Remove the squash from the oven and let it cool enough to handle. Then turn the squash halves over and scoop out the meat. Put it in a blender, and blend until it's smooth. You now have winter squash puree.

Winter squash puree can also be made by boiling cubed squash until they're soft; however, I find that it makes a very thin and watery puree, so I prefer to bake it.

Canning

Winter squash cannot be safely canned in a water bath canner. It can't be pickled like summer squash can, nor can it be used in canned jams, jellies or butters. It's not a big loss, as there are other safe and tasty ways to preserve winter squash.

Winter squash can be pressure canned, but only if it's cubed and loosely put into the jars. There are no approved ways of canning mashed or pureed winter squash. It takes approximately 10 pounds (4.5 kg) of winter squash to fill nine pint (500-ml) jars and 16 pounds (7.3 kg) of winter squash to fill nine quart (1-L) jars. Remember, you need the equivalent of two quart (1-L) jars to properly use the pressure canner.

To pressure can winter squash, rinse the squash, remove the seeds and peel it. Cut the winter squash into 1-inch (2.5-cm) cubes and set them aside.

Fill a medium stockpot about halfway with water and bring it to a boil over medium-high heat. Once the water is boiling, add the squash cubes, return the water to a boil and boil the cubes for 2 minutes. After 2 minutes, remove the pot from the heat. Transfer the squash cubes into the hot jars without mashing or packing down the cubes. Fill the jars with the cooking liquid, leaving 1 inch (2.5 cm) of headspace. If you need more liquid, use boiling water to make up the difference.

When the jars are filled, use the bubble remover tool or a chopstick to remove the air bubbles and recheck the headspace. Wipe the rims of each jar and put a lid and band on the jar. Process the jars, according to the manufacturer's instructions, at 10 psi (69 kPa) for 55 minutes for pints (500 ml) and 90 minutes for quarts (1 L). Adjust for altitude (page 25), if necessary.

Freezing

If you want to preserve winter squash puree or Frozen Winter Squash Butter (page 243), then freezing is the way to do that. I like to make a few jars of pumpkin butter to use during the fall. I also like to keep bags of puree to use for baking, in soups or for making fruit leather (page 44).

Winter squash needs to be cooked and mashed before freezing; spaghetti squash doesn't need to be mashed, just cooked. Winter squash will not hold its shape if you try to freeze it in cubes, so it's better to just go ahead and mash it.

To freeze winter squash, puree it (page 237) by either baking or boiling the winter squash and then pureeing it in a blender or mashing it. Put the puree in labeled freezer bags, put them in the refrigerator to cool overnight, then transfer the bags to the freezer and store them for up to a year.

Dehydrating

Winter squash can be dehydrated in strips or in a puree as fruit leather or roll ups (page 44). The strips need to be blanched before dehydrating; the puree is already cooked.

To dehydrate winter squash strips, wash the squash, cut it open, remove the seeds and peel the squash. Cut the winter squash into ¼-inch (6-mm) strips. Steam-blanch (page 33) the strips for 3 minutes, then put them in an ice bath to cool. Drain the water and pat the squash pieces dry. Lay the squash on a dehydrator tray and dehydrate it at 140°F (60°C) for 2 to 3 hours, then turn the dehydrator down to 130°F (54°C) for another 7 to 10 hours, or until the squash pieces are brittle and crisp. These can be stored for 6 to 9 months; however, if they're stored at room temperature, the flavor may change and deteriorate after only a month. Store them in the refrigerator, freezer or root cellar to preserve the quality.

To rehydrate, put the pumpkin strips in a bowl and pour boiling water over them. Let them soak for about 45 minutes, or until soft. They will have to be cooked to become tender.

Because the flavor may change, I don't preserve winter squash by dehydrating it for long-term storage. However, I do make Dried Spiced Winter Squash Chips (page 247) for snacking.

Fermenting

When fermenting winter squash, you want to use the freshest squash you can find, because winter squash continues to soften while being stored, even in ideal conditions. Old winter squash will usually make a mushy ferment.

Winter squash that are good for fermenting are the dense, sweet varieties, such as acorn, banana, butternut, Cinderella pumpkins, Hubbard, kabocha, Red Kuri and turban.

I've found that grated or thinly sliced winter squash works better in ferments than diced squash. Because winter squash tends to go limp when fermented, it's also a good idea to have other vegetables in the jar instead of just winter squash.

To ferment winter squash, rinse the squash, cut it in half and remove the seeds. Peel the squash and keep a couple of pieces back for inserting into the jar. Grate or thinly slice the squash and put it in a bowl. Sprinkle 1 tablespoon (18 g) of salt for every 2½ pounds (1.2 kg) of grated or sliced winter squash. Massage the salt into the winter squash; the squash should begin to release its juices.

Pack the squash and the juice in a clean wide-mouth Mason jar, put a weight in the jar and screw on a fermentation lid. Put the jar of fermenting squash on a plate or small cookie sheet to catch any overflow and store the jar out of direct sunlight. Let the squash ferment for 5 days, then do a taste test. If the squash needs to ferment more, replace the weight and fermenting lid and let the jar sit for up to 5 more days. When the squash has fermented to your liking, remove the weight and fermenting lid, add a regular storage lid and store the squash in the refrigerator for up to 1 year.

Preserving Winter Squash Cheat Sheet

	Water Bath Canning (Not recommended)	Pressure Canning (Pressure canned plain)	Freezing	Dehydrating	Fermenting 2% brine
How to prepare	N/A	Cubed	Blanching or cooking required; mashed or pureed	Steam blanching or cooking recommended	Grated or sliced
Flavors	N/A	Plain or as a soup base	Plain or seasoned	Plain or seasoned	Seasoned with herbs and other vegetables
Length of processing	N/A	Pints (500 ml): 55 minutes Quarts (1 L): 90 minutes	—	10–12 hours	5–14 days
Storage life	N/A	12 months	8–12 months	6 months for plain but can lose flavor and discolor after just 1 month; 1 month for seasoned	6–12 months

Canned Butternut Squash Soup

If butternut squash doesn't store well in your climate, use the summer harvest to make this canned butternut squash soup concentrate. This gives you a shelf-stable soup for those busy meals—all you need to do is puree, heat and add cream.

Makes 6 pint (500-ml) or 3 quart (1-L) jars

For the Soup

6 cups (1.4 L) water

1½ tsp (9 g) salt

1½ tsp (5 g) garlic powder

4 lbs (1.8 kg) butternut squash, cut into 1-inch (2.5-cm) cubes

1½ cups (240 g) chopped onions, divided

For Serving

¼ cup (59 ml) cream or milk or 1 tbsp (14 g) butter per quart (1 L) of soup

Dried Chili Powder (page 222), bacon bits, cracked black pepper or thyme

Serving Suggestions: *Serve squash soup with baguettes or other bread. It's also tasty paired with an autumn salad of mixed greens, chopped apples and walnuts.*

Note: *If you don't have an immersion blender, empty the squash into a regular blender, blend it until it's smooth, then pour the soup into a stockpot. Then continue following the serving instructions.*

For the soup, rinse the pressure canner and its rack, place the bottom rack inside and fill the canner with a few inches of water, according to the manufacturer's instructions. Put the pressure canner on the stove over low heat. This is a hot-pack recipe, so the water in the pressure canner needs to be 180°F (82°C) before you add the jars.

Wash six pint (500-ml) jars or three quart (1-L) jars in hot, soapy water and check them for any nicks or cracks. Rinse and set them aside. Wash the lids in hot, soapy water, rinse them and set them aside.

Put the water, salt and garlic powder in a medium stockpot and bring it to a boil over medium-high heat. Once boiling, add the squash, return to a boil and boil it for 2 minutes. Remove the pot from the heat.

Divide the onions between the hot jars: each pint (500-ml) jar should get ¼ cup (40 g) of onions and each quart (1-L) jar should get ½ cup (75 g). Transfer the squash into the hot jars without mashing or packing down the cubes. Fill the jars with the cooking liquid, leaving 1 inch (2.5 cm) of headspace. If you need more liquid, use boiling water to make up the difference. Remove the air bubbles using a bubble remover tool or a chopstick, and check the headspace.

Place the filled jars into the pressure canner and, following the manufacturer's instructions for your canner, process pints (500 ml) for 55 minutes and quarts (1 L) for 90 minutes at 10 psi (69 kPa), adjusting for altitude (page 25), if necessary. Let the pressure canner depressurize naturally (page 25). Arrange a folded towel on the counter or table. Open the canner and remove the jars using a jar lifter. Place the jars on the towel and let the jars cool for at least 12 hours. Remove the bands, check the seals and store the jars for up to 1 year. If any jars failed to seal, put them in the refrigerator to use first.

For serving, empty a jar of soup into a medium stockpot and blend the squash, using an immersion blender. Heat the soup over medium heat for 5 to 10 minutes, until it starts to boil, stirring often to make sure it doesn't stick to the pan. Stir in the cream. Garnish the soup with a sprinkle of chili powder.

Dried Pumpkin Pie Roll Ups

Kids need snacks, that's all there is to it. It takes a lot of nutrients and calories to grow strong bones and muscles. At least, that's what I tell myself as I see my kids devouring these pumpkin roll ups by the trayful. Fortunately, they're so easy to make that it's no problem at all to make several batches at a time.

Makes 2 dehydrator trays

2 lbs (907 g) cored and sliced apples

½ cup (118 ml) water

1 tbsp (30 ml) lemon juice

2 cups (474 ml) pumpkin puree (page 237)

½ tsp ground cinnamon

¼ tsp ground nutmeg

¼ tsp ground allspice

⅛ tsp salt

Line two dehydrator trays with silicone mats or parchment paper.

Put the apples in a medium stockpot with the water and lemon juice. Bring the mixture to a boil, then reduce the heat to medium and cover the pot. Cook the apples for about 15 minutes, until they are soft.

Once the apples are cooked, remove the pot from the heat and let the apples cool for 5 minutes. Transfer the apples to a blender and add the pumpkin, cinnamon, nutmeg, allspice and salt. Blend until the mixture is smooth; you want the consistency to be similar to applesauce.

Pour 2 cups (474 ml) of the fruit mixture onto a prepared dehydrator tray. Spread the mixture so that it evenly covers the tray. It should be about ¼ inch (6 mm) thick. Repeat with the remaining fruit mixture and dehydrator tray.

Put the trays in the dehydrator and dehydrate at 135°F (57°C) for 10 to 12 hours, although it can take longer depending on how thick the squash mixture is spread. After 10 hours, check the squash for doneness (page 44); if there are still moist spots, continue dehydrating the leather.

When the leather is completely dry but still pliable, cut it into strips, roll the strips up and store them in a jar with a tight-fitting lid.

Leave the jar of fruit leather on the counter and condition it for a week (page 42) before you put it into storage. Once it's conditioned, you can store the fruit leather in the jar for 4 to 12 months.

Serving Suggestions: *Snack on this right out of the jar! You can also cut the rolls into strips or designs to decorate or garnish cupcakes, cakes, pies, ice cream or cold drinks—you know, the kind with whipped cream on top.*

Frozen Winter Squash Butter

When fall arrives, we start craving all things pumpkin spice, and winter squash is a great way to fulfill those cravings. Since mashed winter squash cannot be canned, use the freezer to preserve pumpkin or winter squash butter.

Makes 4 half-pint (250-ml) jars

4 cups (948 ml) pumpkin or winter squash puree (page 237)

¼–½ cup (59–118 ml) water (optional)

½ cup (100 g) sugar

¼ cup (59 ml) honey

2 tsp (8 g) ground cinnamon

¾ tsp ground nutmeg

½ tsp ground cloves

1 tbsp (15 ml) lemon juice

Put the squash puree in a medium stockpot with a heavy bottom. Depending on how thick your puree already is—you want it to be the consistency of thick applesauce—you might need to add water to the mix. You can always cook it longer to reduce it if you add too much water. I would start with ¼ cup (59 ml) of water and add more, if needed.

Begin to heat the puree over medium heat. Add the sugar, honey, cinnamon, nutmeg, cloves and lemon juice. Mix well, bring the mixture to a boil, then reduce the heat to a simmer. If you don't reduce the heat, the mixture will spatter all over the stove.

Cook the mixture for 20 minutes, stirring often to make sure it doesn't stick to the bottom of the pan. The mixture should caramelize and turn brown and glossy. Once the squash butter is done cooking, remove it from the heat and let it cool.

Put the squash butter into freezer-safe containers, such as 4-ounce (125-ml) Mason jars or plastic freezer bags, and label the containers. If you're using glass jars, be sure to leave ½ inch (12 mm) of headspace for expansion. Put the containers of squash butter into the refrigerator to cool overnight, then transfer them to the freezer. Squash butter can be stored in the freezer for up to a year.

Serving Suggestions: *Spread squash butter on toast or biscuits, serve it with cream cheese and crackers or use it as a filling for turnovers or hand pies.*

Frozen Spaghetti Squash with Pesto

Spaghetti squash makes a fantastic side dish and, unlike other winter squash, keeps its shape when frozen. This is more of a use-what-you-have recipe than an exact recipe, so feel free to use whatever pesto you have on hand and add more or less depending on what your family likes. My favorite way to serve this spaghetti squash is under a piece of grilled chicken.

Makes 6 half-pint (250-ml) jars

4 lbs (1.8 kg) spaghetti squash

1 cup (185 g) Frozen Carrot Top Pesto (page 115), Frozen Radish Top Pesto (page 253) or Sun-Dried Tomato Pesto (page 289)

Preheat the oven to 400°F (204°C) and prepare a baking sheet by oiling it or lining it with parchment paper.

Wash the spaghetti squash, cut it in half and remove the seeds. Put the spaghetti squash halves cut-side down on the prepared baking sheet. Bake for 40 to 45 minutes, or until a fork can easily be inserted into the squash.

When the squash is soft, remove it from the oven and let it cool. Once it's cooled, remove the meat of the squash from the peel using a fork; the squash should come off in strings. Put the cooked squash in a large bowl and mix it with the pesto.

Put the seasoned squash into freezer-safe containers, such as Mason jars or plastic freezer bags, and label the containers. If you're using glass jars, be sure to leave ½ inch (12 mm) of headspace for expansion. Put the squash into the refrigerator to cool overnight, then transfer it to the freezer. Use the seasoned squash within 10 to 12 months.

For serving, thaw the squash in the refrigerator overnight. The next day, transfer the squash to a medium pan and heat it over medium heat for 7 to 10 minutes, or until the liquid has evaporated and the squash is heated through.

Serving Suggestions: *Garnish the spaghetti squash with Parmesan cheese, basil leaves or almond slivers. Serve the squash as a side dish for meat.*

Fermented Winter Squash Chutney

Any sweet winter squash such as butternut, acorn and banana squash will work in this recipe. The combination of winter squash, carrots, warm spices and the tangy flavor of fermentation is fantastic and just what you'd hope for from a winter squash ferment.

Makes 1 quart (1 L)

1½ lbs (679 g) grated winter squash

½ cup (56 g) grated carrots

2-inch (5-cm) piece of fresh ginger, grated

½ cup (70 g) raisins

1 tbsp (18 g) salt

2 cinnamon sticks

8 whole cloves

Filtered water (optional)

In a large bowl, mix the squash, carrots, ginger, raisins and salt. The vegetables should begin to release some of their juices and make their own brine.

Pack the squash mixture and juices into a clean wide-mouth quart (1-L) jar and add the cinnamon sticks and cloves. Make sure all the solids are covered in the brine; if there isn't enough brine to completely cover the solids, add filtered water and stir the mixture. Then put a weight in the jar and put on a fermentation lid.

Put the jar on a plate or small cookie sheet to catch any overflow. Set the jar in a cool place, out of direct sunlight, for 5 to 14 days. You can taste the chutney any time after 5 days. If it needs to ferment longer, replace the weight and fermentation lid and ferment for a few more days.

When the chutney is to your liking, replace the weight and fermentation lid with a plastic storage lid; store the chutney in the refrigerator for up to 9 months.

Serving Suggestions: *Enjoy the chutney straight from the jar or mix it with yogurt or sour cream for a tasty salad.*

Dried Spiced Winter Squash Chips

These light and airy winter squash chips are dehydrated at a high temperature to help create the crunch we so like in chips. And because they're sliced paper thin—I use my mandoline—we can omit the blanching step, which makes these easy to whip up for an afternoon snack.

Makes approximately 1 cup (237 ml)

1 tbsp (15 ml) melted coconut oil

1 tbsp (15 ml) maple syrup

¼ tsp salt

1 tbsp (12 g) ground cinnamon

½ lb (226 g) winter squash, cut into ⅟₁₆-inch (2-mm) or ⅛-inch (4-mm) slices

Mix the coconut oil, maple syrup, salt and cinnamon in a large bowl. Carefully add the squash slices to the bowl, and mix well to coat all of the slices.

Lay the squash slices on dehydrator trays. You can put the pieces close together, as they will shrink considerably. Dehydrate at 155°F (68°C) for 2 to 3 hours, or until the chips are brittle. The chips should easily snap in half when bent.

When the squash chips are fully dry, remove the tray from the dehydrator and let the chips cool for a few minutes. Put the dried squash chips in a glass jar with a tight-fitting lid, and label the jar. Use the chips within 1 month.

These are best eaten within a few days. If they lose their crispiness, they can be put into the dehydrator on high for 15 to 30 minutes to crisp them.

Serving Suggestions: *The chips can be crushed and sprinkled on salads or sandwiches or powdered and mixed with sour cream, yogurt or cream cheese to make a dip or spread.*

radishes
For Salads and Beyond

Most people think of radishes only as fun slices to add to a salad, but radishes can also be cooked. Cooking radishes mellows their flavor. Many people who don't care for raw radishes love cooked radishes.

Like carrots, the entire radish plant is edible. The tops can be used just like any other green (page 174). Radishes contain good amounts of vitamin C, vitamin K and vitamin B_6. And like onions, the roots contain antibacterial and antifungal properties: the spicier the radish, the more antimicrobials in the radish.

Growing

Radishes are the easiest vegetable to grow. If you're a new gardener or gardening with children, growing radishes will be a real confidence booster. Sow some seeds directly in the garden in the spring and, in a few weeks, you're eating radishes.

You can sow radish seeds as soon as the soil can be worked. If you live in the very far north, know that radishes need at least 6 hours of daily sun to correctly develop the root. Unless you want just greens, wait on planting radishes until you have 6 hours of daily sun.

Spring radishes will mature in about 30 days. You can certainly leave them in the ground longer than that, but they will eventually get tough and woody. To have radishes all season long, sow new seeds every 2 to 3 weeks during the growing season.

Radishes that mature in warm weather will be milder than those that mature in hot weather. While some radishes are naturally spicy, those that mature in the heat of the summer will have a bitter or fiery aftertaste. Ideally, you'll want to have the radishes mature before you have consistent 80°F (27°C) daytime temperatures.

For fall and winter radishes, plant varieties that take longer to mature so they mature in the cool of the fall. These longer-maturing radishes are also better for storing.

There are a few pests that bother radishes, with root maggots being the most likely. Root maggots are the larvae that hatch from the root maggot fly; you can deter them by covering the radishes with a floating row cover. That should also take care of any flea beetles that want to munch on the leaves.

Harvesting

Since radishes are at their best for a very short time, I like to make a note on my garden calendar of when I planted them and when they are supposed to be mature. If the root is plump, it's ready to be harvested. If radishes are left in the ground too long, they'll develop a sharp taste and pithy texture, and their roots will eventually split. The greens will be fine to use, but the roots won't be very tasty.

To harvest radishes, gently pull them up by their greens without smashing the greens. It's best to harvest the whole crop at one time, which is why having several small plantings is better than one large planting.

Once the radishes are harvested, wash them in cold water and cut the tops from the root. You can store radish roots in the crisper of the refrigerator for up to 2 weeks. Radish greens can be stored in the refrigerator for 5 to 7 days.

Radish Varieties to Try

Pick radish varieties based on when you want to grow them, spring or fall, and then how spicy you want them.

For spring radishes, Cherry Belle is the classic radish with bright red roots, mildly pungent flavor and a diameter of 1 inch (2.5 cm) or less. It's also shade tolerant and matures in about 24 days. White Icicle radishes mature even faster, in about 20 days, and have a mildly hot flavor. This variety requires deep, loose soil, since its white roots are about 6 inches (15.2 cm) long.

French Breakfast is also a spring radish variety; it has an oblong shape with a pink and white root. It's mildly spicy and withstands early summer heat better than other varieties. It's ready for harvest in about 24 days. The Malaga radish has deep purple skin, white flesh and a very mild flavor; it will mature in about 35 days.

Winter varieties take longer to mature and are larger than spring varieties. Daikon radishes, the mildest of the fall radishes, mature in 60 to 70 days. Sichuan Red Beauty radishes are red all the way through and are most often used in ferments. This variety matures in 50 days.

Many people don't realize that horseradish is a radish, but it is. It's a perennial that spreads, so it's often grown as an annual to prevent spreading. Horseradish takes 140 to 160 days to mature; plant it in the spring and harvest it in the late fall. Horseradish can be added to many foods as a seasoning.

Buying

When buying radishes at the farmers' market, look for radishes that still have their greens attached so that you get double the harvest. The leaves should be crisp and fresh looking and the bulbs should be firm and average size for the variety. You won't know if a radish is woody until you cut into it, but if you know what size that variety is supposed to be, you can avoid buying overgrown radishes.

If you're buying radishes from the grocery store, you might be limited to radishes that have already had their greens removed. Look for radishes that are firm and average size and avoid any that are soft or have mottled skin. If you find some that have the greens attached, you can use them as an indication of how the radishes were stored. Look for radishes whose leaves are fresh-looking with a crisp texture.

When you bring the radishes home, rinse them off in cold water and remove the greens if they're still attached. Store the roots in the crisper of the refrigerator for up to a week and the greens for 3 to 4 days.

Preserving

There are not many ways to preserve radishes, and that's fine because you probably don't need a lot of radish preserves. The radish preserve I make most is the Frozen Radish Top Pesto (page 253). I love filling my freezer with food prepared from an ingredient that most people would just compost or give to the chickens.

The root can also be preserved by pickling, either in vinegar or a saltwater brine, and it can be dehydrated to use as snack or to rehydrate later.

Canning

Radishes can be pickled in a vinegar solution, either by themselves or added to other pickled vegetables. I like to make small jars of Canned Sweet and Spicy Radishes (page 256) when I have radishes that I need to preserve and want them to be shelf-stable.

Radishes need to be sliced before pickling, but that doesn't mean they need to be in circles. Longer radishes, like daikon, are fantastic when they are French-cut and pickled like a cucumber spear.

Radishes cannot be preserved in a pressure canner either by themselves or added to other canned foods. I am assuming this is because they would turn to mush, and who wants that?

Freezing

It is not recommended that radishes be frozen, because they have a high water content and the texture will be very different from that of fresh radishes. However, they can be frozen. As long as you realize that the texture will be different and have a plan for using the frozen radishes, then freezing radish slices might be a good option for you if you have a huge radish harvest.

To freeze radish roots, remove the greens from the root and scrub the root in cold water. Don't peel the radish. Cut it into ⅛-inch (4-mm) slices. The thawed texture will be better in thinly sliced radishes than it will be in thickly sliced radishes. Blanch the slices for 2 to 3 minutes (page 35), then put them in an ice bath. When they're cool, drain the water and pat the slices dry with a clean kitchen towel. Put the slices on a baking sheet lined with parchment paper and put them in the freezer overnight. The next day, transfer the frozen radish slices to a labeled freezer bag and put them back in the freezer.

Radishes can also be made into condiments, like the Frozen Beet and Horseradish Sauce (page 76), and frozen in small quantities to use later.

The radish greens can be frozen just like any other green (page 177). Or they can be blended with herbs, seeds and oil to make a fantastic pesto that can be frozen (page 253).

Dehydrating

Even though I've read and reread preserving guidelines and publications from the USDA and have read the Ball® books on preserving many times, I've never seen suggestions for dehydrating radishes other than horseradish. In fact, none of the books that came with my three dehydrators mention dehydrating radishes.

This leads me to a couple of conclusions. The first is that it's safe to dehydrate radishes, since there are guidelines given for horseradish. The second is that dehydrated radishes are not very practical or useful.

However, if you have a lot of radishes and no plan to use them, then dehydrating them might be a good option for you. We don't dehydrate plain radishes for storage, but when we have extra radishes to use up, I do make Dried Spiced Maple Radish Chips (page 254) for snacking.

To dehydrate radish roots, remove the greens from the root and scrub the root. Slice the radishes paper thin or grate them and lay the pieces on a dehydrator tray. Dehydrate at 125°F (52°C) for 6 to 8 hours or until the pieces are brittle.

The greens can be dehydrated just like other greens and added to your jar of Dried Superfood Green Powder (page 179).

Fermenting

In my opinion, radishes were made for fermenting. The fermenting process mellows their flavor and retains their crispiness. Fermented radishes are truly wonderful.

Radishes can be fermented alone or with other vegetables. To ferment radishes, remove the greens and scrub the roots. You can slice or grate the roots, if you wish, or you can leave them whole. If you leave them whole, they will take longer to ferment.

Put the prepared radishes in a wide-mouth jar and pour 2 percent brine (page 51) over them. Add a weight and screw on a fermentation lid. Let the radishes ferment for 5 to 7 days. Put the jar of fermenting radishes on a plate or small cookie sheet to catch any overflow and store the jar, out of direct sunlight. Let the radishes ferment for 5 days, then do a taste test. If the radishes need to ferment more, replace the weight and fermenting lid, and let the jar sit for up to 2 more days. When the radishes have fermented to your liking, remove the weight and fermenting lid, add a regular storage lid and store the radishes in the refrigerator for up to 1 year.

The radish tops can be fermented using the method for greens (page 178).

Preserving Radish Roots Cheat Sheet*

	Water Bath Canning	Pressure Canning (Not recommended)	Freezing	Dehydrating	Fermenting 2% brine
How to prepare	Rounds or French-cut	N/A	Blanching recommended; slices or grated	Blanching not required; slices or grated	Whole, slices or grated
Flavors	Pickled savory or sweet	N/A	Plain or as part of a sauce	Plain or seasoned	Seasoned with spices
Length of processing	10 minutes	N/A	—	8–10 hours	5–7 days
Storage life	12 months	N/A	8–12 months	12 months for plain; 1 month for seasoned	6–9 months

*The radish greens can be preserved following the same guidelines as other greens (page 178.)

Frozen Radish Top Pesto

I've never understood people who say they don't like pesto, as if there's only one pesto. This radish top pesto is milder than some of the other pesto combinations I make and is the perfect pesto for people who think they don't like pesto.

Makes approximately 2 half-pint (250-ml) jars

½ lb (226 g) radish greens

1-inch (2.5-cm) piece of fresh ginger, sliced

5–10 cloves garlic

½ cup (118 ml) olive oil

2 tbsp (30 ml) lemon juice

¼ cup (33 g) sunflower seeds

1 tsp salt

¼ tsp ground black pepper

¼ cup (20 g) grated Parmesan cheese

Cut the radish greens from the radish root, rinse them and give them a spin in a salad spinner to remove any grit or pests.

Put the radish greens, ginger, garlic, oil, lemon juice, sunflower seeds, salt and pepper in a blender and blend until you have a paste with no large chunks. Stir in the Parmesan and blend again. Add more oil, if needed to achieve your desired consistency for pesto.

Put the pesto into freezer-safe containers, such as 4-ounce (125-ml) Mason jars or plastic freezer bags, and label the containers. If you're using glass jars be sure to leave ½ inch (12 mm) of headspace for expansion. Put the pesto into the refrigerator to cool overnight, then transfer the pesto to the freezer. Pesto can be stored in the freezer for up to a year.

Serving Suggestions: *Use as a condiment for pizza, sandwiches, bruschetta and flatbread wraps. Add to canned seasoned tomatoes and tomato paste to make a light pasta sauce.*

Dried Spiced Maple Radish Chips

Dehydrating radishes takes some of the bite out while leaving the zesty flavor. Combine them with spices and maple syrup, and you have a healthy snack your family will love. I use my mandoline to get paper-thin slices.

Makes 1 pint (500 ml)

2 tbsp (30 ml) maple syrup

1½ tbsp (11 g) ground cinnamon

1 tbsp (15 g) sugar

½ tsp ground cloves

½ tsp ground allspice

1 lb (453 g) radishes, cut into ⅟₁₆–⅛-inch (2–4-mm) slices

In a large bowl, mix the maple syrup, cinnamon, sugar, cloves and allspice. Carefully add the radishes to the bowl, and mix to coat all of the pieces with the syrup mixture.

Lay the radish slices on a dehydrator tray. Dehydrate at 125°F (52°C) for 8 to 10 hours, or until brittle. The chips should easily snap in half when bent.

When the radish slices are fully dry, remove the tray from the dehydrator and let the slices cool. Put the dried radish slices in a glass jar with a tight-fitting lid and label the jar. Use the radish chips within 1 month.

These are best eaten within a few days. If they lose their crispiness, they can be put into the dehydrator on high for 15 to 30 minutes to crisp them.

Serving Suggestions: *Serve as a snack or use as a chip with dip. These can be lightly crushed and sprinkled on salads or soups instead of croutons. They can also be powdered and mixed with sour cream for a dip or with cream cheese for a spread.*

Canned Sweet and Spicy Radishes

Zesty pickled radishes are a fantastic addition to salads, sandwiches, flatbread wraps and any other food to which you want to add a zing. If you want the radishes to retain their color, then use red wine vinegar instead of white wine vinegar.

Makes 4 half-pint (250-ml) jars

1½ cups (356 ml) white wine vinegar (5% acidity)

2 tsp (12 g) salt

1 cup (200 g) sugar

1 tsp black peppercorns

2 tsp (8 g) mustard seed

1 tsp red pepper flakes

1 lb (453 g) radishes, cut into ¼-inch (6-mm) slices

Prepare the water bath canner by filling it halfway with water and putting it on the stove to simmer. Check four half-pint (250-ml) jars for any nicks or cracks, wash them in hot soapy water and rinse them in hot water. Keep the jars hot until it's time to use them. Wash the lids in hot soapy water, rinse them and set them aside.

Combine the vinegar, salt, sugar, peppercorns, mustard seed and red pepper flakes in a stockpot and bring the mixture to a boil, stirring occasionally.

Divide the radish slices among the hot jars.

When the brine begins to boil, remove it from the heat and ladle it into the jars, leaving ½ inch (12 mm) of headspace. Remove the air bubbles with a bubble remover tool or chopstick and recheck the headspace; add more brine if necessary. Wipe the rims with a clean cloth, put the lids on the jars and screw on the bands. Place the jars in the prepared hot water bath canner, making sure that the jars are covered by at least an inch (2.5 cm) of water.

Bring the water to a full rolling boil and put the lid on the canner. Process the jars for 10 minutes, adjusting for altitude (page 17), if necessary. Arrange a folded towel on the counter or table. Remove the jars, using a jar lifter, and place them on the towel. Let the jars cool for at least 12 hours.

Once the jars are cooled, remove the bands and check the seals. If any jars failed to seal, put them in the refrigerator to use first. Wipe the jars with a clean cloth and store them for up to a year.

Serving Suggestions: *Use to add crunch to salads, on sandwiches and in flatbread wraps. The brine can be mixed with a little olive oil to make a salad dressing.*

Fermented Radish Slices with Dill

Fermenting radishes takes the sharp bite out of the radishes and in its place, you'll find a zesty, pickled crunch. Radishes will transfer the pink color from their skin to the brine, so don't be worried when the brine turns pink. Don't forget to reserve the radish tops for pesto (page 253).

Makes 1 pint (500 ml)

½ lb (226 g) radishes, cut into ¼-inch (6-mm) slices

Sprig of fresh dill

¼ tsp caraway seeds

½ tsp black peppercorns

1 tbsp (18 g) salt

1 cup (237 ml) filtered water

Put the radishes into a clean wide-mouth pint (500-ml) jar. Add the dill, caraway seeds and peppercorns to the jar.

Mix the salt into the water to make the brine. Fill the jar with the saltwater brine, making sure to cover the radish slices but leaving room for the weight and expansion.

Put a weight in the jar to keep everything under the brine and top the jar with a fermentation lid. Put the jar on a plate or small cookie sheet to catch any overflow. Set the jar in a cool place, out of direct sunlight, for 5 to 7 days. You can taste the radishes any time after 5 days. If they need to ferment longer, replace the weight and fermentation lid and ferment for a few more days.

When the radishes are to your liking, replace the weight and fermentation lid with a plastic storage lid and store the radishes in the refrigerator for up to 9 months.

Serving Suggestions: *These fermented radish slices add a nice crunch to salads, sandwiches and flatbread wraps. The radishes will lose their color to the brine, so be sure to use the brine, too, to get all the nutrients. The brine is tasty with fish or tuna salad or mixed with a little olive oil for a salad dressing.*

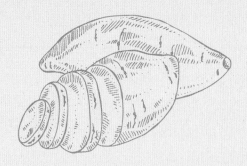

sweet potatoes
Not-Your-Average Spud

Sweet potatoes are often called *yams*, but true yams are rarely found in US grocery stores. They are mainly grown in tropical climates in Africa and South America. They are a starchy, dry tuber that has scaly skin and, usually, white flesh.

Sweet potatoes are a moist root vegetable with smooth, thin skin and, typically, orange flesh. They're a heat-loving plant that grows well in most climates of the US.

Sweet potatoes are incredibly nutritious and, even though they are sweet, they're lower on the glycemic index than Irish or white potatoes. If you're concerned about feeding your family nutrient-dense food, then sweet potatoes need to be on your menu regularly.

Growing

Unlike Irish potatoes, you don't plant a piece of the potato to grow more potatoes; instead, you plant sweet potato slips. You can either buy sweet potato slips or grow them from an organic sweet potato saved from a previous harvest or purchase. If you choose to grow the slips, you'll need to start 2 to 3 months before you want to plant sweet potatoes outside, and you need a seed potato.

To grow sweet potato slips, cut the seed sweet potato in half and put it cut side down in a jar with water. Some people suspend the sweet potato half in the jar by inserting three toothpicks about halfway down the potato, then resting the toothpicks on the rim of the jar. You can also just plant the sweet potato in soil with the pointy side up; don't put soil on top of the potato. In a few days, you'll notice buds and, in a few weeks, you'll have leafy greens and roots.

The greens are the slips, and they can be removed and planted. If a slip doesn't have roots attached to it when you remove it from the potato, put the slip in a glass of water and it will root. Plant the slips in loose, well-draining soil after all danger of frost has passed. Sweet potatoes like warmth, so they are the last thing I plant in our spring garden.

As the vine trails along the ground, it will often re-root itself at various places along the vine. This will make more roots and more sweet potatoes to harvest. I don't grow sweet potatoes on trellises, but you could if you have very little space; just know that you'll get a smaller harvest.

Sweet potatoes also grow well in large, deep containers where there's plenty of room for their roots to spread. If you have a short growing season, this allows you to bring them inside if you get a late frost at the beginning of the season or an early frost at the end of the season.

Sweet potatoes are an annual plant and, depending on the variety, they need 100 to 160 days to mature. In climates that don't freeze, sweet potatoes can be grown as a perennial. Even though sweet potatoes are more drought tolerant than most vegetables, you'll get a larger harvest if you water them regularly, especially once the roots start developing.

We have not had any pest or disease trouble with sweet potatoes. The foliage is so vigorous that it can usually thrive even when insects are eating the leaves. In some areas, the sweet potato weevil is a problem, as are wireworms and nematodes.

Most of the pests and diseases that plague sweet potatoes can be controlled by building healthy soil, rotating crops and attracting beneficial insects.

Harvesting

Unlike Irish potatoes, sweet potatoes have edible leaves that can be harvested once the plant has eight to ten leaves on it. I usually harvest the leaves to cook fresh, making sure to take only a couple of leaves from each plant. Unless the plants were huge, I would not harvest the leaves for preserving.

The roots can be harvested 3 to 4 months after planting and can be left in the ground until the first frost. Usually the leaves and ends of the vines will begin to yellow when the sweet potatoes are ready to be harvested.

To harvest the roots, use a garden fork to gently loosen the soil, being careful to not puncture the roots. Then lift the plants out of the soil; most of the roots will come up with the plants. The roots will grow 4 to 6 inches (10 to 15.2 cm) deep, so you might need to dig around a bit with your hand to find them all.

Handle the roots carefully, because they bruise easily. Dust the dirt off and let them sit in a warm, humid place for 10 to 14 days to cure. Even if you are not storing the sweet potatoes, they need to be cured in order to develop their sweet flavor. A good way to cure them is to place them, not touching each other, on a table in the shade.

Once they're cured, store the sweet potatoes in a dark place at 55°F (13°C) for up to 6 months.

Sweet Potato Varieties to Try

There are thousands of varieties of sweet potatoes worldwide and they can be orange, white, red or purple. Most people will need to plant an early-season variety in order to harvest before the first frost. All these varieties will mature in less than 110 days.

Beauregard originally comes from Louisiana but is widely adaptive and is a good choice for cooler climates, too. It produces a high percentage of marketable roots that have dark red-orange skin and orange flesh.

Centennial, another widely adapted variety with copper skin and pale orange flesh, is one of the most popular sweet potato varieties. It's often the variety sold in grocery stores. If you have heavy soil, Centennial will probably produce better for you than other varieties will.

Vardaman and Bush Porto Rico are both short-vine varieties that are good for gardeners who have limited space or are growing sweet potatoes in containers. They both have orange flesh and produce high yields.

Purple sweet potatoes tend to be drier and not as sweet as orange sweet potatoes; however, they are highly nutritious and a fun addition to the garden if you have room. Some purple varieties to consider are All Purple, Molokai Purple and Purple Delight.

The popular White Yam variety, also called Southern Queen or Choker, isn't a yam at all. It's a white-fleshed sweet potato and one of the oldest known sweet potatoes grown in the US. Frazier White is a high-yielding white variety that produces uniform roots.

Most yellow-fleshed sweet potatoes are more modern varieties. Heirloom yellow varieties, such as Nancy Hall, tend to be poor yielders. Hannah is a high-yielding yellow sweet potato that has a consistency similar to Irish potatoes.

Buying

Look for unblemished, firm roots with no soft spots or bruises; avoid any potatoes with signs of sprouting. Choose small to medium potatoes that are heavy for their size; large sweet potatoes can be fibrous.

Orange-fleshed sweet potatoes should have evenly colored skin, while the skin of potatoes with lighter flesh will be more mottled.

If you're buying local sweet potatoes, talk to the farmer about when he harvested them and whether he cured the potatoes before he brought them to market. If he didn't cure them, then you'll want to cure them before cooking them so their flavor is fully developed.

When you bring sweet potatoes home, store them in a cool, dark place for up to a week. Don't refrigerate sweet potatoes or you run the risk of them developing a permanently hard center.

Preserving

Once you've harvested sweet potatoes or have bought them from a local farmer, you don't have to rush to preserve them, as you do with other vegetables. The flavor and sweetness of sweet potatoes tends to develop more fully after they've been cured for at least a week.

Before preserving sweet potatoes, they will need to be rinsed and scrubbed with a vegetable brush.

There is a large range of texture for sweet potatoes. Some are dry and similar in texture to Irish potatoes, and some are moist and fibrous. You might need to play around with a few varieties before finding the variety that works best for your preserving needs.

Canning

To can sweet potatoes, you need to use a pressure canner, as there are no approved methods for canning sweet potatoes in a water bath canner.

It takes an average of 11 pounds (5 kg) of unpeeled sweet potatoes to fill nine pint (500-ml) jars and an average of 17½ pounds (8 kg) of unpeeled sweet potatoes to fill seven quart (1-L) jars. To safely use a pressure canner, you need to have at least four filled pints (500 ml) or two quarts (1 L) to process.

Choose small to medium potatoes that are mature but not so big they're fibrous. It's best to can them within 2 months of harvesting them. Sweet potatoes can be canned in water or in syrup.

To can sweet potatoes, boil them whole for 15 to 20 minutes, until they are partially soft but not cooked all the way through. Put the partially cooked sweet potatoes in a bowl to cool. When they are cool enough to handle, remove the skins and cut the potatoes into pieces that are no larger than 2¼-inch (5.7-cm) cubes.

Put the sweet potato cubes into prepared jars without mashing or packing them down. You can add 1 teaspoon of salt per quart (1 L) or ½ teaspoon of salt per pint (500 ml), if you wish. Pour fresh boiling water into each jar, leaving 1 inch (2.5 cm) of headspace. When the jars are filled, use the bubble remover tool or a chopstick to remove the air bubbles. Wipe the rims of each jar, and put a lid and band on the jar. Process the jars, according to the manufacturer's instructions, at 10 psi (69 kPa) for 65 minutes for pints (500 ml) and 90 minutes for quarts (1 L). Adjust for altitude (page 25), if necessary.

Be aware that sweet potatoes will get very soft when canned at home; they will also discolor a bit. This isn't a bad thing; it's just how it is. Canned sweet potatoes can be used as mashed potatoes or in pies. I like to add canned spiced sweet potatoes (page 268) to lentil soup. The spices add warmth to the soup and the potatoes fall apart and thicken the soup.

Freezing

Freezing sweet potatoes offers the most options for preserving them. They can be frozen sliced, cut in half, mashed or whole, depending on how you want to use them.

To freeze sweet potatoes, choose medium to large sweet potatoes that have been cured for at least a week. They need to be cooked until almost tender and then peeled. You can cook them in boiling water, in steam, in a pressure cooker or in the oven; just don't cook them all the way through. Let the sweet potatoes cool, then peel and cut or mash them. Put the potatoes into labeled freezer containers, seal the containers and freeze the sweet potatoes.

Sweet potato slices or whole peeled sweet potatoes can be dipped in a solution of ½ cup (118 ml) of lemon juice per 1 quart (1 L) of water to prevent darkening. To keep mashed potatoes from darkening, mix 2 tablespoons (30 ml) of orange juice or lemon juice into each quart (1 L) of mashed sweet potatoes.

To freeze whole sweet potatoes for serving as baked sweet potatoes, bake clean, unpeeled sweet potatoes for an hour at 375°F (191°C). Poke a few venting holes in them with a fork before baking them. When they are soft but not completely cooked all the way through, remove them from the oven and let them cool. When they're cool, wrap them in aluminum foil and put them in a freezer bag

to freeze. To serve, put the frozen or thawed sweet potatoes in an oven at 375°F (191°C) and bake for 30 to 60 minutes, or until they are cooked all the way through. Leave the sweet potatoes wrapped in the foil while cooking them.

Sweet potatoes can be stored in the freezer for 8 to 12 months.

Dehydrating

Because canning sweet potatoes makes them very soft, dehydrating them is a good option for shelf-stable sweet potatoes that will be firm when cooked.

There are a couple of different ways to prepare sweet potatoes for the dehydrator; one is the recommended way and one is the fast way. They both work fine for me, but long-term sweet potato storage is not one of my food-preserving goals. I don't know how well the methods compare to each other for dried sweet potatoes stored for more than 6 months.

The recommended way to dehydrate sweet potatoes is to peel the sweet potato and cut it into ¼-inch (6-mm) slices. If the sweet potato is 3 inches (7.6 cm) or more in diameter, cut the slices into half circles. Put the sweet potato slices into a bowl of water as you cut the potatoes. Blanch the sweet potato slices for 5 minutes, then put them into an ice bath made with ½ cup (118 ml) of lemon juice per quart (1 L) of water. When the sweet potatoes are fully cooled, transfer them to the dehydrator trays and dehydrate them at 125°F (52°C) for 10 to 12 hours.

The easy way to prepare the sweet potatoes for the dehydrator is to bake unpeeled sweet potatoes at 400°F (204°C) for 50 to 60 minutes, or until they are soft enough that a knife can be easily inserted. Remove the sweet potatoes from the oven, and let them cool until they are cool enough to be peeled; the peels should slip right off the potatoes, since they've been cooked. Once they're peeled, cut the potatoes into ¼-inch (6-mm) slices and dehydrate them just as you would if you were using the recommended method above.

Mashed sweet potatoes can also be dehydrated; many backpackers call it sweet potato bark. Spread the mashed sweet potatoes on fruit leather trays and dehydrate as you do slices. It probably won't take quite as long, though.

Fermenting

While fermenting sweet potatoes isn't as common as fermenting carrots, they respond and look very similar in ferments. You can use sweet potatoes as you would carrots in ferments.

Sweet potatoes can be grated, sliced, diced or French-cut before fermenting; it just depends on what you want to do with the ferment once it's done. To ferment sweet potatoes, scrub and peel the potato. Very thin slices or grated are my favorite

ways to cut them for ferments. Sprinkle the grated or thinly sliced sweet potato with salt at the rate of 1 teaspoon of salt per pound (453 g) of sweet potato. Massage the salt into the sweet potato as you do for sauerkraut (page 50). Then put the potatoes in a clean, wide-mouth jar, add a fermentation weight to keep the solids below the brine, screw on a fermentation lid and put the jar on a plate or small cookie sheet to catch any overflow. Let the potatoes ferment for 5 to 7 days. If you're making thick sweet potato slices or pickles, then put the sliced sweet potato in a clean, wide-mouth jar and pour a 2 percent brine (page 51) over them. Add a fermentation weight and lid and ferment for 5 to 7 days.

You can test the sweet potato ferment any time after 5 days. When it's fermented to your liking, replace the weight and fermentation lid with a storage lid, and store the ferment in the refrigerator for up to 12 months.

Preserving Sweet Potatoes Cheat Sheet

	Water Bath Canning (Not recommended)	Pressure Canning	Freezing	Dehydrating	Fermenting 2% brine
How to prepare	N/A	Cubed no larger than 2¼ inches (5.7 cm)	Cook until almost tender; slices or mashed	Blanching required; slices or puree	Grated, slices, spears
Flavors	N/A	Plain or seasoned	Plain or seasoned	Plain, seasoned, with fruit for fruit leather	Seasoned with herbs
Length of processing	N/A	Pints (500 ml): 65 minutes; Quarts (1 L): 90 minutes	—	10–12 hours	5–7 days
Storage life	N/A	12 months	8–12 months	12 months for plain; 1 month for seasoned	6–9 months

Dried Sweet Potato and Apple Roll Ups

If I could make a fruit leather out of every vegetable, I would, just to be sure I am well-stocked for my children's snacking needs. By adding low-glycemic vegetables, such as sweet potatoes, to fruit leather, you add interesting flavors while reducing sugar. For this recipe, I added cardamom to create a warm fall flavor, but if you don't have it, feel free to swap it out with another warming spice, such as nutmeg or allspice.

Makes 2 dehydrator trays

2 lbs (907 g) sweet potatoes, chopped

1 lb (453 g) apple slices

⅔ cup (158 ml) water

1 tsp ground cinnamon

½ tsp ground cardamom

2 tbsp (30 ml) maple syrup

Line the dehydrator trays with silicone mats or parchment paper.

Put the sweet potatoes, apples and water in a medium stockpot. Bring the water to a boil, then reduce the heat to medium and cover the pot. Cook the sweet potatoes and apples for 25 to 30 minutes, until they are very soft.

Remove the pot from the heat and let the mixture cool for 5 minutes. Transfer the mixture to a blender. Add the cinnamon, cardamom and maple syrup. Blend the mixture until it's smooth; you want the consistency to be similar to applesauce.

Pour 2 cups (474 ml) of the mixture onto a prepared dehydrator mat. Spread the mixture so that it evenly covers the tray. It should be about ¼ inch (6 mm) thick. Spread the remaining mixture on the second dehydrator tray.

Serving Suggestions: Snack on this right out of the jar! You can also cut the roll ups into strips or designs to decorate or garnish cupcakes, cakes, pies, ice cream or drinks with whipped cream.

Put the trays in the dehydrator and dehydrate at 135°F (57°C) for 10 to 12 hours, although it can take longer depending on how thick the fruit leather is spread. After 10 hours of dehydrating, check the leather for doneness (page 44); if there are still moist spots, continue dehydrating the leather.

When the leather is completely dry but still pliable, cut it into strips, roll up the strips and store them in a jar with a tight-fitting lid.

These don't last long in my house, so I don't worry about them sticking together. If you are making these for long-term storage, then put the sheet of fruit leather on plastic wrap or parchment paper before cutting it. When you cut the fruit leather, cut the plastic or paper with it and then roll it. The plastic or paper will keep the fruit leather from sticking to itself.

Leave the jar of fruit leather on the counter and condition it for a week (page 42) before you put it into storage. Once it's conditioned, you can store the fruit leather in the jar for 4 to 12 months.

Frozen Sweet Potato Balls

Sweet potato balls might just be our favorite way to preserve sweet potatoes. The combination of bacon, sweet potatoes and pecans reminds me of the "yams" we had growing up, but these taste better. I use pecans because we grow them; if you don't have a good source for pecans, try rolling the balls in another nut, or even breadcrumbs.

Makes approximately 50 balls

½ lb (226 g) pecan pieces, chopped

3½ cups (700 g) mashed sweet potatoes, made from 2 lbs (907 g) of sweet potatoes

¼ cup (28 g) cooked, crumbled bacon, made from ¼ lb (113 g) of bacon

2 tbsp (30 ml) orange or lemon juice

¼ tsp ground black pepper

1 tsp salt

½–1 cup (28–56 g) panko or bread crumbs (optional), divided

4 tbsp (59 ml) melted butter

Line a baking sheet with parchment paper and spread the pecans on a plate.

In a large bowl, stir together the sweet potatoes, bacon, orange juice, pepper and salt until they are well combined. The mixture should be the consistency of thick mashed potatoes. If it's not, add ½ cup (28 g) of the panko and stir it into the mixture. Let the mixture sit for 5 minutes, then check the consistency again. If needed, add the remaining ½ cup (28 g) of the panko, stir it in and let the mixture rest again.

To make the balls, scoop approximately 1 tablespoon (16 g) of the sweet potato mixture and form it into a ball about the size of a large marble.

Dip the ball into the butter, then roll it in the pecans to coat the ball. Place the ball on the prepared baking sheet. Repeat with the remaining mixture.

Put the baking sheet into the freezer and freeze it overnight. The next day, transfer the frozen sweet potato balls to freezer-safe containers in serving-sized portions. Zippered freezer bags or vacuum-sealed bags work well for this recipe.

To cook the sweet potato balls, preheat the oven to 400°F (204°C), and lightly oil a baking sheet. Put the frozen sweet potato balls on the baking sheet and bake them for 20 to 25 minutes, or until the outside has browned and the inside is warm.

Serving Suggestions: *Garnish the sweet potato balls with chopped fresh parsley and serve them with a sauce. To make a sauce, blend orange juice into Canned Banana Pepper and Mint Jam (page 217) or mix plain yogurt with powdered Dried Seasoned Onion Crisps (page 193) or Dried Spiced Winter Squash Chips (page 247).*

Fermented Sweet Potatoes with Ginger

A tangy yet sweet slaw is how I would describe this ferment. Of course, it's wonderful right out of the jar, but it also pairs well with pork carnitas tacos. Serve as a side dish for grilled meats and fish or even for a snack with cheese and crackers.

Makes 1 quart (1 L)

4 lbs (1.8 kg) sweet potatoes, grated

1 tbsp (7 g) grated fresh ginger

Juice and zest from ½ lemon

1 tbsp (18 g) sea salt

In a large bowl, combine the sweet potatoes, ginger, lemon juice and zest and the salt. The vegetables should begin to release some of their juices and make their own brine.

Pack the sweet potato mixture and juices into a clean wide-mouth quart (1-L) jar. Put a weight in the jar, make sure all the solids are covered in brine and put on a fermentation lid. Put the jar on a plate or small cookie sheet to catch any overflow.

Set the jar in a cool place, out of direct sunlight, for 5 to 10 days. You can taste the sweet potatoes any time after 5 days. If they need to ferment longer, replace the weight and fermentation lid and ferment for a few more days.

When the ferment is to your liking, replace the weight and fermentation lid with a plastic storage lid and store the jar in the refrigerator for up to 9 months.

* In the photo, the fermented sweet potatoes are shown in the jar on the left.

Serving Suggestions: *Enjoy straight from the jar or mix with yogurt or sour cream for a tasty salad.*

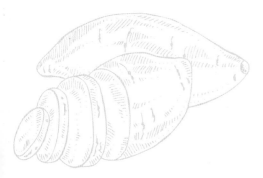

Canned Sweet Potatoes in Spiced Syrup

I love these spiced sweet potatoes for adding to lentil soup, but they also make a quick and delicious side dish when heated and mashed. You can also use these to make quick breads or pies.

Makes 5 pint (500-ml) jars

3 lbs (1.4 kg) sweet potatoes, washed

5 tbsp (75 g) sugar, divided

5 tsp (25 ml) lemon juice, divided

1¼ tsp (7 g) salt, divided

2½ tsp (10 g) ground cinnamon, divided

*See photo on page 267 (this recipe is shown in the jar on the right).

Serving Suggestions: *Mash these sweet potatoes to use in a casserole or as a side dish. These potatoes can also be used to make a quick fruit leather.*

To prepare the pressure canner, rinse it and its rack, place the bottom rack inside and fill the canner with a few inches of water, according to the manufacturer's instructions. Put the pressure canner on the stove over low heat while you prepare the jars. This is a hot-pack recipe, so the water in the pressure canner needs to be about 180°F (82°C) before you put the jars into the canner.

Wash five pint (500-ml) jars in hot, soapy water and check them for any nicks or cracks. Rinse the jars in clean water and set them aside. Wash the lids in hot, soapy water, rinse them and set them aside. Fill a teakettle or medium stockpot with water and put it on to boil.

Fill a large stockpot halfway with water and bring to a boil. Boil the sweet potatoes for 15 to 20 minutes, until they are just soft enough to make peeling easier. Use tongs to take the potatoes out of the water and put them on a platter until they are cool enough to handle. Remove the skins. Cut the potatoes into cubes no larger than 2¼ inches (6 cm).

While the sweet potatoes are boiling, divide the sugar, lemon juice, salt and cinnamon among the jars. Each pint should get approximately 1 tablespoon (15 g) of sugar, 1 teaspoon of lemon juice, ¼ teaspoon of salt and ½ teaspoon of cinnamon.

Carefully put the sweet potato cubes into the jars. Pour fresh boiling water into each jar, leaving 1 inch (2.5 cm) of headspace. Remove the air bubbles using the bubble remover or chopstick, and check the headspace.

Process the jars, according to the manufacturer's instructions, at 10 psi (69 kPa) for 65 minutes for pints (500 ml), adjusting for altitude (page 25), if necessary. Let the pressure canner depressurize naturally (page 25). Arrange a folded towel on the counter or table. Open the canner and remove the jars, using a jar lifter.

Place the jars on the towel, and let them cool for at least 12 hours. Remove the bands and check the seals. If any jars failed to seal, put them in the refrigerator to use first. Wipe the jars with a clean cloth, label them and store them for up to a year.

tomatoes

Creative Flavors for Everyone's Favorite Garden Veggie

Tomatoes are THE most popular home-grown vegetable in the US and for good reasons. Fresh-from-the-vine tomatoes are so much more flavorful than tomatoes that were picked early and shipped hundreds of miles.

There are hundreds of tomato plants to choose from. Some will be bushy plants that grow to be about 3 to 4 feet (91 cm to 1.2 m) tall, produce most of their fruit in a short time period and then fizzle out. hese are called *determinate* tomatoes. Other tomato varieties will grow all season long and can easily grow to 6 to 8 feet (1.8 to 2.4 m). They'll produce tomatoes until the first frost, if climate conditions allow. These are called *indeterminate* tomatoes. Most heirloom tomatoes are indeterminate varieties.

Tomatoes are typically classified as slicing tomatoes, canning or plum tomatoes and snacking or cherry tomatoes. Slicing tomatoes come in all sizes and colors, but are generally bigger than a ping pong ball and have a high-water content. These are the tomatoes we put on sandwiches and burgers. Canning or plum tomatoes are usually oblong in shape and have more flesh and less moisture than slicing tomatoes. This makes them great for canning

or sauce making. Snacking or cherry tomatoes are small tomatoes that you can often eat in one bite. These come in various colors and are great for salads and snacking.

Growing

Ideally, tomatoes should be grown in the ground, however, some varieties produce well in containers and in greenhouses. They can be started indoors about 6 weeks before your average last frost date and then transplanted in the garden after all danger of frost has passed. Tomatoes are very frost tender.

When you plant the tomato plants, dig a very deep hole and plant them all the way up to their first set of true leaves. All the little hairs on the stem will grow into roots that will feed and support the plant. When the plant is about 6 inches (15.2 cm) tall, you can prune the bottom set of leaves to keep the leaves from touching the ground.

Tomatoes are heavy feeders that like rich, loose soil with some compost worked in. If you plant indeterminate tomatoes, add more compost around the base of the plant midseason.

There are some determinate tomatoes that are bushy enough to not need any staking or cages, but the vast majority of tomatoes need support of some kind. If you're growing indeterminate varieties, make sure the support is tall and sturdy.

Tomatoes need to be watered deeply; this will encourage the roots to grow deep in search of water. If you water shallowly every single day, the roots will be content to stay close to the surface. When you water tomatoes, water the soil and not the plant. Like most fruiting vegetables, tomatoes are more susceptible to disease if the leaves are wet.

There are quite a few pests and diseases that can bother tomato plants. Many can be controlled by rotating your crops, which builds healthy soil, and not planting tomatoes where you've planted other nightshades, such as eggplant, peppers or potatoes, the previous season. Also, attracting beneficial insects, such as parasitic wasps, to your garden will help control some of the biggest tomato pests.

The pests that bother our tomatoes the most are tomato hornworm and tomato moth caterpillars and leaf-footed bugs.

I always start the season with just handpicking these pests off the tomatoes and dropping them in a bucket of soapy water. If that doesn't control them, I will use *Bt* on the plants to control the caterpillars and diatomaceous earth to help with the leaf-footed bugs.

Blossom-end rot can happen at any time during the season, but most often happens early in the season. This problem is caused by uneven watering or a calcium deficiency. Don't let tomato plants completely dry out before watering; they need about 2 inches (5 cm) of water a week. When it's hot, water them several times a week. Mulching around the tomato plants will help conserve moisture and reduce the risk of blossom-end rot. You can also add crushed oyster shells or bonemeal to the soil to give the plant calcium. *Blight* is the common name of several fungal diseases that quickly spread through tomato and potato plants, usually during wet weather. There are different symptoms for each type of blight, but the result is the same; left untreated, the plant will stop producing and die. If you notice leaves that are turning yellow or gray, cut them off and burn them. Then wash the garden clippers and your hands to help prevent spreading the fungal spores. Some of these fungal spores can survive in the soil over the winter, which makes rotating crops especially important.

Harvesting

There is much debate about when it's best to harvest tomatoes. My rule of thumb is after they've started turning from green to whatever color they'll be at maturity and before the birds find them. This means that we will pick tomatoes that are more green than red at times.

The great thing about tomatoes is that they will continue to ripen and develop their flavor once they've been picked, as long as they are kept at room temperature and not refrigerated. Of course, it's better if the tomatoes can be left on the vine to ripen, but if the birds are going to get them before they're ripe, you might as well pick them a little underripe and enjoy them.

Ripe tomatoes should easily come off the vine when they are gently pulled; this is especially true of snacking tomatoes. For larger tomatoes, you might need to clip the stem with garden shears but usually a little twist and a tug is all that's needed.

After harvesting, bring the tomatoes in the house and store them at room temperature.

Tomato Varieties to Try

The best tomato varieties are the ones that will produce well in your climate. There are hundreds to choose from, and each one has positives and negatives. If you're new to growing tomatoes, talk to your local gardening friends or folks at the local nursery to find out what grows well for them.

I try to plant tomato varieties that I know will do well in my area and then a few just-for-fun varieties. This ensures that I'll have plenty of tomatoes for eating fresh and preserving, while satisfying my desire to experiment and try new tomatoes.

Ideally, for canning you want tomatoes that have a small seed cavity and low moisture, as these tomatoes will hold their shape when canned. This makes paste tomatoes ideal for canning, but there are some slicing tomatoes that are thick, meaty and good for canning.

Amish Paste is an heirloom tomato that will mature in 80 days and produce high yields. San Marzano is also a paste tomato that matures in 80 days; it's a low-acid hybrid that is a traditional Italian favorite and a high-producer. These make excellent dried tomatoes. Marglobe is an heirloom slicing tomato that will mature in 73 days. It's a determinate tomato and will have large yields ripening at once, making it great for large-batch canning.

The best tomatoes for drying are small, solid and meaty varieties, which means snacking and paste tomatoes make good dehydrated tomatoes. Juliet is an indeterminate hybrid that will mature in 60 days. Juliet tomatoes are sometimes called *mini-Romas* because they look just like small Roma tomatoes; however, they set fruit in clusters and are heavy producers. Speckled Roman is an open-pollinated variety that will mature in 85 days and has a sweet, meaty flesh.

Green tomatoes are any unripe tomatoes; they all start out green. However, many people call tomatillos, which are a related, but different plant, "green tomatoes." Green tomatoes and tomatillos can be used interchangeably in recipes such as Fermented Green Tomato Relish (page 284), but tomatillos will not work well as Frozen Breaded Green Tomatoes (page 283).

Buying

When they're in season in your area is the best time for buying tomatoes. You should be able to find many different varieties at the farmers' market, compared to just a few varieties at the grocery store.

When buying tomatoes, look for ripe but firm tomatoes that have good color and weight for their variety. Avoid very ripe or soft tomatoes, unless you are using them for making sauce. If that's the case, try to find a farmer who will sell you his "seconds" at a bulk price.

I've found that many farmers in our area will pick and set aside however many pounds of tomatoes or other vegetables you want to buy for preserving. You just need to give them a few days' notice. This helps them and you speed things along on market day; don't be shy about asking for this.

Preserving

Tomatoes are not only the most beloved vegetable grown in home gardens; they are also the most loved vegetable preserved at home. Who can resist putting up jar after jar of salsa, marinara, soup and stewed tomatoes? But canning isn't the only way to preserve tomatoes and, in some cases, isn't the best way. Tomatoes can also be dehydrated, fermented and frozen.

When I bring tomatoes in from the garden, I sort through them and pull out the ones that still need to ripen more. For the rest of the tomatoes, I decide right then what to do with each ripe tomato.

Before preserving, the tomatoes will need to be rinsed and have any stems and bad spots removed. Depending on how they are being preserved, they might need to have the skins removed.

How to Remove Tomato Skins

Tomato skins tend to get tough and bitter when cooked, so it's important to remove them before canning. There are a couple of ways to do this: the correct way and the easy way.

The correct way to remove tomato skins is by blanching the tomatoes and then peeling them. To blanch tomatoes, fill a large stockpot about halfway with water and bring the water to a rolling boil. Cut a shallow X on the blossom end of each tomato, just deep enough to cut through the skin. When the water is boiling, dip the tomatoes in the boiling water for 30 to 60 seconds, or until the skin splits. Then dip the tomatoes in cold water to cool them enough to be handled.

The skins should slip right off the tomatoes when you gently pull them. If there is a spot that is stuck, use a paring knife to peel off the skin. If the skin is not coming off easily, put the tomato back into the boiling water for another 15 to 30 seconds.

Once the tomatoes are peeled, you can remove the cores and process them according to the recipe directions.

The other way to remove the skin is easier, but you sacrifice some texture in the process. I don't use this method when I'm canning whole tomatoes, but I do use it for all my other canned tomato recipes.

When we're sorting through the tomatoes after harvesting them, any tomatoes that I cannot preserve that day or the next get put in the freezer. I'll share exactly how I do this in the freezing tomatoes section. For now, just know that when they thaw out, the skins will slip right off.

Regardless of how you peel the tomatoes, the skins can be dehydrated using the instructions in the dehydrating section and powdered. I use this powder as a tomato bouillon and add it to soups, sauces and rice.

Some people also like to remove the seeds when they can chopped tomatoes; you can do this by running them through a food mill.

Canning

Canning tomatoes is most people's first experience with canning vegetables. It's no wonder, since tomatoes are the only vegetables that can be safely water bath canned without being pickled or made into a jam or jelly.

Because there's such a wide variety of acidity among tomatoes—some are low-acid and some are high-acid—it is recommended that tomatoes be acidified by adding citric acid, lemon juice, lime juice or vinegar to each jar. Tomatoes that are pressure canned have the same recommendation. For plain tomatoes, I prefer citric acid as it doesn't alter the flavor of the tomatoes.

The preparation for canning whole or halved tomatoes is the same regardless of whether they will be canned in a water bath canner or a pressure canner. You'll need approximately 21 pounds (9.5 kg) of tomatoes to fill seven quarts (1 L) or approximately 13 pounds (5.9 kg) of tomatoes to fill nine pints (500 ml).

The tomatoes need to be skinned and have the cores removed. If you froze the tomatoes, you'll need to put the skinned tomatoes and their juice into a stockpot of water and bring it to a boil before packing the tomatoes into the jars. This ensures that the tomatoes aren't cold and won't cause the hot glass jars to break. If you didn't freeze the tomatoes, they will be warm enough from the blanching and peeling that you don't have to worry about the jars breaking.

Before packing the tomatoes into the jars, add ½ teaspoon of citric acid or 1 teaspoon of lemon or lime juice to each quart (1-L) jar and ¼ teaspoon of citric acid or ½ teaspoon of lemon or lime juice to each pint (500 ml). You can also add 1 teaspoon of salt per quart (1 L) and ½ teaspoon of salt per pint (500 ml) to each jar. Pack the tomatoes into the prepared jars, pushing them down so they release their juices. Leave ½ inch (12 mm) of headspace.

Using the bubble remover tool or a chopstick, remove any air bubbles from the jars. Wipe the rims, add the lid and screw on a band. Process the jars in a water bath canner for 85 minutes or in a pressure canner at 10 psi (69 kPa) for 25 minutes; make sure to adjust for altitude (page 25), if necessary.

Freezing

Some people have strong opinions against freezing tomatoes but, for me, freezing tomatoes allows me to can tomatoes later and focus my canning time on fruits and vegetables that need to be canned right after harvesting.

I mainly freeze tomatoes for short-term storage, but every summer I make several batches of Frozen Roasted Tomato and Herb Sauce (page 287) for the freezer. These are easy to put together as I'm sorting through that day's tomato harvest.

It's recommended that tomatoes be blanched and peeled before they're frozen, just like when they are canned. I don't do this, since the skin will easily slip off the tomato once it thaws. To me, there isn't any difference in the flavor or texture of a blanched and peeled tomato and a tomato that has been frozen with the skin intact. Early in the tomato season, try freezing a few tomatoes both ways and decide which way is best for you.

To freeze tomatoes with the skins on, rinse the tomatoes and remove the core where the stem attaches. Put the tomatoes in a labeled freezer-safe container and put them in the freezer. If the tomatoes are large, cut them in half to fit more tomatoes in each container.

Thaw the tomatoes in the refrigerator overnight. If you used a plastic freezer bag to freeze the tomatoes, put it in a bowl before thawing. The tomatoes will release their liquid as they thaw, and if the bag has a small hole in it the liquid will leak out. The next morning, transfer the tomatoes and any juice to a bowl and remove the skins. Use as you would any other peeled tomatoes, but realize that the texture will be a bit mushier, which is fine for most recipes.

Dehydrating

Tomatoes are one of the easiest vegetables to dehydrate because they don't need to be blanched first. It's recommended that the tomato skin be removed before dehydrating. You can do that by following the previous instructions (page 272), but I don't.

It's also recommended that tomatoes be pretreated by dipping them in citric acid and water for 10 minutes before dehydrating. This is a quality and safety recommendation. There are two ways to make a pretreatment solution. Mix 1 teaspoon of citric acid in 1 quart (1 L) of water. The second option is to mix equal parts lemon juice and water.

To dry snacking tomatoes, cut them in half, pretreat them and put them skin-side down on the dehydrator trays. Dehydrate them at 125°F (52°C) for 8 to 10 hours. This is easy to do while sorting through that day's tomato harvest.

Larger tomatoes can be dehydrated in ¼-inch (6-mm), ½-inch (12-mm) or ¾-inch (19-mm) slices using the same procedure as for snacking tomatoes. The slices can be dehydrated plain for long-term storage (page 39) or with seasonings for short-term storage and snacking.

I dehydrate only snacking or cherry tomatoes for long-term storage and save the larger tomatoes for canning, because the smaller tomatoes are more work to can. I use the dehydrated cherry tomatoes to make Sun-Dried Tomato Pesto (page 289) and to make a powder to add to soups, sauces and rice. Don't forget: the peels can also be dehydrated and turned into a tomato powder.

Fermenting

Fermenting ripe tomatoes is challenging, since the sugars in the tomatoes can easily turn into alcohol, leaving you with tomato wine, which really isn't a thing. However, green tomatoes and firm snacking tomatoes make nice ferments.

To ferment green tomatoes, rinse the tomatoes and remove the core. You can slice or dice the tomatoes; I like to dice them and make them into a Fermented Green Tomato Relish (page 284). Put the cut tomatoes into a clean wide-mouth Mason jar and pour a 3 percent brine (page 51) over them. Add the fermentation weight and lid and put the jar on a plate or small cookie sheet to catch any overflow. Let the tomatoes ferment, out of direct sunlight, for 3 to 7 days. You can check the tomatoes any time after 3 days. If you're happy with the flavor, replace the fermentation lid with a storage lid and store the ferment in the refrigerator for 4 to 6 months. If the tomatoes need more fermenting time, return the fermentation weight and lid to the jar and give them another day or two.

Preserving Tomatoes Cheat Sheet

	Water Bath Canning (Needs to be acidified for safety)	Pressure Canning (Needs to be acidified for safety)	Freezing	Dehydrating	Fermenting (Green tomatoes or very firm cherry tomatoes) 3% brine
How to prepare	Peeling recommended; whole, sliced, puree	Peeling recommended; whole, sliced, puree	Peeling recommended; whole, sliced, puree	Peeling recommended; halves or slices	Cherry tomatoes, whole; green tomatoes, sliced or diced
Flavors	Plain or with herbs	Plain or with herbs	Plain, with herbs or as a sauce	Plain or seasoned	Seasoned with herbs
Length of processing	85 minutes for tomatoes in their own juices	25 minutes for tomatoes in their own juices	—	10–12 hours	3–7 days
Storage life	12 months	12 months	8–12 months	12 months for plain; 1 month for seasoned	4–6 months

Canned Tomatoes, Onions and Garlic

Most of my tomatoes end up in this recipe because I can use it to make so many other things. It can be added to soups or beans or it can be made into pasta sauce or salsa by adding just a few more ingredients. At the height of tomato season, this is the recipe I reach for.

Makes 6 pint (500-ml) jars

20 lbs (9 kg) tomatoes, peeled (page 272), seeded if desired (page 272) and roughly chopped

1 cup (150 g) chopped onions

8 cloves garlic, chopped

1½ tsp (6 g) citric acid or 6 tbsp (90 ml) lemon juice, divided

Serving Suggestions: *Add tomato paste and your favorite pesto to a jar of this to make a quick pasta sauce. Or add grilled peppers, cilantro and lime juice to turn a jar into salsa. These tomatoes can also be added to canned kidney or black beans, browned hamburger meat and chili powder (page 222) to make a quick chili con carne.*

To prepare the pressure canner, rinse it and its rack, place the bottom rack inside and fill the canner with a few inches of water, according to the manufacturer's instructions. Put the pressure canner on the stove over low heat while you prepare the jars. This is a hot-pack recipe, so the water in the pressure canner needs to be about 180°F (82°C) before you put the jars into the canner.

Wash six pint (500-ml) jars in hot, soapy water and check them for any nicks or cracks. Rinse the jars in clean water and set them aside. Wash the lids in hot, soapy water, rinse them and set them aside.

Put the tomatoes, onions and garlic in a large stockpot. Bring the tomato mixture to a boil, then turn down the heat and simmer the mixture for 20 minutes. If you want, you can use an immersion blender to break up the tomatoes a bit. Or you can leave them in larger chunks.

Put ¼ teaspoon of the citric acid or 1 tablespoon (15 ml) of lemon juice in each pint (500-ml) jar.

After 20 minutes, remove the stockpot from the heat and ladle the tomato mixture into the prepared jars, leaving 1 inch (2.5 cm) of headspace. Remove the air bubbles using the bubble remover tool or a chopstick and check the headspace.

Process the jars, according to the manufacturer's instructions, at 10 psi (69 kPa) for 25 minutes, adjusting for altitude (page 25), if necessary. Let the pressure canner depressurize naturally (page 25). Arrange a folded towel on the counter or table. Open the canner and remove the jars, using a jar lifter.

Place the jars on the towel and let them cool for at least 12 hours. Remove the bands, check the seals and store the jars for up to 1 year. If any jars failed to seal, put them in the refrigerator to use first.

Canned Marinara

Yes, there's a difference between marinara sauce and spaghetti sauce. Marinara sauce is a quickly cooked sauce with a sweet, bright flavor, while spaghetti sauce is slow cooked and has a more complex flavor. Traditionally, marinara has a bit of sugar in it. You can leave it out if you wish, but don't leave out the balsamic; that's what gives this marinara a richer flavor than is found in most marinara sauces.

Makes 6–8 pint (500-ml) jars

15 lbs (6.8 kg) tomatoes, peeled (page 272), seeded if desired (page 272) and roughly chopped

2 cups (300 g) chopped onions

10 cloves garlic, chopped

1 tsp dried oregano

2 tbsp (30 ml) balsamic vinegar

4 tbsp (60 g) sugar

1 tsp salt

½ tsp ground black pepper

2 bay leaves

6–8 stems (18 g) of fresh basil, tied together with twine

1½–2 tsp (6–8 g) citric acid or 6–8 tbsp (90– 120 ml) lemon juice, divided

Serving Suggestions: Serve over pasta or as a dipping sauce for bread, cheese sticks or Frozen Breaded Squash Fries (page 298).

Prepare the water bath canner by filling it halfway with water and putting it on the stove to simmer. Check eight pint (500-ml) jars for any nicks or cracks, wash them in hot soapy water and rinse them in hot water. Keep the jars hot until it's time to use them. Wash the lids in hot soapy water and rinse them.

In a large stockpot, combine the tomatoes, onions, garlic, oregano, balsamic vinegar, sugar, salt, pepper and bay leaves. Add the basil stems to the stockpot.

Bring the sauce to a boil, then turn down the heat and simmer the sauce for at least 20 minutes. If you want a thicker sauce, let it simmer until it is the consistency you like. When the sauce is ready, remove the stockpot from the heat and take out the basil stems and the bay leaves.

Meanwhile, put ¼ teaspoon of citric acid or 1 tablespoon (15 ml) of lemon juice into each jar.

Blend the marinara sauce with an immersion blender or ladle it into a blender and blend it in batches. Ladle the tomato mixture into the prepared jars. Remember to leave ½ inch (12 mm) of headspace. Remove the air bubbles from each jar with a bubble remover tool or a chopstick. Wipe the rims with a clean cloth, put on the lids and screw on the bands. Place the jars in the prepared hot water bath canner, making sure the water covers the jars by at least 1 inch (2.5 cm). If it doesn't, add more hot water. Process the jars for 40 minutes.

After 40 minutes, turn off the heat, remove the lid and let the jars sit for 5 minutes. Arrange a folded towel on the counter or table. Remove the jars from the water bath canner, using a jar lifter, and place them on the towel. Let them cool for at least 12 hours.

Once the jars are cooled, remove the bands and check the seals. If any jars failed to seal, put them in the refrigerator to use first. Wipe the jars with a clean cloth, label them and store them for up to a year.

Canned Mexican Salsa

Salsa shouldn't taste like vinegar, but most canned salsas do. By substituting bottled lime juice for vinegar, you get a salsa that has a fresh Mexican flavor instead of a vinegar flavor. Use a combination of sweet and hot peppers to make the salsa as hot or as mild as your family likes.

Makes 8–10 pint (500-ml) jars

10 lbs (4.5 kg) tomatoes, peeled (page 272), seeded if desired (page 272) and roughly chopped

2 lbs (907 g) onions, chopped

4 cloves garlic, chopped

1 cup (16 g) chopped fresh cilantro

¼ lb (113 g) chopped sweet or hot peppers, seeds removed from hot peppers if you prefer a milder flavor

1 tbsp (18 g) salt

1 tsp ground black pepper

2 cups (474 ml) lime juice

Serving Suggestions: *Use as a dip for tortilla chips. Add to tacos and burritos. Use to add a tangy punch to chili or taco soup.*

Prepare the water bath canner by filling it halfway with water and putting it on the stove to simmer. Check ten pint (500-ml) jars for any nicks or cracks, wash them in hot soapy water and rinse them in hot water. Keep the jars hot until it's time to use them. Wash the lids in hot soapy water and rinse them.

In a large stockpot, combine the tomatoes, onions, garlic, cilantro, peppers, salt, black pepper and lime juice.

Bring the salsa to a boil, then turn down the heat and simmer the salsa for at least 20 minutes. If you want a thicker salsa, let it simmer until it has reduced to the consistency you like.

When the salsa is finished simmering, remove the stockpot from the heat. If you want a less chunky salsa, blend it a bit using an immersion blender or regular blender. If you use a regular blender, you'll need to work in batches.

Ladle the tomato salsa into the prepared jars, leaving ½ inch (12 mm) of headspace. Remove the air bubbles with a bubble remover tool or chopstick and recheck the headspace. Wipe the rims with a clean cloth, put the lids on the jars and screw on the bands. Place the jars in the prepared hot water bath canner, making sure that the jars are covered by at least an inch (2.5 cm) of water.

Bring the water to a full rolling boil and put the lid on the canner. Process the jars for 35 minutes, adjusting for altitude (page 25), if necessary. Arrange a folded towel on the counter or table. Remove the jars, using a jar lifter, and place them on the towel. Let the jars cool for at least 12 hours.

Once the jars are cooled, remove the bands and check the seals. If any jars failed to seal, put them in the refrigerator to use first. Wipe the jars with a clean cloth and store them for up to a year.

Dried Cheesy Tomato Crisps

When I was testing recipes for this book, I pulled these out of the dehydrator, asked my husband and son if they wanted to taste them and left the room. When I came back, the last few tomato crisps were being eaten with cream cheese and crackers. I knew then that this simple recipe had to be shared.

Makes 1 pint (500 ml)

½ tsp citric acid

2 cups (474 ml) water

2 lbs (907 g) tomatoes, cut into ¼-inch (6-mm) slices

⅓–½ cup (80–118 ml) pesto (basil, carrot top [page 115] or radish top [page 253])

Grated Parmesan cheese

Mix the citric acid and water together in a large bowl, then add the tomato slices to the bowl. Let them sit in the mixture for 10 minutes.

Working with one tomato slice at a time, pat the slice dry on a clean kitchen towel. Spread a small amount of the pesto on top of a tomato slice and put it on a dehydrator tray. When all the tomato slices have pesto on them and are on the dehydrator tray, sprinkle the slices lightly with the Parmesan cheese.

Put the tray in the dehydrator and dehydrate at 135°F (57°C) for 8 to 12 hours. These will be leathery when dry. When the tomato slices are done, remove the tray from the dehydrator and let the slices cool for a few minutes. Put the dried tomatoes in a glass jar with a tight-fitting lid and label the jar.

These will need to be conditioned. Leave them out on the counter for 7 days. Shake the jar daily and look for condensation in it. If, after 7 days, there's no condensation, put the jar in storage and use it within a month.

Serving Suggestions: *These are fantastic on top of a Triscuit-type cracker with cream cheese. They can be crushed and used to garnish Frozen Summer Squash Soup (page 301). And, of course, they can be eaten just as they are.*

Canned Tomato-Basil Soup

This is a grown-up tomato soup, but not so grown-up that you can't dip your grilled cheese in it. The addition of basil and garlic create a soup that your family will be begging for on cold winter days.

Makes 4–6 pint (500-ml) jars

For the Soup

8 lbs (3.6 kg) tomatoes, peeled (page 272), seeded if desired (page 272) and roughly chopped

12 cloves garlic, chopped

2 cups (300 g) chopped onions

1 cup (100 g) chopped celery

½ cup (24 g) chopped fresh basil

½ tsp ground black pepper

4 tsp (24 g) salt

2 tbsp (30 g) sugar (optional)

6 bay leaves

For Serving

Splash of cream or milk

1 tsp butter

Serving Suggestions: *Garnish the soup with fresh basil and serve it with grilled cheese sandwiches or toasted baguettes. You can also use this as a sauce for Frozen Cabbage Rolls (page 103).*

For the soup, prepare the pressure canner. Rinse it and its rack, place the bottom rack inside and fill the canner with a few inches of water, according to the manufacturer's instructions. Put the pressure canner on the stove over low heat while you prepare the jars. This is a hot-pack recipe, so the water in the pressure canner needs to be about 180°F (82°C) before you put the jars into the canner.

Wash six pint (500-ml) jars in hot, soapy water and check them for any nicks or cracks. Rinse the jars in clean water and set them aside. Wash the lids in hot, soapy water, rinse them and set them aside.

In a large stockpot, combine the tomatoes, garlic, onions, celery, basil, pepper, salt and sugar, if desired. Bring the tomato mixture to a boil, then turn down the heat and simmer for at least 15 minutes. For a thicker soup, continue simmering for up to 60 minutes.

When the soup is done simmering, remove the pot from the heat. Use an immersion blender to blend the soup or transfer the soup in batches to a blender and blend it until it's smooth. Put a bay leaf in each jar and ladle the soup into the jars, leaving 1 inch (2.5 cm) of headspace. Remove any air bubbles from each jar with a bubble remover tool or a chopstick. Wipe the rims of each jar, top with the lids and screw on the bands.

Place the filled jars in the pressure canner and process for 20 minutes at 10 psi (69 kPa), adjusting for altitude (page 25), if necessary, and following the manufacturer's instructions for your canner. Let the pressure canner depressurize naturally (page 25). Arrange a folded towel on the counter or table. Open the canner and remove the jars, using a jar lifter.

Place the jars on the towel and let them cool for at least 12 hours. Remove the bands, check the seals and store the jars for up to 1 year. If any jars failed to seal, put them in the refrigerator to use first.

For serving, put the contents of the jar in a saucepan and heat over medium heat for about 10 minutes. Stir in the cream and butter to deepen the flavor.

Frozen Breaded Green Tomatoes

Fried green tomatoes are a Southern staple that are typically made at the beginning of the tomato season, when you just can't wait to eat a fresh tomato. But they can also be made at the end of the season when the tomato plants still have green tomatoes and an early frost is on its way. This is the perfect time to make a bunch of breaded green tomatoes for the freezer.

Makes 4–6 servings

For the Tomatoes

1 lb (453 g) green, unripe tomatoes, cut into ⅓-inch (8.5-mm) slices

1 tbsp (18 g) salt

1 large egg

½ cup (118 ml) buttermilk

¾ cup (98 g) all-purpose flour, divided

½ cup (60 g) cornmeal

1 tsp salt

½ tsp ground black pepper

⅛ tsp chili powder (page 222) (optional)

Pinch of cayenne (optional)

For Serving

Oil

For the tomatoes, sprinkle the tomato slices with salt and lay them in a colander to sweat for 20 minutes. Put a plate under the colander to catch the juices.

While the tomatoes are sweating, prepare a baking sheet by lining it with parchment paper and pull out three bowls. In one bowl, beat the egg and buttermilk together. In another bowl, place ½ cup (65 g) of the flour. In the last bowl, mix together the remaining ¼ cup (33 g) of flour, the cornmeal, salt, pepper and, if desired, the chili powder and cayenne.

After 20 minutes, gently pat the tomatoes with a clean kitchen towel to remove most of the salt and the excess liquid.

Working in batches, bread the tomato slices by dredging them in the flour to lightly dust them and then dipping them in the egg mixture. Lastly, press them into the cornmeal mixture and coat them well. Lay the slices on the prepared baking sheet.

When all of the tomato slices are coated, put the baking sheet in the freezer overnight. The next day, transfer the frozen tomato slices to a freezer container and label and date it. Use them within 6 months.

For serving, pour enough oil—whatever oil you normally fry in—into a skillet to have ¼ inch (6 mm) of oil in it. Heat the oil over medium-high heat until bubbles form around a wooden spoon or chopstick inserted into the oil; if the oil smokes, it's too hot. Put the frozen breaded tomato slices in the skillet and fry them for 3 to 5 minutes on each side. The crust should be crispy and golden brown.

Serving Suggestions: *Serve as a side for sandwiches, burgers or wraps. Serve with a dipping sauce, such as Frozen Cucumber Tzatziki (page 158).*

Fermented Green Tomato Relish

Fermented green tomato relish is a probiotic-rich version of salsa verde. When you serve this, squeeze some fresh lime over it for an authentic Mexican flavor. You can use green tomatoes or tomatillos interchangeably in this recipe.

Makes 1 quart (1 L)

1 lb (453 g) green tomatoes or tomatillos

¼ lb (113 g) chopped onions

2 cloves garlic, minced

1 tsp crushed coriander seed

1 tbsp (18 g) salt

1½ cups (355 ml) filtered water

Rinse and finely chop the tomatoes. If you're using tomatillos, remove the husks and wash them with a cloth to remove the sticky substance on the peel. Put the chopped tomatoes or tomatillos in a clean wide-mouth quart (1-L) jar.

Add the onions, garlic and coriander to the jar.

Mix the salt into the water to make the brine. Fill the jar with the saltwater brine, making sure to cover the tomatoes, but leaving room for the weight and expansion.

Put a weight in the jar to keep everything under the brine and top the jar with a fermentation lid. Put the jar on a plate or small cookie sheet to catch any overflow.

Set the jar in a cool place, out of direct sunlight, for 4 to 7 days. You can taste the relish any time after 4 days. If it needs to ferment longer, replace the weight and fermentation lid and ferment for a few more days.

When the relish is to your liking, replace the weight and fermentation lid with a plastic storage lid and store the ferment in the refrigerator for up to 6 months.

* In the photo, the relish is in the jar on the right.

Serving Suggestions: *Enjoy with tortilla chips. Add to eggs, tacos, burritos or burgers.*

Fermented Cherry Tomatoes

When cherry tomato plants are at their height of production, you'll be bringing in small tomatoes by the basketful. There are not many practical ways of preserving cherry tomatoes, so fermenting them is a great option. Use firm cherry tomatoes—those that are just barely ripe are perfect for this recipe—as mature cherry tomatoes tend to get mushy over time.

Makes 1 quart (1 L)

1 lb (453 g) cherry tomatoes

2 cloves garlic

6–10 fresh basil leaves

1 tbsp (18 g) salt

2 cups (474 ml) water

Put the tomatoes, garlic and basil in a clean, wide-mouth quart (1-L) Mason jar.

Mix the salt into the water to make the brine. Fill the jar with the brine, making sure to cover the tomatoes but leaving room for the weight and expansion.

Put a weight in the jar to keep everything under the brine and top the jar with a fermentation lid. Put the jar on a plate or small cookie sheet to catch any overflow.

Set the jar in a cool place, out of direct sunlight, for 3 to 6 days. You can taste the tomatoes any time after 3 days. If they need to ferment longer, replace the weight and fermentation lid and ferment for a few more days.

When the cherry tomatoes are to your liking, replace the weight and fermentation lid with a plastic storage lid and store the ferment in the refrigerator for up to 6 months.

*See photo on page 285 (this recipe is shown in the jar on the left).

Serving Suggestions: *Add the fermented cherry tomatoes to salads. Or mix them with goat cheese and pepper and spread the mixture on a baguette.*

Frozen Roasted Tomato and Herb Sauce

When I'm sorting tomatoes from the garden, there are always some that are perfectly ripe and can be preserved that day. I put those tomatoes in a baking dish with a few spices and pop it in the oven while I finish sorting through the rest of the garden harvest. By the time I'm done sorting, the tomatoes are ready to come out of the oven and get preserved for the freezer. It's almost like cheating.

Makes 3 half-pint (250-ml) jars

1–2 tbsp (15–30 ml) olive oil

3 lbs (1.4 kg) paste tomatoes

¼ lb (113 g) onions, cut into quarters

7 cloves garlic

1 tsp fresh thyme

1 tsp chopped fresh oregano

½ tsp chopped fresh rosemary

1 tbsp (1.5 g) chopped fresh basil

Preheat the oven to 350°F (177°C).

Oil a cast-iron skillet or baking sheet with olive oil and put the tomatoes, onions and garlic in it. Lightly brush the vegetables with the olive oil. Sprinkle the thyme, oregano, rosemary and basil on top of the vegetables.

Put the pan in the oven and bake the mixture for 45 minutes. When the vegetables are soft, remove the pan from the oven and allow the vegetables to cool.

There are several things you can do with the cooled vegetables, depending on how you want to use them. You want to remove the tomato skins; they should easily slip off. You can put the vegetables and herbs in a bowl and slice through them with two knives. Or you can blend the vegetables and herbs into a chunky or smooth sauce. Or you can leave them as they are.

Put the tomatoes and herbs in freezer-safe containers, label them and put them in the refrigerator overnight to cool. The next day, transfer the containers to the freezer and store them for up to a year.

Serving Suggestions: *Thaw the tomatoes and herbs overnight in the refrigerator. Serve them on bruschetta, rice or pasta. You can add them to hot sandwiches, such as grilled cheese. If you froze them in blended form, use them as a dipping sauce for Frozen Breaded Squash Fries (page 298).*

Sun-Dried Tomato Pesto

Pesto doesn't have to be green; it can be red, yellow or whatever color your dried tomatoes are. And tomatoes don't have to be dried in the sun to be used in this pesto recipe; any dehydrated tomato will work. I like to use dehydrated cherry tomatoes, since I always have an abundance of them.

Makes 1 cup (250 ml)

2 cloves garlic

½ cup (65 g) dehydrated or sun-dried tomatoes

¼ tsp salt

⅛ tsp ground black pepper

¼ cup (20 g) pecans, approximately 8 halves

Pinch of red pepper flakes

¼ cup (25 g) grated Parmesan cheese

⅓ cup (79 ml) olive oil

Put the garlic, tomatoes, salt, pepper, pecans, red pepper flakes and Parmesan in a small food processor. Turn on the food processor, and add the olive oil in a small stream through the feed tube. You might not need all of the oil, or you might need to add a bit more. Just use your judgment about how thick you like pesto to be.

When the pesto is well-blended, transfer it to a small jar and label it. This pesto will keep for a week in the refrigerator and for 12 months in the freezer.

Serving Suggestions: *Mix the pesto with pasta or add it to soups. This pesto also makes a good spread for sandwiches, flatbread wraps or toasted bread. You can also spread it on chicken before you roast it.*

zucchini and other summer squash

Making the Most of the Overachiever Veggie

Most people recognize yellow squash and zucchini as summer squash, but any squash variety that is harvested when it's small and has edible seeds and skin is summer squash.

Summer squash isn't the nutritional powerhouse that some other vegetables are, but they're low in calories and extremely versatile. Their mild flavor enables them to replace cucumbers in pickling recipes and just as easily replace pasta in pasta recipes.

While most of use eat just the fruit, the bloom and the leaves of summer squash are also edible.

Growing

Most people plant too many summer squash plants and harvest them too late, so they end up with crazy amounts of large overgrown squash that no one really wants. Fortunately, there's a tasty way to preserve overgrown squash (page 292).

Summer squash is very frost tender, so you'll need to plant after all danger of frost has passed. If you have a short growing season or are just anxious to harvest summer squash, seeds can be started indoors 4 to 6 weeks before the average last frost date. However, the seeds are large enough that they do well being direct seeded in the garden.

Squash flowers are either male or female and there are both types on each plant. The female flowers are the ones that have a tiny fruit at the base. A squash plant will usually bloom several male flowers first and then start producing female flowers. These flowers need pollinators to carry pollen from the male blooms to the female blooms; the early male flowers attract the pollinators and get them in the habit of visiting the squash plants. Then, when the female blooms open, there are pollinators already visiting the plant.

Sometimes the plants need a little help with pollinating, especially if you don't have many pollinators in your area. Whenever I notice that female flowers have bloomed, I use a small paintbrush to collect pollen from the male flowers and paint it inside the female flowers. I usually do this only at the very beginning of the season. After a while, the bees will find the squash flowers and visit them each day.

Squash plants are heavy feeders and like rich, well-draining soil. They need consistent water, about an inch (2.5 cm) a week. When you water squash, it's super important to water the soil and not the leaves. Squash often struggles with powdery mildew and wet leaves will make it even worse.

If you notice white powder on the squash leaves, that's powdery mildew. I usually cut the leaves off and burn them. This opens the plant up and allows airflow, which helps reduce future powdery mildew. Obviously, you can't cut off all the leaves but you can prune some. You can also sprinkle them with wood ash or spray with a mixture of 3 tablespoons (45 g) of baking soda and 1 gallon (4 L) of water.

Squash bugs and cucumber beetles can wreak havoc on summer squash. Because I'm concerned about harming the bees that visit squash, I don't use any pesticides, even organic ones, to control these. I simply pick them off and put them in a bucket of soapy water. I also check the undersides of the leaves for egg clusters and squish them. I'm OK with there being some bug damage on the squash leaves.

If you go out to your garden in the morning and notice that the squash plants are limp, as if they are dehydrated, then you probably have vine borers, which are the larvae stage of the vine bore moth. The moth lays eggs in the soil, and, when they hatch, the worms bore into the vines and eat them from the inside out. If you notice a little pile of what looks like sawdust on the plant's stem near the soil, a vine borer is inside. If you catch it early enough, you can dig the borers out of the stem and mound up more soil over the cut. I also like to inject the stem with some liquid *Bt* and pour some around the base

of the plant to kill any that are still in the soil. You can also try sprinkling diatomaceous earth or crushed eggshells around the base of the plant to kill the worms before they get to the stem.

Harvesting

Summer squash can truly be harvested at any time since the blooms, fruit and leaves are edible. However, most squash is harvested just after the bloom falls off or when the squash is about 6 inches (15 cm) long. This is when the skin and seeds will be most tender and digestible.

The more you harvest, the more the plant will produce, so harvest early and often. I think it's better to harvest squash a little early rather than a little late. There will always be a squash or two that are hiding under leaves that you miss when you harvest. Many times, these will grow to be 2 or 3 pounds (1 or 1.4 kg) each before you find them.

To harvest squash, cut it off the vine with a knife, leaving about an inch (2.5 cm) of stem attached. If you try to twist or pull it off the stem, you run the risk of damaging the plant or breaking off the top of the squash.

Summer squash has a high water content, so try to use harvested squash right away. If necessary, you can store them in the crisper of the refrigerator for a few days.

Summer Squash Varieties to Try

Summer squash either grows on a bush-type plant or a vining plant. Fortunately, summer squash is so prolific that you need only two to three plants to feed most families, which means you don't necessarily need to pick a variety based on available space. However, vining varieties tend to be more resistant to vine borers.

Probably the most popular summer squash is zucchini. Black Beauty zucchini is extremely prolific and takes about 55 days to mature. This zucchini can grow very large, very fast, so check them often. Golden zucchini is a yellowish-orange zucchini variety that produces in about 65 days. This variety tends to be a little sweeter than regular zucchini. Cocozelle zucchini is a dark and light green striped zucchini that matures in about 58 days. This variety isn't as prolific as the Black Beauty, but the plants are smaller so they take up less space. Also, the fruit stays tender as long as it's harvested at 12 inches (30 cm) or less.

When my husband was in graduate school, I shopped in a Mexican grocery store that was in our neighborhood. They sold a light green squash labeled *calabaza* much cheaper than regular green zucchini. This is a popular summer squash variety in Mexico, Texas and New Mexico that is usually called *Calabacita larga,* meaning long little squash, or *Calabacita bola,* meaning round little squash. The long variety and Gray zucchini are similar in color and both have tender skin and small seeds. The round variety is Tatume squash, which is a vining squash.

Another vining variety that would be good to grow if you struggle with vine borers is Cucuzzi squash. This squash can get up to 4 feet (1.2 m) long, but are usually harvested when they are 6 to 24 inches (15 to 61 cm) long.

There are far fewer varieties of yellow squash than there are of zucchini. For the most part, you have the choice of crookneck squash or straight-neck squash. They both mature in about 65 to 70 days, and they taste the same.

Patty Pan squash, also called *scalloped squash,* look like little flying saucers and come in several colors. These plants are prolific and are more compact than other summer squash varieties. They will mature in about 50 days.

Chayote is another vining squash that tastes similar to jicama. The vines can reach up to 50 feet (15.2 m) and need 120 to 150 frost-free days to mature. This variety is good for those who live in tropical or subtropical climates, as it is more resistant to powdery mildew than other summer squash varieties.

Buying

It's best to limit your summer squash purchases to small, firm squash. Most summer squash is going to get stringy and pulpy once it's 8 to 10 inches (20.3 to 25.4 cm) long. The optimal size for Patty Pan squash is about 3 inches (7.6 cm) in diameter; the skin gets thick and tough in anything larger.

The squash should be heavy for its size; if it's light, it has lost moisture and is probably pulpy inside. The skin should be glossy and bright and should be easy to prick with a thumbnail. Now, I wouldn't go around pricking squash at the farmers' market or grocery store—there will be other indicators to tell you if the squash is fresh—but thin skin is one of the things to look for. Withered or limp squash will have lost its texture and probably flavor.

Ideally, the squash would have been refrigerated or kept in cold coolers after it was harvested. If your buying from a farmers' market, ask the farmer when it was harvested and how it was stored.

When you get the squash home, you can store it in the crisper of the refrigerator for a few days, but it's best to use it as soon as possible.

Preserving

Because summer squash is picked when it's immature, it doesn't store well at all. My personal opinion is that summer squash is best enjoyed fresh. However, I do like to preserve it various ways to reduce my grocery bill and to make the most of the harvest our garden has given us.

Unlike tomatoes or corn, I would never go buy bushels of summer squash just to preserve it. I would, however, beg a local farmer to let a few zucchinis grow really big for me because my kids want fruit chews and my zucchini was wiped out from vine borers. Yes, I would do that.

Summer squash can be pickled in a vinegar brine and water bath canned. It can also be frozen, dehydrated and fermented.

Before preserving summer squash, rinse it and remove the stem. After that, it can be sliced, diced or grated, according to the recipe's instructions.

Canning

Squash is usually canned as a relish or pickle, just like cucumbers are. In fact, squash can be substituted for cucumbers in water bath canning recipes. They can also be mixed with fruit or other acids and made into a jelly or glaze (page 19). The flavor of summer squash is so subtle that it takes on the flavor of the other ingredients.

As a general rule, summer squash cannot be pressure canned; it's both a quality and safety issue. The pressure in the canner would turn the contents of the jar to a very dense mush. And there's no guarantee that the heat from the canner could penetrate all the way to the center of the dense mush. When foods are pressure canned, they need to be loosely packed, with room for liquid to be around every piece.

That being said, there is a tested recipe on the National Center for Home Food Preservation website for pressure canning tomatoes and zucchini together. There is also a tested recipe in the most recent *Ball® Blue Book® Guide to Preserving* for canning zucchini with other vegetables. However, I think it's easier to make Frozen Summer Garden Mix (page 170) than mess with the pressure canner and end up with mushy summer squash mixed in with firmer vegetables.

Freezing

To freeze summer squash slices, use small tender squash for the best results. Blanch the slices for 3 minutes (page 35). When the slices are cooled, put them on a kitchen towel and pat them dry. Then lay them on a baking sheet lined with parchment paper and put the pan in the freezer overnight. The next day, transfer the frozen squash slices to a labeled freezer bag and store it in the freezer for up to 12 months.

For grated summer squash, it's recommended that you grate the squash and blanch it for 1 to 2 minutes, just until it's translucent. Then pack it into freezer-safe containers. I prefer to not blanch grated squash. I've found that the thawed unblanched squash is just fine for my baking and fritter-making needs. I reserve the liquid that the thawed unblanched squash releases and add that to the baked goods, since I don't sweat fresh grated squash before baking with it. I drain the liquid when I use the unblanched thawed squash for making fritters, since I do sweat the fresh grated squash before making fritters. If you don't know, sweating the squash means to salt it and let the salt draw out the liquid in the squash.

Fully cooked squash can also be frozen, although it will be mushy when it thaws.

Dehydrating

Since summer squash can't be canned by itself, dehydrating it is a great way to have plain, shelf-stable squash to use through the winter. Every summer, I dehydrate summer squash slices to add to winter soups, and I dry grated summer squash to add to spaghetti sauce. Summer squash can also be added to fruit leather mixtures and dehydrated.

To blanch summer squash, cut the squash into ¼-inch (6-mm) slices and blanch them for 3 minutes. Drain the water, let the squash cool until it's cool enough to handle and lay the slices on the dehydrator trays. Dehydrate at 125°F (52°C) for 10 to 12 hours, or until the squash is leathery or brittle.

It's recommended that grated squash also be blanched before dehydrating; however, I've found that it doesn't really make a difference in the quality of the dried squash if I'm reconstituting it in water or soup.

I like to use the smaller squash for dehydrating in slices and larger squash for grating. I remove any large seeds from the squash before I grate it.

Fermenting

For fermenting summer squash, start with the freshest and smallest squash possible. Very small squash can even be fermented with their unopened bloom intact. Ideally, squash used for fermenting will be 1¼ inch (3 cm) in diameter or smaller; save the baseball bat–sized zucchini for dehydrating.

Because summer squash is a tender vegetable, the brine needs to be a little stronger. I use a 3 percent cucumber brine (page 51) for fermenting squash instead of the general 2 percent vegetable brine (page 51).

When you ferment whole, sliced or diced summer squash, put the squash in a clean wide-mouth Mason jar along with any spices and pour a 3 percent brine (page 51) over it. Add a weight and the fermentation lid and ferment for 5 to 7 days. You can ferment them longer, just check them every few days to see when they taste good to you. I like to make Fermented Squash Relish (page 302) for at least a week before testing it.

If you're fermenting grated squash, massage the salt into the grated squash like you would sauerkraut (page 50). Grated squash will ferment faster than whole, sliced or diced squash, so test grated squash after 3 or 4 days.

Preserving Summer Squash Cheat Sheet

	Water Bath Canning	Pressure Canning (Not recommended)	Freezing	Dehydrating	Fermenting 3% brine
How to prepare	Slices or diced	N/A	Blanching recommended; slices or grated	Blanching recommended; slices or grated	Whole, sliced, diced or grated
Flavors	Pickled or as a jam	N/A	Plain or added to other vegetables	Plain or seasoned	Seasoned with herbs
Length of processing	15 minutes	N/A	—	10–12 hours	3–7 days
Storage life	12 months	N/A	8–12 months	12 months for plain; 1 month for seasoned	6–9 months

Dried Squash Fruit Chews

If you like fruit chews, you'll love these chews made from overgrown zucchini. I know, it sounds weird, but once you have these, you'll never go back to regular fruit chews. And you'll be begging every farmer you know to call you when he finds an overgrown zucchini in his field. I usually use store-bought frozen fruit juice concentrate for this recipe. You can also use home-processed fruit juice, but you'll want to boil it down to concentrate the flavor.

Makes 1 pint (500 ml)

1½ cups (355 ml) fruit juice concentrate

1½ cups (355 ml) water

2 lbs (907 g) overgrown zucchini, seeded, peeled and chopped into 1-inch (2.5-cm) cubes

In a large stockpot, combine the fruit juice concentrate and the water. Bring it to a gentle boil over medium-high heat.

When the juice mixture is boiling, add the zucchini to the stockpot, turn the heat down and simmer the mixture for 30 minutes, or until the cubes are translucent.

Remove the pot from the heat and strain out the zucchini cubes. I like to pour the juice mixture through a mesh strainer with a clean bowl underneath to save the juice for a second batch.

Put the zucchini cubes on a dehydrator tray and dehydrate at 125°F (52°C) for 8 to 10 hours, or until they are chewy.

When the zucchini chews are done, remove the tray from the dehydrator and let the chews cool for a few minutes. Put the chews in a glass jar with a tight-fitting lid and label the jar. These will need to be conditioned (page 42). Leave them out on the counter for 7 days, shake the jar each day and look for condensation in it. If, after 7 days, there's no condensation, put the jar in storage and use the chews within 3 months.

Serving Suggestions: *Eat these as is for a snack or mix the chews with granola for a simple trail mix.*

Canned Squash and Pepper Chutney

Chutney or relish? I'm not sure what category this falls into, but we call it chutney to differentiate it from pickle relish. Regardless of its name, this dish is a fun and useful way to preserve zucchini. This chutney is mildly sweet, and since it uses white wine vinegar instead of distilled white vinegar, it has a tangy, not harsh, flavor. This chutney makes a great addition to meat dishes or can be used as a condiment. My favorite way to use it is to blend it up and use it as a dip or salad dressing.

Makes 4 pint (500-ml) jars

2 cups (474 ml) white wine vinegar (5% acidity)

½ cup (100 g) sugar

5 allspice berries, crushed

1 tsp black peppercorns, crushed

2 lbs (907 g) zucchini, finely diced or grated

½ cup (75 g) finely diced sweet or hot peppers, seeds removed from hot peppers if you prefer milder flavor

1 cup (150 g) chopped onions

Serving Suggestions: *Serve on sandwiches, tacos, flatbread wraps or hot dogs. This chutney is really great blended until smooth and used as a dipping sauce for fried foods, such as eggrolls and samosas. We also enjoy it with cheese and crackers.*

Prepare the water bath canner by filling it halfway with water and putting it on the stove to simmer. Check four pint (500-ml) jars for any nicks or cracks, wash them in hot soapy water and rinse them in hot water. Keep the jars hot until it's time to use them. Wash the lids in hot soapy water and rinse them.

Combine the vinegar, sugar, allspice and peppercorns in a nonreactive stockpot (such as stainless steel) and bring the mixture to a boil, stirring occasionally. If you don't have a mortar and pestle, you can use the back of a spoon and a bowl to crush the allspice and peppercorns.

When the vinegar mixture boils, add the zucchini, peppers and onions to the stockpot. Bring the brine back to a boil, then boil the mixture gently for 5 minutes.

After 5 minutes, remove the pot from the heat and ladle the chutney into the prepared jars, leaving ½ inch (12 mm) of headspace. Remove the air bubbles with a bubble remover tool or chopstick and recheck the headspace; add more brine if necessary. Wipe the rims with a clean cloth, put the lids on the jars and screw on the bands. Place the jars in the prepared hot water bath canner, making sure that the jars are covered by at least an inch (2.5 cm) of water.

Bring the water to a full rolling boil, and put the lid on the canner. Process the jars for 15 minutes, adjusting for altitude (page 25), if necessary. Arrange a folded towel on the counter or table. Remove the jars, using a jar lifter, and place them on the towel. Let them cool for at least 12 hours.

Once the jars are cooled, remove the bands and check the seals. If any jars failed to seal, put them in the refrigerator to use first. Wipe the jars with a clean cloth and store the chutney for up to a year.

Frozen Breaded Squash Fries

At the height of zucchini season, breaded fries become one of my go-to sides for burgers and snacks. By freezing them, I can serve them the rest of the year, too. This recipe is best made with small zucchini that are under 2 inches (5 cm) in diameter.

Makes 6 servings

2 lbs (907 g) small zucchini, cut lengthwise into ½-inch (12-mm) strips

2 tbsp (36 g) + 2 tsp (12 g) salt, divided

2 eggs

2 cups (112 g) panko or plain bread crumbs

½ cup (50 g) grated Parmesan cheese

1 tbsp (9 g) garlic powder

½ tsp ground black pepper

Sweat the zucchini: put it in a colander with a bowl under it, add the 2 tablespoons (36 g) of salt and toss to coat all of the pieces. The salt will draw out the water in the zucchini, which will make a crispier fry. Let the zucchini sweat for 20 to 30 minutes.

Line a large baking sheet with parchment paper.

Beat the eggs in a medium bowl and set it aside. In another bowl, mix the panko, Parmesan, garlic powder, the remaining salt and the pepper.

When the zucchini fries are done sweating, rinse them with fresh water and blot them dry with a clean towel.

Working in small batches, dip the zucchini fries in the eggs, then dredge them in the panko mixture, pressing to coat them. Lay them on the prepared baking sheet.

When all the fries are coated, put the baking sheet in the freezer overnight. The next day, transfer the fries to a freezer container and label it. Vacuum sealer bags and plastic freezer bags work great for this recipe. Use the fries within 6 months.

To cook the fries, preheat the oven to 425°F (218°C). Place a cooling rack in a rimmed baking sheet and oil the rack. You can also bake the fries directly on an oiled baking sheet, but they will be less crispy. Bake the fries for 25 to 30 minutes, or until they are browned and crispy.

Serving Suggestions: *Garnish with chopped fresh parsley or basil. Serve with dipping sauces, such as Frozen Cucumber Tzatziki (page 158) or Canned Marinara (page 277).*

Frozen Summer Squash Soup

I love summer squash soup, a creamy soup that reminds me a of a blended creamy broccoli soup, a true comfort food. Besides being a comfort food, summer squash soup is a great way to preserve a lot of summer squash and fill your freezer with ready–made food.

Makes 4 half-pint (250-ml) jars

For the Soup

3 tbsp (45 ml) olive oil

1 cup (150 g) chopped onions

6–8 cloves garlic, roughly chopped

½ tsp chopped fresh thyme

1 tsp chopped fresh rosemary

2 lbs (907 g) summer squash, cut into ¼-inch (6-mm) slices

1½ tsp (9 g) salt

½ tsp ground black pepper

For Serving

¼ cup (59 ml) cream or milk (optional) per 2 cups (474 ml) of soup

In a medium stockpot over medium heat, heat the olive oil. Sauté the onions and garlic in the oil for 5 minutes, until the onions are translucent. Add the thyme and rosemary and cook for just a minute or two, until the spices begin to release their aroma.

Add the summer squash, salt and pepper to the pot and stir well. Cover the pot and cook the squash over medium-low heat for 15 to 20 minutes, until the squash is soft.

Remove the pot from the heat and blend the soup until it's smooth. You can use an immersion blender or transfer the hot soup in batches to a blender. Let the soup cool, put it into serving-sized freezer-safe containers and label the containers. If you're using glass jars, be sure to leave 1 inch (2.5 cm) of headspace for expansion. Put the soup into the refrigerator to cool overnight, then transfer it to the freezer. The soup can be stored in the freezer for up to a year.

For serving, thaw the soup in the refrigerator overnight. Heat the soup over medium heat in a medium stockpot for 10 minutes, until the soup comes to a boil. Stir in the cream, if you are using it.

Serving Suggestions: *Garnish with chopped herbs such as cilantro or basil, grated Parmesan or croutons.*

Fermented Squash Relish

This is a savory relish that is reminiscent of sour pickle relish without the vinegar flavor. You can make this ferment spicy or mild, depending on what peppers you choose to use. The cloves are the secret ingredient in this fermented summer squash relish; they add a rich spiced flavor that mellows the ferment.

Makes 1 quart (1 L)

¾ lb (340 g) diced zucchini or yellow squash

¼ cup (30 g) diced sweet or hot peppers, seeds removed from hot peppers if you prefer milder flavor

¼ cup (40 g) chopped onion

5 black peppercorns

¼ tsp mustard seed

2 cloves

1 tbsp (18 g) salt

2 cups (474 ml) filtered water

Put the zucchini, peppers and onion in a 1-quart (1-L) jar. Add the peppercorns, mustard seed and cloves to the jar.

Mix the salt into the water to make the brine. Fill the jar with the saltwater brine, making sure to cover the vegetables but leaving room for the weight and expansion.

Put a weight in the jar to keep everything under the brine and top the jar with a fermentation lid. Put the jar on a plate or small cookie sheet to catch any overflow.

Set the jar in a cool place, out of direct sunlight, for 8 to 14 days. You can taste the relish any time after 8 days. If it needs to ferment longer, replace the weight and fermentation lid and ferment for a few more days.

When the relish is to your liking, replace the weight and fermentation lid with a plastic storage lid. Store the relish in the refrigerator for up to 9 months.

* In the photo, the squash relish is in the jar on the right.

Serving Suggestions: *This relish is great on hot dogs or served with link sausage. Use it to top hamburgers or add it to a flatbread wrap.*

Canned Rosemary–Squash Glaze

Summer squash doesn't have much flavor on its own, which makes it great for combining with flavorful herbs and fruits to make a glaze. I like to use organic fruit for this recipe, so I can use the orange peel to flavor the glaze and shred the apple with its skin. This glaze has a distinct rosemary flavor with a tangy punch provided by the oranges and apple cider vinegar, making it perfect for chicken, pork and salmon.

Makes 8 half-pint (250-ml) jars

5 cups (620 g) shredded zucchini or yellow squash

½ lb (226 g) thinly sliced oranges, peel chopped and placed in a muslin bag, if desired

1 cup (130 g) shredded tart apple

2 tbsp (15 g) chopped fresh ginger

½ cup (118 ml) apple cider vinegar

1 tbsp (3 g) chopped fresh rosemary

4 cups (800 g) sugar

In a medium stockpot, combine the zucchini, oranges, apple, ginger, vinegar, rosemary and sugar. Add the bag of peels, if you are using it. Bring the mixture to a boil over medium-high heat, then reduce the heat to medium and simmer the mixture uncovered for 45 minutes, stirring often. The mixture will thicken as it simmers.

While the glaze is simmering, prepare the water bath canner by filling it halfway with water and putting it on the stove to simmer. Check eight half-pint (250-ml) jars for any nicks or cracks, wash them in hot soapy water and rinse them in hot water. Keep the jars hot until it's time to use them. Wash the lids in hot soapy water and rinse them.

After about 45 minutes, remove the pan from the heat and gently remove the bag of orange peels, if you used one, scraping the glaze off the bag. Ladle the glaze into the hot jars, leaving ¼ inch (6 mm) of headspace.

Wipe the rims with a clean cloth, put on the lids and screw on the bands. Place the jars in the prepared hot water bath canner and process for 10 minutes, adjusting for altitude (page 17), if necessary.

Arrange a folded towel on the counter or table. Remove the jars, using a jar lifter, and place them on the towel. Let the jars cool for at least 12 hours.

Once the jars are cooled, remove the bands and check the seals. If any jars failed to seal, put them in the refrigerator to use first. Wipe the jars with a clean cloth, label them and store the glaze for up to a year.

* See photo on page 303 (this recipe is shown in the jar on the left).

Serving Suggestions: *Blend the glaze until it's smooth to make a dipping sauce for fried foods, such as egg rolls and samosas. You can also serve this with soft cheese and crackers.*

herbs

Adding Flavor to Your Food

Herbs are such a great way to add flavor to food. They can take a good dish and elevate it to a fantastic dish without adding work for you. Fortunately, herbs are easy to grow and easy to preserve.

Whole books have been written on growing and preserving herbs. For this book, we'll concentrate on the most common culinary herbs used in preserving vegetables.

Growing and Harvesting Herbs

When I think of growing herbs, I tend to think of herbs in four groups: those that prefer cool temperatures, those that prefer warm temperatures, those that like a lot of water and those that like to dry out before being watered. For sure, there's some overlap between those groups, but thinking of herbs in these groups helps me know when and where to plant herbs to get the best harvest.

Herbs can be annuals or perennials and some are annuals in cold climates but perennials in warm climates. For the most part, all herbs like to be planted in well-draining soil and in full sun, although most can tolerate part sun. Herbs also like to be harvested regularly; the more you harvest, the more the plant will produce.

Basil is an annual herb that loves the heat and is frost tender. Basil is somewhat drought tolerant, but will grow better when it's watered regularly. Plant basil in full sun when all danger of frost has passed. Harvest individual leaves whenever they're needed and cut the plants back a couple of times during the growing season. After the basil has flowered, let the seeds dry out on the plant and collect them for planting next year.

Chives are a member of the onion family and are cold and heat hardy. As long as the ground doesn't freeze, chives will come back each spring. Harvest chives by cutting the greens whenever you need them. After about 3 or 4 years, they will have formed a root clump that can be divided and replanted to grow more chives.

Cilantro, also called *coriander*, is an annual, cool-weather herb that will go to seed when it gets too warm. In zones 8 and above, plant cilantro in the fall and grow it over the winter. In other zones, plant cilantro as soon as the ground can be worked. Plant cilantro in full sun and water it regularly. Harvest cilantro leaves as you need them, and harvest a large amount several times during the season. After the cilantro flowers, allow the seed pods to dry on the plant, then harvest them for planting next year and using in pickled recipes. In the US, cilantro is the green plant and coriander is the seed; in some other countries, coriander is used as the name of both the plant and seeds.

Dill is another cool-weather herb that is used in pickling recipes. Technically, dill is a biennial but is usually grown as an annual. In zones 8 and above, plant dill in the fall and grow it over the winter months. In zones 3 to 7, plant dill as soon as the ground is workable. Plant dill in full sun and water it regularly; once the plants are established, let them dry out between watering. Harvest the dill leaves, or fern, as needed but also harvest large amounts a couple of times during growing season. Once the dill flowers, let the seeds dry on the plant and harvest them before they start dropping. The seeds are also used in pickling recipes. Sometimes the dill leaves are called *dill weed* and the seeds are called *dill heads*.

Mint is a perennial herb that loves water. If you have a place on your property that's often damp, plant mint there, and it will thrive. Mint is also invasive; plant it in a pot if you don't want it to spread. Harvest mint leaves as needed, but also harvest several large amounts through the growing season. In most climates, mint will die back in the winter and re-emerge in the early spring. In hot climates, it might also die back during the heat of the summer and then flourish when the cooler temperatures of fall arrive.

Parsley is related to cilantro and is another biennial plant that is grown as an annual. In zones 8 and above, parsley can be planted in the fall and grown over the winter months. In colder zones, plant parsley as soon as the ground is workable. Plant

parsley in full sun and water it regularly. Harvest parsley as needed, and harvest several large cuttings during the growing season. Unlike cilantro, the seeds are not used in cooking, but they can be collected for replanting.

Oregano is a perennial plant that thrives in hot weather. Plant oregano after all danger of frost has passed and plant it in full sun. After oregano is established, let it dry out between watering. Harvest oregano regularly to encourage the plant to become bushy and not grow leggy. There are two main types of oregano, Mexican oregano and Mediterranean oregano. They can be used interchangeably, but have distinct flavors, with the Mediterranean variety being milder than the Mexican. It's worth it to grow both varieties.

Rosemary is an evergreen perennial herb that is cold hardy in zones 7 and above; in other zones, you will need to protect the rosemary during the winter months. Rosemary thrives in full sun and likes to dry out between watering. Plant rosemary after all danger of frost has passed. There are two kinds of rosemary, a shrub and a creeping plant; both need similar growing conditions. The creeping variety is ideal for those with limited space or for growing in containers. You can harvest rosemary leaves whenever you need them, but also plan on doing a couple of large harvests each season.

Sage is a perennial herb that is cold hardy in zone 4 and above. Not all sage plants are used for food, so be sure to get culinary or garden sage, not the drought tolerant landscape sage. Plant sage in full sun and allow it to dry out between watering. Sage leaves can be harvested at any time, but the plant will benefit from a few large harvests during the growing season.

Thyme is another evergreen perennial herb that is cold hardy in zone 5 and above. Plant thyme in full sun after all danger of frost has passed, and let it dry out between watering. Thyme, rosemary and oregano are all Mediterranean plants that grow well together. Harvest thyme leaves as needed, but also harvest several large amounts during the growing season.

Preserving Herbs

There are many ways to preserve herbs, so don't get stuck in a rut just dehydrating everything. As with vegetables, I like to think about how I'm going to be using the end product before I start preserving. Am I going to be cooking with this herb or making infusions with it? Does the herb lose some of its flavor when it's dried but retains it when it's frozen, like cilantro? The more questions you ask, and answer, the more likely you'll preserve your herbs in a way that you'll use throughout the year.

You can preserve herbs as single herbs or as combinations. Again, think about how you already use herbs to decide if you want to preserve them in combinations or singly.

Before preserving herbs, you'll want to wash and dry them. Wash the herbs in cold water and either pat them dry with a kitchen towel or spin them in a salad spinner. Some herbs, like sage, are a bit fuzzy, and dirt tends to really stick to these herbs. Others, such as basil, are smooth, and dirt doesn't seem to stick on them as much.

Dehydrating Herbs

Any herb can be dehydrated and most should be, because dehydrating herbs is a great way to make sure you always have herbs available for cooking, medicine making and other uses. Most herbs retain their flavor when dehydrated but some, such as cilantro and basil, don't.

Dehydrating herbs can be as simple as tying up small bundles and hanging them in a cool, dark place. Or you can use a dehydrator on low (95 to 115°F [35 to 46°C]). The most important part of drying herbs is to not use much heat. The flavor is in the aromatic oils in the plant, and the oils will evaporate when herbs are exposed to high heat, leaving you with herbs that don't have much flavor.

You can also dehydrate herbs in the oven. Lay the herbs out on a baking sheet lined with a towel and turn the light on. The light in an electric oven or the pilot light in a gas oven should provide enough heat to dehydrate herbs in a timely manner.

If I have only a small herb harvest, I'll often lay the leaves out on a towel in a dark corner on my kitchen counter and let them sit out until they're dry; it usually takes just a couple of days.

Once the herb is completely dry, store it in an airtight jar and label it. Herbs do lose some of their potency when exposed to air and light, so some people prefer to store herbs in colored jars. I'm too frugal for that. I keep my herbs in a closed cabinet in my kitchen and I preserve only enough for a year, so I don't worry about them losing potency because they're in clear glass jars. If you are trying to preserve enough for more than a year, you should store them in colored jars.

Herbs that dehydrate well are chives, dill, mint, parsley, oregano, rosemary, thyme and sage. Dried herbs will remain good for years, but their potency will diminish over time, which is why I try to preserve only enough for a year.

Freezing Herbs

There are many ways to freeze herbs, but I'm going to share my favorite way first . . . put the herbs in a freezer bag, remove the air and label the bag. Now, toss it in the freezer. Yep, that's it. When you want to use it, just break off a chunk.

The proper way to freeze herbs is to chop them, put them in an ice cube tray, then cover the herbs with water or oil. When they're frozen, you just pop them out of the ice cube tray, put them in a freezer bag or other freezer-safe container and put them back into the freezer until you're ready to use them. In my opinion, the downside of this method is dealing with the extra water or oil that is covering the herbs. It's fine if you are going to use the herbs in soups or sautéed vegetables where it will just blend in or evaporate. But if you want to use the herbs for dips or things that you don't want extra liquid in, you will lose some flavor by not incorporating the liquid.

I've heard of people blanching herbs before freezing, as you would do with fresh greens (page 177). I have no idea why someone would do this; it might help retain the herb's color, but the flavor is diminished in the blanching process.

Herbs frozen in these ways work great for cooking and salsa making, but not so great for garnishing, because they will be limp.

Herbs that freeze well are basil, chive, cilantro, mint, parsley, oregano and sage. Herbs can be safely stored in the freezer for about a year.

Fermenting Herbs

Herbs can be preserved by fermenting, just like most vegetables and some fruits. I have not fermented very many herbs, so I'm certainly no expert. However, I do use herbs in many of my vegetable ferments. I find this easier and more useful than having jars of fermented herbs stored in the refrigerator.

If you make fermented herbs, it's best to make them in small batches of 1 cup (237 ml) or less. While they can be stored for several months in the refrigerator, once they're opened, they really need to be used within a week or two.

There are two ways to make herbal ferments: a brine ferment and a paste ferment. For a brine ferment, make a brine solution of 1 cup (237 ml) of non-chlorinated, filtered water and 1 teaspoon of sea salt. Remove the herb leaves from the stems and loosely fill a jar with them. Pour the brine solution over the herbs, add a fermentation weight, making sure all the herb solids are under the weight, then put on a fermentation airlock. Let the herbs ferment for 5 to 10 days, until the liquid stops bubbling and the brine tastes tangy. Remove the fermentation weight and lid and replace it with a plastic storage lid. Store the ferment for up to 6 months in the refrigerator.

You can make an herbal paste ferment just like you make sauerkraut, by massaging salt into the herbs and letting them ferment in their own juices. You'll want to use herbs that were just picked, so they have a high moisture content. Put the herbs in a bowl and sprinkle them with 2 grams of salt for every 100 grams of fresh herbs. Toss the herbs with the salt.

Using a kraut pounder or your hands, mash (or bruise) the herbs with the salt. The herbs will start to release their juices. Put the herbs with the juice in a small jar; if there isn't enough liquid to cover the herbs, add enough 2 percent brine (page 51) to cover them. Add a fermentation weight, making sure that all the herb solids are under the weight, and a fermentation airlock lid. Put the jar on a plate or small cookie sheet to catch any overflow. Put the ferment in a dark cabinet or corner for 5 to 10 days, or until it stops bubbling and tastes tangy. Remove the airlock system and replace it with a plastic storage lid. Store the ferment for up to 6 months in the refrigerator.

Sometimes herbs will oxidize and turn black; this is normally just fine. However, go with your own judgment and if the herbs smell off, don't use them.

Herbs that are good for a brine ferment are chives, dill, garlic and rosemary.

Herbs that are good for a paste ferment are basil, cilantro, chives, mint, parsley and thyme.

Canning Herbs

Using herbs while canning other fruits and vegetables is a good way to preserve herbs. However, I've never come across a canning recommendation for canning just herbs in a jar. I assume it could be done if you add enough vinegar, but you'd lose some of the herb's flavor and most of its health benefits due to the excessive heating. If you want to preserve herbs in vinegar, an herbal infusion is a better choice.

When using herbs in canning recipes, it's important to use only dried herbs, unless the recipe specifically calls for fresh herbs. However, if it calls for fresh herbs, you can substitute dried herbs. The water content in fresh herbs takes the herb from a seasoning to a low-acid ingredient; this can lead to inadequate processing times.

For the most part, any dried herb can be added as a seasoning to any canned vegetable without affecting safety. I find this very liberating!

There is conflicting information about using sage in canned goods; it's not a safety conflict, but a taste conflict. Sage has been known to cause bitterness once it's been processed. This doesn't always happen, and some authorities recommend sage when canning fish, for instance. However, it can happen and I want you to be aware of it.

Herbal Paste

Herbal pastes are all the rage in high-end grocery stores, but you don't need to spend an arm and a leg to have herbal pastes to cook with. Herbal pastes are simply herbs and oil blended together into a paste. Olive oil is the most commonly used oil, but you can use any oil with which you normally cook.

Using a blender or food processor, blend the herb and just enough olive oil so the chopped herbs and oil make a paste. Once you have the herb and oil blended, you can spoon the mixture into ice cube trays and freeze the trays overnight. Once the cubes are frozen, pop them out of the ice cube trays and put the cubes into a freezer bag or other freezer-safe container. I've found this is the best way for long-term storage, since oil can go rancid over time. When I'm ready to use the herbal paste, I just grab a cube and put it in a small Mason jar to thaw.

Herbal pastes can also be frozen in small jars, such as 4-ounce (125-ml) Mason jars or baby food jars. If you freeze the herbal paste in jars, you'll need to allow time for it to thaw before you want to use it. The jar can be thawed on the counter, but if you don't use it all, store the rest in the refrigerator. Because we use pesto weekly, this is how I freeze it.

Herbs that make a good paste are basil, cilantro, chives, dill, parsley and oregano.

Herbal Butter

Herbal butters, also called *compound butters*, are made by combining butter with fresh herbs. These are so wonderful for cooking and spreading on bread. They make seasoning a whole chicken a snap. To make an herbal butter, combine one stick of softened butter (½ cup [110 g]) with 2 to 3 tablespoons of chopped fresh herbs (the weight will vary depending on the herb). You can use a fork and bowl or a food processor to combine the butter and herbs. Put the herbal butter on a piece of plastic wrap, roll it into a log and put the log in a freezer bag or freezer-safe container. You could also freeze herbal butter in ice cube trays, then transfer the frozen cubes into a freezer bag or freezer-safe container to store. Herbal butter can be stored in the freezer for up to a year and in the refrigerator for about 5 days.

Herbs that make good herbal butters are basil, cilantro, chives, dill, garlic, parsley, oregano, rosemary, sage and thyme.

Herbal Salt

If you tend to use the same herb combinations over and over when you cook, having herbal salts in the cabinet will save you a bit of time. Plus, they make really great gifts. Herbal salts can be made with dehydrated herbs or fresh herbs. If you use fresh herbs, you'll have an extra step at the end.

If I'm using fresh herbs, I like to use a ratio of about 3 cups of fresh herbs (the weight will vary depending on the herb) to ½ cup (144 g) of salt. Put the herbs in a small bowl and mix them with the salt. You can use a food processor and pulse it, but it's easy to over process and make a paste, so be careful if you choose to use a food processor.

Once you have the herbs and salt mixed well, spread the mixture on a baking sheet lined with parchment paper. Put the baking sheet in the oven and turn the light on, or turn the oven on its lowest setting and leave the door ajar. Let the mixture dehydrate. This should take anywhere from an hour to a day, it just depends on how much moisture was in the herbs and how warm the oven is. Once the herbal salt is completely dry, put it in a jar, label the jar and store it in the pantry.

If you really don't want to dehydrate the herbal salt, then it can be stored in the refrigerator for up to 6 months.

Dehydrated herbs can also be used to make herbal salts. I like to crush the dried herbs first, especially if they are bulky like sage or basil, to have more consistent measuring. I use a ratio of ½ cup (144 g) of coarse salt and 2 tablespoons of dried herbs (the weight will vary depending on the herb) to begin, then I add more herbs if I need to. I like to put the salt and dried herbs in a coffee mill that I use only for herbs and give it a whirl a few times. You can also use a mortar and pestle to crush the herbs into the salt. Once it's mixed, put the herbal salt in a jar and label it. It can be stored indefinitely in the pantry.

Herbs that are good for herbal salts are basil, chives, dill, garlic, parsley, oregano, rosemary, sage and thyme.

Herbal Vinegar

Making herbal vinegar is a simple way to preserve herbs. For culinary purposes, herbal vinegar doesn't need to be as precise as when you're using herbal vinegars medicinally and need to figure out dosing.

To make a culinary herbal vinegar, wash and dry the herbs and then put them in a jar. For every 1 cup of fresh herbs (the weight will vary depending on the herb), pour 2 cups (474 ml) of vinegar into the jar. The vinegar needs to have 5 percent acidity for the herbal vinegar to be shelf-stable. Set the jar out of direct sunlight and shake it every day for a week. After a week, check the flavor and, if it is flavorful enough, strain the herbs out of the vinegar, replace the lid and store the vinegar in a cool, dark place for up to a year.

Herbal vinegars are good for salad dressings, marinades and sauces, and in anything you add vinegar to.

Herbs that are good for herbal vinegars are basil, chives, dill, garlic, parsley, oregano, rosemary, sage and thyme.

resources

I truly hope this book helps you get a little further along on your journey of growing and preserving food. There are so many places to get help and supplies for growing and preserving food, but I always recommend starting in your local community.

Local Community Resource—The most helpful local organization is going to be your County Extension Office; call and make new friends. You can find them with a quick Google search. This office has ties to a State University and will often have a Master Food Preserver on staff. This is a great place to ask about altitude and to get the dial gauge of your pressure canner checked.

Seed Companies—Small seed companies abound and are doing the important work of keeping heirloom and open pollinated seeds available. Some of my favorite seed companies are: MIgardener, Baker Creek Heirloom Seed Company, Seeds for Generations, Seed Savers Exchange, Southern Exposure Seed Exchange, Fedco Seeds, Territorial Seed Company and Seeds of Change. Look locally to see if there are any small seed companies or seed exchange groups in your area.

Preservation Equipment—AllAmericanCanner. com, NourishedEssentials.com, Excaliburdehydrator. com, Amazon.com, Walmart, Tractor Supply Co. and local hardware stores.

USDA Guidelines for safe food preserving can be found on the National Center for Home Food Preservation website. This is an amazing resource and you should spend a lot of time on this website.

Gardening Books—*The All You Can Eat Gardening Handbook* by Cam Mather is a fantastic general gardening book. You should also look for gardening books that are specific to your area.

Other Preservation Books—It might seem funny to list other preservation books as a resource, but we've only touched the tip of each of the preservation methods in this book. These books are specific for each preservation method: *Ball® Blue Book® Guide to Preserving* by Jarden Home Brands, *Wild Fermentation* by Sandor Ellix Katz, *Fermented Vegetables* by Christopher and Kirsten K. Shockey and *The Dehydrator Bible* by Jennifer MacKenzie.

acknowledgments

Thank you, Page Street Publishing, for bringing what was in my head to life. I've thought about this book for years, but it wasn't until you came along that it became a reality. Your team is so professional, patient and kind; you have been a pleasure to work with. With special thanks to Sarah Monroe, my editor, who is making me a better writer, and Dianne Cutillo, my copyeditor, who has impressive error-catching skills. You ladies are amazing.

For the photography duo who so graciously shared their gifts and talents to take preserved food and make it look as pretty as it is delicious, thank you. Dennis, your ability to stay focused on the hero and bring to life my simple recipes is truly a gift. Darcy, your patience and commitment to get the food pretty but "not too styled" is inspiring. The excitement you both shared for the recipes was more encouraging than you will ever know. I loved turning around and seeing you sample the food. I enjoyed having you in our home, and I hope we get to work together on future projects. I am truly blessed by both of you.

To the readers of my blog, SchneiderPeeps, this book is for you. The feedback and encouragement you've given me set the foundation for this book and gave me the courage to write it. You are amazing.

A special thanks to my fellow blogging buddies: Kathie, Chris, Susan, Kris, Ashley, Jessica, Meredith, Tessa, Amy F., Megan, Tanya, Devon, Jan, Amy D., Dawn, Amy S., Amanda, Ann, Shelle, Janet, Rachel, Connie, Quinn, Colleen and Teri. Y'all are the most generous bloggers I've ever met. Thank you for your savvy business hacks, your mad spreadsheet-making skills and your willingness to cheer each other on toward our goals. Colleen, thank you for mentioning me to Page Street and getting this project started. Kathie, thank you for talking me off the ledge more than once and helping me to see truth when I felt like believing lies.

So many of my "in-real-life" friends have encouraged me and been subjected to impromptu taste testing; thank you for your support! D'Ann, thank you for always being ready to pray for and with me when life is crazy and I feel overwhelmed. To Georgia and Julie, thank you for all the extended play dates you made for Esther with your daughters so I could write and not feel "mommy guilt."

To my sister, Michelle, thank you for always encouraging me. Also, thanks for finding me some overgrown zucchini when my kids ate the zucchini fruit chew photo props.

To my kids, Christian, Josiah, Gabriel, Phoebe, Benjamin and Esther, as well as my daughter-in-law, Nychelle, and grandson, Nik, y'all are amazing, and I'm not just saying that because I'm your Mom and Grandma. I see each of you boldly following your dreams and not letting self-doubt hold you back. Y'all inspire me to do the same. Thank you for being so very wonderful. Oh, and for doing the dishes, over and over and over and over. . . . To my husband, Carl, who knew that the little blackberry patch would lead us to where we are now? I love the life we've built together, and I look forward to growing old with you. Thank you for believing in me, even when I don't believe in myself. Thank you for giving me the time and space to write for hours on end. Thank you for tasting every recipe that didn't have vinegar, and a few that did, and giving honest but kind suggestions. You are truly the love of my life.

Most importantly, I want to thank God for using this journey to grow me as a person and to help me realize more fully that part of my worship of the Creator is taking care of His creation. And that doing my part to reduce my family's impact on the Earth by growing and preserving food is a way to honor You.

about the author

Angi Schneider has been gardening and preserving food for over 25 years. She lives on 1.5 acres along the Texas Gulf Coast with her husband and children, a flock of chickens and a few beehives. She is the writer behind SchneiderPeeps, a blog where she shares her gardening and preserving adventures. When she's not in the garden or writing, Angi can be found cooking, sewing or chauffeuring and always trying to live a simple handmade life.

index